The Early Advantage

The Early Advantage

Early Childhood Systems That Lead by Example

A Comparative Focus on International Early Childhood Education

Sharon Lynn Kagan, Editor

Foreword by Marc Tucker

TEACHERS COLLEGE PRESS

TEACHERS COLLEGE | COLUMBIA UNIVERSITY

NEW YORK AND LONDON

NCEE

National Center On
EDUCATION
And The Economy ®

2121 K Street NW, Suite 700
Washington, DC, www.ncee.org

Published simultaneously by Teachers College Press, 1234 Amsterdam Avenue, New York, NY 10027 and National Center on Education and the Economy, 2121 K Street NW, Suite 700, Washington, DC 20037, www.ncee.org

The study undergirding this book has been funded by the National Center on Education and the Economy (see p. xii: "About the Sponsoring Organizations")

Figure 1.1 was previously published, in modified form, on p. 22 of Kagan, S. L., & Gomez, R. E. (Eds.). (2015). *Early childhood governance: Choices and consequences*. New York, NY: Teachers College Press. Reprinted by permission of the publisher.

Library of Congress Cataloging-in-Publication Data is available at loc.gov

ISBN 978-0-8077-5941-7 (paper)
ISBN 978-0-8077-7715-2 (ebook)

Printed on acid-free paper
Manufactured in the United States of America

25 24 23 22 21 20 19 18   8 7 6 5 4 3 2 1

This book is dedicated to the cherished memory of
Collette Tayler, Ed.D.
Scholar, Pioneer, Friend, and Colleague.

Photo Credit: University of Melbourne

Honoring her, all proceeds from this volume will be donated to the Collette Tayler Indigenous Education Fund at the University of Melbourne, to provide scholarships to Indigenous Australians pursuing degrees in early childhood or early years education.

Contents

Foreword

The organization I head, the National Center on Education and the Economy, has been studying the countries that have been doing the best job of educating their young people for almost 30 years. Differences in politics, culture, and many other things mean that a policy that works well in one country often does not work well in another. But this does not mean that everything is situational and culture-bound, making it impossible for one nation to learn anything useful from another. It turns out that certain broad strategies and principles underlie the world's most successful systems, strategies and principles that are more likely to be found in the top performers than elsewhere, not in isolation, but in harness, together, working in harmony. These principles can be used by other nations to build their own harmonious systems, different in their details, but no less powerful and effective.

So, a few years ago, we distilled the findings from our research into a conceptual framework titled *The Nine Building Blocks for a World-Class Education System*. Subsequently, we decided to ask a leading scholar in each of the fields defined by these nine building blocks to undertake what we hoped would be a landmark international comparative study of the strategies used by the top performers to get to excellence in the arena defined by that building block. Our aim was to build a library of resources that policymakers and practitioners all over the world interested in building top-performing education systems at the scale of an entire nation could turn to for the research they needed to do exactly that.

This study is the second in that series. The first was a study of teacher quality led by Linda Darling-Hammond, emeritus professor at Stanford University, now head of the Learning Policy Institute. We knew that we wanted the next big international comparative study to be on what the top performers do for families with young children in general and early childhood education in particular.

There was no question as to who we would ask to do it. Sharon Lynn Kagan is a giant in this field. One of the world's leading scholars and thinkers in early childhood, Kagan had access to a worldwide circle of leading experts in the field, enabling her to form a research team of noted professional scholars from every corner of the globe who had deep experience in the policy realm.

Given the range of her experience, I had imagined that little she en-countered as this research progressed would surprise her. I was wrong. Her enthusiasm became excitement. As you will see when you read the first chapter, Kagan had the ability to stand outside established constructs and see it all afresh.

Looking at a familiar world through the lens of systems analysis, Kagan saw a rich variety of programs, initiatives, and activities and a growing conviction on the part of many governments that investments in this arena will pay off in many ways. But these programs, initiatives, and activities had their origins in a great variety of historical contexts. She concluded that what is needed now is good thinking not so much about the individual parts and pieces as about the designs of the larger systems of which they are a part.

Taking a page, as it were, from NCEE's effort to distill the experience of the countries with the most effective school systems into a set of building blocks for effective school systems, Kagan and her team drew on their own broad experience, enriched by this very comprehensive international com-parative study, to create a similar framework, an array of what they take to be the essential building blocks for constructing high-quality systems of early childhood education that are equitable, efficient, and sustainable.

Kagan and her team describe a field at a very important inflection point, and they provide a framework for pushing on to the next stage. My guess is that this book will be remembered not just for incisive reporting and analy-sis, but as the book the field needed to get to the other side of that inflection point.

—Marc Tucker

Acknowledgments

The authors gratefully acknowledge the contributions of Jessie Roth (USA), Naomi Eisenstadt (England), Dr. Maggie Koong (Hong Kong), Dr. Stephanie Chan (Hong Kong), and Moon Jeong Kim (Republic of Korea). In addition, we are most appreciative of the inspiration and technical and fiscal support from Marc Tucker, Betsy Brown Ruzzi, and their talented team at the National Center on Education and the Economy (USA).

About the Sponsoring Organizations

This work is made possible through a grant by the Center on International Education Benchmarking® at the National Center on Education and the Economy, and it is part of a study of early childhood education and care systems around the world. For a complete listing of the material produced by this research program, please visit www.ncee.org/cieb.

The Center funds and conducts research around the world on the most successful education systems in order to identify the strategies those countries have used to produce their superior performance. Through its books, reports, website, monthly newsletter, and a weekly update of education news around the world, CIEB provides up-to-date information and analysis on those countries whose students regularly top the Programme for International Student Assessment (PISA) league tables. Visit www.ncee.org/cieb to learn more.

NCEE was created in 1988 to analyze the implications of changes in the international economy for American education, formulate an agenda for American education based on that analysis, and seek wherever possible to accomplish that agenda through policy change and development of the resources educators would need to carry it out. For more information, visit www.ncee.org.

CHAPTER 1

Changing the Narratives

Sharon Lynn Kagan

On Saturday, August 27, 2016, Yale President Peter Salovey addressed an anticipant group of incoming freshmen. No one missed the fact that Salovey was speaking to the class of 2020, a number associated with perfect vision. Yet Salovey elected not to dwell on either perfection or vision; rather, he focused on the narrative stories that propel and encase these visions. Noting the advent of a national zeitgeist characterized by inflamed skepticism, exaggerated emotions, and the stubborn simplification of social and political issues, Salovey begged for disciplined, reasoned, and careful searches for light and truth. Predictable, you might say.

What wasn't predictable was Salovey's focus on personal narratives—those majestically constructed, tenaciously guarded, and often instantaneously transmitted "truths" we each hold and cherish. Calling on those present to acknowledge narratives' predictive power over us, he implored students to use their college years to forego "drenched ideologies and entrenched assumptions" and think afresh. Salovey provided strategic guidance as he advised students to rethink "the heart and soul of the [democratic] enterprise": to carefully examine and use empirical data wisely and cautiously; to engage honestly in challenging discourse and tough controversial exchanges; and to ask themselves tenacious, unanswered, and yet-to-be-imagined questions.

Though seemingly remote from early childhood education, Salovey's call to the class of 2020 is the very call that prompted this volume. In an era characterized by rapid change, unbridled rhetoric, and scattered policy action, early childhood education has lived off entrenched narratives that have prevailed for decades, narratives that this volume contends are stale and must be revisited. Defining early childhood education and care (ECEC) as a critical component of the panoply of comprehensive early development (CED) services for children aged 0–8 and their families, this work audaciously reconsiders the "heart and soul of the enterprise," seeking to learn from diverse countries around the world that have exemplary services for young children. It explicates and challenges prevailing discourses as it confronts deeply held assumptions and historic narratives; moreover, it privileges judicious inquiry, unconventional data, and intellectually unbounded discourse. Using the contemporary context, advanced knowledge, and fresh ways of knowing, this volume offers a revisionist stance regarding what matters for young children and the individuals and institutions who serve them. Grounded in lessons from six jurisdictions (Australia, England, Finland, Hong Kong, the Republic of Korea, and Singapore), it offers a set of stories that posit fresh perspectives and narratives, along with the requisite ingredients for leaders working to design and usher in a new era of ECEC.

To travel this essentially re-contoured journey, this book, the first of two based on this inquiry, will proffer alternate paths for consideration. Chapter 1 begins by reviewing entrenched narratives that frame contemporary ECEC as a prelude to reconstructing them. Each of the six chapters that follow (Chapters 2–7) tell individual country/jurisdictional narratives. Leading scholars who are also renowned for their policy work share their distinct and expressive stories, analyzing how and why their countries/jurisdictions hold and enact contemporary services to young children and their families. In the final chapter (Chapter 8), common themes are extracted and restructured to suggest a set of emerging narratives that are both empirically grounded and, hopefully, helpful and prescient. Using these emerging narratives as the path, the book creates a new approach to envisioning and enacting early childhood education and care services.

To do so and to render cohesion to the volume, several frequently used terms warrant explication. First, as briefly noted, CED is used as an umbrella term that includes health, mental health, nutrition, protective, education, and care services provided to young children from birth to age 8. ECEC, in turn, is the subset of CED that focuses on care and education services, typically serving children from birth and continuing until they enter formal primary education. Second, for ease of understanding, and because five of the six jurisdictions presented herein are independent countries, we take the liberty of referring to all six as countries. Throughout this volume, though sometimes termed a country in the aggregate, Hong Kong is understood as a special administrative region of China. Third, for the sake of brevity, the Republic of Korea is frequently abbreviated to simply "Korea," with the two terms being used interchangeably throughout.

MULTIPLE NARRATIVES: HISTORIC, EXISTING, AND EMERGING

Historic Narratives: The Seminal Rationales for ECEC

Throughout the episodic history of ECEC globally, three significant rationales have shaped the early childhood discourse and its services. Sometimes functioning in isolation and sometimes in union, each emanates from a different time and place, and offers a distinct lens for enlivening early childhood education and care. Notably, these rationales have produced quite distinct and often durable approaches for serving young children around the world.

Empirical Rationales. Collectively, empirical rationales emanate from the long-held premise that science can and should contribute to the general public good (Lindblom & Cohen, 1979). Deposing the philosopher-king as the primary bearer and user of knowledge, they suggest that research in diverse fields is obligated to inform the public and, hopefully, the public good. So much the better if such science is predicated on interventions that have proven their effectiveness and if the results are used to create wise, efficient, and cost-effective policy.

Moving to ECEC specifically, this rationale is eminent. Years' worth of policies and programs to serve young children and their families have been catapulted to prominence predicated on an empirical rationale and the evaluation results that attest to the benefits of specific interventions for children, families, and society (Marope & Kaga, 2015). More specifically, early childhood evaluation research has played a prominent role in advancing pedagogical efforts at the classroom level, particularly when such research demonstrated gains in children's academic and social competence. Moreover, the holy trinity of longitudinal American early childhood evaluations (the Abecedarian Project, High Scope/Perry Preschool, and Chicago Child-Parent Centers) has served as the basis for preschool program expansion in this country and globally (Barnett, 1995; Nores & Barnett, 2015; Reynolds & Temple, 2008). Data, particularly drawn from well-constructed longitudinal studies of interventions, have solidified empirical results as a critical elixir of ECEC domestically and internationally.

Social Need Rationales. Another, and very different, rationale also undergirds the imperative for establishing services for young children. Predicated on addressing broader social and economic conditions, the inspiration for this rationale emanates from societal needs, either temporary crises or more trenchant phenomena (Kamerman & Kahn, 2001). In social need rationales, children are not the *raison d'être* for policy creation; rather, policies for children are established as a means of addressing broader, more contextualized problems (e.g., wars and their aftermaths, economic depressions). In some countries, such as the United States, commitment to young children burgeoned at times when female labor force participation was deemed essential to mitigating broader social and economic ills. Evoked both by the Great Depression and two World Wars, child care was seen as a means to free up women's time and thereby incentivize their labor force participation; to meet these social crises, universal and ubiquitous child care was established (Cahan, 1989).

Alternatively, in World War II–ravaged Europe, depleted citizenries gave rise to widespread pronatalist maternal and child policies that incentivized population growth, including liberal parental leave and child care provisions. These social need rationales elicited some of the most comprehensive and fast-paced expansions of services to the young. Interestingly, while European war-borne efforts came to serve as the bedrock of many contemporary policies, efforts predicated on other social crises were short-lived in the United States, quickly disbanding after the crises had passed (Grubb & Lazerson, 1982).

Obligation-Rights Rationales. Emanating from a totally different stance, some countries—primarily the Nordic nations—began their commitments to children and families with a primary premise grounded neither in science nor social or economic needs; rather, ECEC was regarded as a part of the natural repertoire of services that countries owed their citizens. ECEC services constituted a cornerstone of the social contract, based in the fundamental obligation to serve all citizens and to serve them well. If such obligations were the duty of the government, they were entitlements for all citizens. This rationale fueled the provision of broader, more comprehensive, and more durable systems and services for young children as a part of normative and essential social obligations (Organisation for Economic Co-operation and Development [OECD], 2000).

Existing Narratives: A Revised Story

As seminal as they are, the historic rationales convey only part of today's early childhood story. Layered on top of these fundamentally different and highly formative rationales are a set of existing narratives, etched from the contemporary context, that contour the services provided to young children worldwide. Pervasive, these evoke their own challenges, with which current early childhood services—no matter where located—are contending. Five existing narratives, discussed here, offer both a frame within which to understand ECEC in the countries in this volume and a magnifying glass that provides a clear prelude to the emerging narratives that these country stories will reveal.

Globalization Narrative. The young children of today will grow up in a world that is totally different from that of their parents. Whether talking about a "flat" and globalized world where ease of transport and interconnected economies prevail or the technological revolution through which instant communication, handheld technologies, and online learning are ubiquitous, it is an unequivocal reality that the world is changing, and changing rapidly. Environmental changes are inescapable, as are transformations of gender roles that are propelling women into leadership and same-sex partnerships into legitimacy. Global migration means that once comparatively homogeneous societies and cultures are becoming more diverse, posing new challenges for leaders and citizens. For young children and those who serve them, these 21st-century realities raise fundamental questions regarding if and how old narratives and strategies will prepare children for the worlds of flux they will encounter. Such questions beckon ECEC to consider how to best serve the changing needs of young children.

Services Imperative Narrative. Gone are the days when children were to be seen and not heard and "babysitting" was the vernacular associated with caring for young children. Under a deluge of economic evidence that investment in the early years pays off, policymakers globally have solidified their commitments to young children. Today's existing narrative beckons investment in and support of the young, with services to children no longer a social nicety but a social and political imperative. Work by Nobel laureate economist James Heckman has shown that early investments in young children yield durable benefits, made manifest, for example, in higher adult earnings and reduced welfare dependence and criminal rates (Heckman, 2006). Thus, for many countries, investments in young children are the mark of prudent thinking and wise resource allocation, often approaching the top of the list of requisite investments. Nary a politician would reject a call to improve the well-being of young children, with much of the political rhetoric being matched by significant increases in social investments in low-, middle-, and upper-income countries worldwide (OECD, 2001, 2006; U.N. General Assembly, 2015; UNESCO, 2006). In short, the contemporary narrative proclaims young children as an essential arena for investment, beckoning policymakers toward quickly launched and often less than meticulously planned and implemented services.

New Sciences Narrative. Building on the historical need for and use of empirical data, new evidence from several research disciplines has provided a broadened scientific basis for service expansion to the young. From widely popularized neuroscience comes recognition of the importance to human development of the first 3 years of life. Eyes widen as policymakers hear that young children's brains grow to 80% of their adult size by age 3 and 90% by age 5; pulses quicken as they understand brain fragility and that without consistent nurturing and protecting stimuli, such development can be durably impaired (Shonkoff, 2010; Shonkoff & Phillips, 2000).

Yet neuroscience is not the only science that is changing the contemporary early childhood narrative. From a content perspective, cultural psychologists are dramatically reshaping how the early childhood field understands and honors diversities (Nisbett, 2003; Rogoff, 2003). From the process perspective, implementation scientists are informing early childhood practitioners about strategies that promote effective and efficient program implementation; they examine, for example, practice-borrowing (adoption and adaptation), scaling-up strategies, and policies that promote durability and sustainability.

And perhaps most potently, systems scientists have recognized that early childhood is fertile ground for bringing the new political and social imperatives to reality. Systems science looks at early childhood education and care contextually and holistically (Joachim & May, 2010). That is, it squarely situates itself in both historic and existing narratives (the context) while acknowledging that a focus on individual programs and services is insufficient to marshal the kinds of changes being demanded of the field in the contemporary era (Urban, Vandenbroeck, Van Laere, Lazzari, & Peeters, 2012). Altogether, such reliance on scientific rationales moves early childhood from the informal domain to one that is more rigorously scrutinized and held to new accountability standards.

Pedagogical Quality Narrative. Emanating from increasingly diverse ideologies, pedagogies, and sciences, ideas about what constitutes quality for young children are taking diverse shapes. For some, group size, staff-to-child ratios, and teacher preparation continue to frame quality gold standards. Others feel these need to be accompanied by additional elements of structural quality augmented with a heavy dose of process quality variables (Bowman, Donovan, & Burns, 2011). Still others—the postmodernists—contend that such variables require malleability and defy any universal definition that is applicable to all; rather, they argue, quality is constructed within time and place, privileging variation (Dahlberg, Moss, & Pence, 1999; Myers, 2006). These diametrically opposed views of quality—one constant, definable, and measurable and the other contextually driven, fluid, and malleable—beg for reconciliation as increasingly varied early childhood efforts take hold. Beyond that, however, all quality narratives must be constructed to accommodate the needs of diverse children, with diverse abilities, who speak diverse languages. Indeed, the perennially difficult task of defining quality has been reframed in the existing narrative as a challenge to define *multiple* ideas about, and conceptions of, quality(ies).

Equal Access to Services Narrative. In recent years, children's rights have escalated to prominence through the international human rights and early childhood agendas. Although an obligation-rights narrative has long prevailed in a few countries globally, the equal services narrative is being positioned front and center on the global stage, with the Sustainable Development Goals enunciated by the United Nations now addressing the need to provide services for all young children. This reconstructed narrative calls on nations to serve all children—regardless of religion, race, ethnicity, family economic conditions, language spoken, or legal status—all the time. It demands the expansion of services numerically, a movement that is gaining speed worldwide.

Emerging Narratives: Looking Forward

This volume suggests that, intentionally or not, narratives play a key role in shaping how we think about and enact early childhood programs, services, and policies. Three historic rationales and five existing narratives conspire to create the current ECEC zeitgeist. Important to acknowledge and understand, they form the base from which contemporary and future ECEC narratives will emerge. The country stories in this volume, however, reveal that entirely new ECEC narratives are taking shape, ones that are grounded in the past, responsive to the present, and prescient for the future. They capitalize on early childhood's contemporary political momentum and the new sciences informing it, while fully acknowledging that the unit for change is not only the settings where children are present (e.g., family child care homes, early childhood classrooms/programs), but the institutional structures and infrastructure elements that encase the services. Moreover, these emerging narratives seek to honor two inescapable and often overlooked realities that characterize what early childhood is and always will be: (a) inherently multidisciplinary in orientation; and (b) composed of a complex set of loosely configured delivery mechanisms. Emerging narratives transcend classrooms and pedagogy to incorporate systems thinking. In so doing, they reset the focus, embrace beyond-the-cusp thinking, and provide a platform to design ECEC for the future.

Any emerging narrative demands contextualization in contemporary realities and, as Salovey admonished, requires bringing judiciously curated knowledge and fresh perspectives to bear on conventional or commonly accepted "truths." This volume aims to do just that. It adopts a fresh approach to empirical work, one that engages leading scholars as they critically examine early childhood practices, policies, and systems in six diverse countries around the world. Unique in approach, the analysis:

1. adopts a systems approach to considerations of ECEC services, drawing on a range of new sciences;
2. examines services across numerous sectors and across the 0–8 age range;
3. accords heavy emphasis to the critical role of culture in shaping personal and societal values, and the nature and quality of services afforded to young children; and
4. employs a comprehensive methodology that augments descriptive statistics with in-depth document reviews, high-profile policy interviews, and validity analyses.

In short, it is a new approach that yields a reformulated narrative, appropriate for its time and place.

As noted earlier, this volume tells the stories of six countries/jurisdictions that have made considerable innovative commitments to young children and their families. Through this process, new narratives emerge. We will see, for example, how each country's approaches and commitments to young children mirror their unique contexts. This volume will unveil the gnawing persistence of the quality, equity, efficiency, and sustainability challenges and will delineate how these countries have triumphed in their distinct efforts to address them. In so doing, this comparative analysis will traverse the globe as it investigates the inherent realities (including its multidisciplinary focus and its complex delivery mechanisms) that shape all ECEC policy and practice. In the end, it will blend successful experiences and theory to unveil and explicate new and emerging narratives. This entire story is intended to serve leaders across the globe, and especially in the United States, as they seek to improve services to young children and their families by constructing, and then implementing, new narratives.

PREPARING FOR EMERGING NARRATIVES:
THE FRAMING ARCHITECTURE

That emerging narratives must necessarily be grounded in systems work is well understood (Bruner, Stover-Wright, Gebhard, & Hibbard, 2004; Gallagher, Clifford, & Maxwell, 2004; Goffin, Martella, & Coffman, 2011; Kagan & Cohen, 1996; Sugarman, 1991; Vargas-Barón, 2013), as it is clear that no one program or intervention can be a proxy for ECEC. No single approach to pedagogy can begin to explicate the complicated and fascinating panoply of policies that converge to create services for young children. And no single country or jurisdiction has a monopoly on the singular right way to construct ECEC systems. In that sense, the orientation of this analysis is postmodernist; it accepts multiple constructs of the emerging system and multiple approaches to its achievement.

This makes studying and deeply understanding ECEC difficult. It is challenging structurally, because most countries do not consolidate all their comprehensive early development services in a single ministry or at a single level of government. It is challenging from a temporal perspective, because ECEC policies can emerge during one year or under one political regime, often to disappear with the next. It is challenging fiscally, because countries use different approaches (both market and non-market) to fund their efforts. And finally, it is challenging ideologically, because country rationales for services vary dramatically, as do the values that surround service delivery. With ECEC not yet deemed a right in most countries, inconsistent and sporadic practices and policies are gamed on ideological playgrounds amidst changing rules, funds, and governance structures. To make sense of ECEC systems across six distinct jurisdictions, to render thoughtful and consistent analysis, and to evoke new narratives, the study that undergirds this volume understood that conceptual or analytic frameworks were necessary, as was framing research questions. Explicated below, these set the context for the individual country chapters that follow.

Conceptual Framework

A number of conceptual frameworks, building blocks, organizational theories, and explanatory tools are available to ease the challenge of untangling complex, highly interactive systems. The National Center on Education and the Economy, the sponsor of this work, has proffered the helpful *9 Building Blocks for a World-Class State Education System* (Tucker, 2016). The World Bank's *Systems Approach for Better Education Results* (SABER) and its early childhood iteration, SABER-ECE (Neuman & Devercelli, 2013), are particularly helpful. These and other frameworks underscore the salience of systems thinking, including the importance of policy goals and levers, human variables (e.g., leadership, professional development), and accountability factors (e.g., standards, data, compliance).

Considering the holistic nature of early development, the modal lack of consistent and durable ECEC policies, and the need for systems analyses, the country stories that comprise this volume build on prior conceptual grounding (Kagan & Gomez, 2015; Kagan, Araujo, Jaimovich, & Aguayo, 2016). The framework laid out in Figure 1.1 provisionally suggests that positive child and family well-being (F) are predicated on systemic (high-quality, equitably distributed, sustainable, and efficient services) (D) and family supports (E), which are achieved only in the presence of an effective system (C). Such a system is based on a clearly delineated infrastructure (B) that supports diverse programs (A), sometimes linked by boundary-spanning mechanisms (BSMs) that integrate programs and services across ministerial boundaries. All malleable, these factors are encased in both temporal (political, economic, environmental) (G) and sociocultural (values, beliefs, heritages, religions) contexts (H).

Research Questions

Using the framework above, this analysis addressed three sets of research questions that describe, compare, and analyze ECEC systems. The first set, largely descriptive in nature, sought to discern *what* understandings about each country's ECEC system actually exist, as well as the current status of the ECEC system. Comparative in nature, the second set of research questions sought to understand *how* differences in ECEC systems have evolved, are structured, and produce their intended outcomes. The final, analytic set sought to explain or conjecture *why* the systems have evolved and function as they do. All of the research questions, a sample of which are included

Figure 1.1. Theory of Change

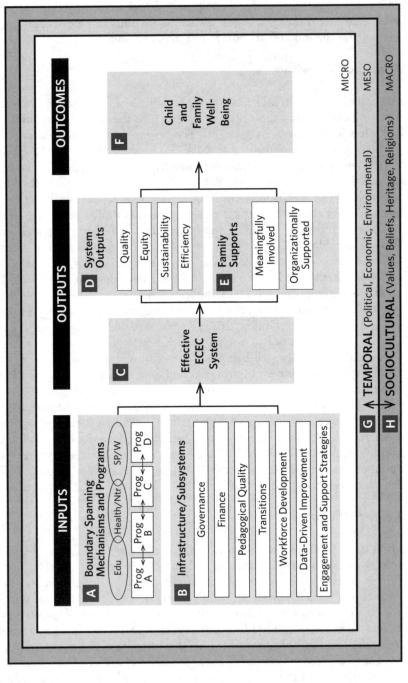

below, were designed to understand the nature and contributions of ECEC systems to high-quality, equitably districted, sustainable, and efficient service provision (Kagan, 2017).

Descriptive Questions—The What. What does the country perceive its commitment to young children to be, and what contextual variables evoked this stance? What are the major CED policies, frameworks, programs, and services in place (e.g., parental leave, perinatal services, home visiting, child care, preschool, transition, health and mental health services, and services for developmentally and economically at-risk children)?

Comparative Questions—The How. How does the country value or "hold" young children, and how do these values frame policies and practices? How do country policies vary over time as a result of changes in economic, political, and governmental (centralized/decentralized) conditions and structures? How do these changes affect patterns of implementation and the evolution of the ECEC system?

Explanatory Questions—The Why. Why does an evolving ECEC system reflect durable country values and more transient country economics and politics? Why, and under what conditions, do ECEC systems evolve? Can, and under what conditions can, the contemporary support for young children be mobilized to yield greater effectiveness in quality, equitable distribution, sustainability, and efficiency?

UNDERSTANDING EMERGING NARRATIVES: GUIDING METHODOLOGY

Armed with the conceptual framework and research questions presented above, the challenge of collecting richly informative data across multiple countries needed to be addressed so as to evoke reliable and valid work. This section outlines the process of selecting the participating countries, followed by a presentation of the study methodology that guided all authors.

Country Selection

Two diverse constructs guided the jurisdictional selection: (a) PISA performance rankings for mathematics and/or (b) ECEC performance rankings for quality. More specifically, this study divided the top 30 PISA 2012 countries into three groups (high, 1–10; medium, 11–20; and lower, 21–30), ranked according to their mathematics results (OECD, 2012). To discern the quality of ECEC programs, the study used composite scores from the 2012 Economist Intelligence Unit report "Starting Well," which examined

Table 1.1. Country Rankings Typology

	PISA High	PISA Medium	PISA Lower
Economist high	Netherlands	Finland	Denmark
	Republic of Korea	Belgium	New Zealand
			Norway
			UK—England
			France
Economist medium	Hong Kong	Germany	Czech Republic
	Switzerland	Austria	
Economist lower	Japan	Canada	
	Singapore	Australia	
	Taiwan		

four criteria of ECEC systems: (i) social context; (ii) availability; (iii) afford-ability; and (iv) quality. The top 30 countries from this report were then divided into the same three groups (high, 1–10; medium, 11–20; and lower, 21–30). Ultimately, the constructs and each of their three categories were cross-mapped to form nine cells, in which overlapping countries were listed (Table 1.1).

Given these different performance profiles, and given that only five to six countries could be involved in this study due to fiscal and temporal constraints, one country from each cell of the three PISA high-performing countries and one country from each of the three Economist high-perform-ing countries was selected. Using these criteria, five jurisdictions that were high-performing, either on the PISA or the Economist ECEC rankings, but not necessarily on both, were selected: the Republic of Korea, Hong Kong, Singapore, Finland, and the UK (ultimately, this was narrowed to England, the largest country in the UK). One additional country, Australia, was add-ed for three reasons: first, it represented a totally different profile (medium PISA and low Economist rankings); second, it demonstrates unprecedented quality work; and third, its mixed market and highly differentiated state approaches to early childhood remarkably parallel the United States.

Data Sources

Following country selection, the quest for relevant data was guided by the conceptual framework and the research questions presented previously. Three sources of data were reviewed to discern elements and/or variables that might contribute to the evolution of emerging narratives: cross-coun-try systems analyses, country-specific documents and policies, and key

respondent interviews. Taken together, these sources constitute the most recent comparative data on ECEC systems available.

Cross-Country Systems Studies. A literature review of multicountry systems analyses was undertaken to identify key lessons and unanswered di-
lemmas. Gleaning lessons from 16 research studies, most of which were
conducted after 2010 and which together represent all regions of the world,
the review of the literature helped procure information that pertained to
one or more elements of the infrastructure. Subsequently compiled into a
compendium (Neuman, Roth, & Kagan, in press), the review contributed
to both the individual country analyses and to coalescing the scholarship on
comparative ECEC policy more generally. Specifically, as the first attempt
to collate and synthesize global ECEC research using a systems lens, it provided rich information on diverse analytic methodologies, tools, and results.
Data from this review helped to refine the provisional research questions
and the methodological approach to this study.

Country-Specific Documents. To obtain a detailed overview of the evolution and contemporary status of ECEC in each country, numerous sources
were reviewed, including government and policy documents and legislation,
published reports, media coverage, ECEC frameworks and curricula, and
empirical research conducted in or about each country's ECEC services and
systems. Additionally, while many of the documents were well known, in
order to capture failed and visionary efforts, additional unpublished litera-
tures were also reviewed.

Key Respondent Interviews. In order to garner the most recent information
regarding the status of the ECEC system in each country, a series of key respondent interviews was conducted. The sample selection of interviewees was
guided by a commitment to including diverse voices so that even a comparatively small sample could deliberately capture contrasting perspectives and,
in some cases, disconfirming evidence. For all countries, the sampling frame
included individuals from the government and representative governmental
bodies, the private sector, and the academic community. In most countries,
senior ministry personnel were interviewed, as were representatives from the
ECEC community and individuals from more marginalized communities. In
each country, between 12 and 27 interviews were conducted in total, all in
accord with a common protocol. Taken together, the interviews provided diverse perspectives on ECEC history, policies, services, trends, and challenges.

Data Collection, Analysis, and Validation

Data Collection. As outlined above, document review preceded the
key respondent interviews and served as the basis for the development of

interview protocols. Each document was reviewed for its salience to the research questions, with all key data summarized. Roughly hour-long respondent interviews were then collected over a 3- to 6-month period. In all cases, notes were taken during interviews. Two verification strategies were used: multiple interviewees compared their notes to avoid misinterpretations and/or respondents were provided with summaries for validation.

Data Analysis. With the goal of producing an accurate and revealing story, a systematic process was used to analyze the data. Since the data are both quantitative and qualitative in nature, the country teams used different strategies to analyze each dataset and then integrate the key lessons. The quantitative data were reported as they were extracted from primary sources; all quantitative data are attributed. The qualitative data were summarized into field notes, which were then reviewed for policy and practice trends and concrete examples. Data were integrated to discern key convergent and divergent themes that were expanded as the analysis was written. Primary source documents were regularly consulted as the chapters were written.

Validation. The creation of new narratives means that new ideas and facts are being assembled and considered. There is, then, an obligation to verify the information. Further, because the authors whose work is presented herein are all committed to the highest standard of research, each chapter was validated at several points in its evolution. First, the international team, consisting of lead investigators from each of the six jurisdictions and the study's principal investigator, co-developed the data collection instruments. Second, categories of interview respondents were reviewed and confirmed by the international team with the goal of fostering a breadth of diverse, yet informed, interviewees. Agreed upon by the full team, the interviewee categories were then content-validated. Third, the final draft of each of the case studies was subjected to an internal review by knowledgeable ECEC country experts who were not affiliated with the study. Finally, the study was reviewed by external experts from the staff and board of the National Center on Education and the Economy.

CONSTRUCTING EMERGING NARRATIVES:
AMALGAMATING THE LESSONS

Any undertaking as complex and ambitious as the construction of new narratives is laden with limitations and challenges. In the spirit of transparency, three limitations are presented below, followed by a discussion of the value of analytically driven new narratives.

Limitations

Three limitations characterize this work. First, ECEC systems throughout the world are in a state of flux. Over the 2-year course of the study, each country faced profound changes in its ECEC system. Discussed individually in the forthcoming chapters, these changes differ by country, with some being quite modest and others revolutionary; impact must be considered by looking at both the nature and magnitude of the change itself as well as the country predispositions and readiness for such change. Whatever the case, the stories that follow present useful insights on change, but they may not reflect policy or practice reforms that have been implemented since the study concluded in late 2017. This suggests that this analysis, although broadly reflective of the overall countries, presents a snapshot in time, which must be understood within the dynamic contextual realities that encase ECEC systems.

Second, as is the case for any qualitative research, the positionality of the investigators influences the interpretation of the data. Although efforts have been made to validate the accuracy of the information provided, some of the content of the stories told herein is subject to the interpretation of the lead investigator and team, most of whom are research scholars. Such positionality is somewhat mitigated by the reality that the authors have conducted previous cross-national work and by the fact that numerous international and external reviewers have examined the content of this study.

Finally, this study is based on a conceptual framework that specifies the outputs of systemic work in four areas: quality, equitable distribution, sustainability, and efficiency of services. The efficacy of the systems is, therefore, predicated on achievements in these outputs. Unlike many other ECEC studies, this one cannot and does not make any attributional claims or suggest correlations with, much less causality for, specific *child* outcomes, either in the short or long term. In this analysis, however, the four areas are conjectured to be both an output of the system and, along with families, an input to child outcomes. Although this lack of direct focus on child outcomes may be regarded as a limitation of the study, the authors regard the work as groundbreaking in that it contributes to discerning key systemic variables that foster quality, which in turn directly relates to child outcomes.

The Value of Emerging Narratives

To return to Salovey's welcoming remarks to the class of 2020, the construction of new narratives is as inevitable as it is wise. Forward-looking country leaders avoid the complacency associated with an overreliance on the past, but recognize history's critical role in informing both the present and the future. History, like past narratives, constitutes the bedrock for future—hopefully more nuanced and germane—narratives.

But only in part. Reconstructing history is not an effort in exorcising past demonic values or in blithely acquiescing to new knowledge; rather, the construction of new narratives, when done well, demands rigorous thought, careful curation, and judicious analysis. It is in that spirit that this study, and these country stories, are being told. Each country's chapter represents a new narrative, a new way to understand ECEC systems and a new way to interpret future trajectories for young children. No one narrative fits all the countries; no one narrative trumps others. Collectively, they demonstrate that in leading countries around the world, ECEC is being conceptualized in ways that transcend past narratives, and in ways that lead to a broader vision for the field. ECEC is more than an individual program, a loose set of services, or errant policies or erstwhile classroom practices. In the following pages, the new narratives, told with different voices, all reflect the value of fresh, empirically driven thinking that expands conceptions and beckons reinterpretation of what ECEC is and what it should be. Inherent in this discourse is some 20/20 thinking; it reflects a future vision of what ECEC can be if it is to fulfill the promises it claims. To that end, it humbly proffers and hopefully inspires new narratives.

REFERENCES

Barnett, W. S. (1995). Long-term effects of early childhood programs on cognitive and school outcomes. *The Future of Children, 5*(3), 25–50.

Bowman, B. T., Donovan, M. S., & Burns, M. S. (Eds.). (2001). *Eager to learn: Educating our preschoolers.* Washington, DC: National Academy Press.

Bruner, C., Stover-Wright, M. S., Gebhard, B., & Hibbard, S. (2004). *Building an early learning system: The ABCs of planning and governance structures.* Des Moines, IA: State Early Childhood Policy Technical Assistance Network, Child & Family Policy Center.

Cahan, E. (1989). *Past caring: A history of U.S. preschool care and education for the poor, 1820–1965.* New York, NY: National Center for Children in Poverty.

Dahlberg, G., Moss, P., & Pence, A. (1999). *Beyond quality in early childhood education and care: Postmodern perspectives.* Philadelphia, PA: Falmer Press, Taylor & Francis. Retrieved from files.eric.ed.gov/fulltext/ED433943.pdf

Economist Intelligence Unit. (2012). Starting well: Benchmarking early education across the world. Retrieved from graphics.eiu.com/upload/eb/lienstartingwell.pdf

Gallagher, J. J., Clifford, R. M., & Maxwell, K. (2004). Getting from here to there: To an ideal early preschool system. *Early Childhood Research and Practice, 6*(1).

Goffin, S. G., Martella, J., & Coffman, J. (2011). *Vision to practice: Setting a new course for early childhood governance.* Washington, DC: Goffin Strategy Group.

Grubb, W. N., & Lazerson, M. (1982). *Broken promises: How Americans fail their children.* New York, NY: Basic Books.

Heckman, J. J. (2006). Skill formation and the economics of investing in disadvantaged children. *Science, 312,* 1900–1902.

Joachim, A., & May, J. R. (2010). Beyond subsystems: Policy regimes and governance. *Policy Studies Journal, 38*(2), 303–327.

Kagan, S. L. (2017). Proposal to the National Center for Education and the Economy. The National Center for Children and Families, Teachers College, New York, NY.

Kagan, S. L., Araujo, M. C., Jaimovich, A., & Aguayo, Y. C. (2016). Understanding systems theory and thinking: Early childhood education in Latin America and the Caribbean. In A. Farrell, S. L. Kagan, & E. K. M. Tisdall (Eds.), *The SAGE handbook of early childhood research* (pp. 163–184). London, England: SAGE.

Kagan, S. L., & Cohen, N. E. (Eds.). (1996). *Reinventing early care and education: A vision for a quality system.* San Francisco, CA: Jossey-Bass.

Kagan, S. L., & Gomex, R. E. (Eds.). (2015). *Early childhood governance: Choices and consequences.* New York, NY: Teachers College Press.

Kamerman, S. B., & Kahn, A. J. (2001). Child and family policies in an era of social policy retrenchment and restructuring. In K. Vleminckx & T. M. Smeeding (Eds.), *Child well-being, child poverty and child policy in modern nations: What do we know* (pp. 501–525). Chicago, IL: University of Chicago Press.

Lindblom, C. E., & Cohen, D. K. (1979). *Usable knowledge: Social science and social problem solving.* New Haven, CT: Yale University Press.

Marope, P. T. M., & Kaga, Y. (2015). *Investing against evidence: The global state of early childhood care and education.* Paris, France: UNESCO.

Myers, R. G. (2006). *Quality in program of early childhood care and education (ECCE).* Paris, France: UNESCO.

Neuman, M. J., & Devercelli, A. E. (2013). *What matters most for early childhood development: A framework paper.* Systems Approach for Better Education Results (SABER) Working Paper No. 5. Washington, DC: World Bank.

Neuman, M. J., Roth, J., & Kagan, S. L. (in press). A compendium of international early childhood systems research.

Nisbett, R. E. (2003). *The geography of thought: How Asians and Westerners think differently . . . and why.* New York, NY: Free Press.

Nores, M., & Barnett, W. S. (2015). Investment and productivity arguments for ECCE. In P. T. M. Marope & Y. Kaga (Eds.), *Investing against evidence: The global state of early childhood care and education* (pp. 53–90). Paris, France: UNESCO.

Organisation for Economic Co-operation and Development. (2000). Early childhood education and care policy in Finland. *Background report prepared for the OECD thematic review for early childhood education and care policy.* Retrieved from oecd.org/finland/2476019.pdf

Organisation for Economic Co-operation and Development. (2001). *Starting strong: Early childhood education and care.* Paris, France: Author.

Organisation for Economic Co-operation and Development. (2006). *Starting strong II: Early childhood education and care.* Paris, France: Author.

Organisation for Economic Co-operation and Development. (2012). *PISA 2012 results in focus.* Paris, France: Author.

Reynolds, A. J., & Temple, J. A. (2008). Cost-effective early childhood development programs from preschool to third grade. *Annual Review of Clinical Psychology, 4*, 109–139.

Rogoff, B. (2003). *The cultural nature of human development*. New York, NY: Oxford University Press

Salovey, P. (2016). Countering false narratives [freshman address]. New Haven, CT: Yale University. Retrieved from president.yale.edu/speeches-writings/speeches/countering-false-narratives

Shonkoff, J. (2010). Building a new biodevelopmental framework to guide the future of early childhood policy. *Child Development, 81*(1), 357–367.

Shonkoff, J., & Phillips, D. (2000). *From neurons to neighborhoods: The science of early childhood development*. Washington, DC: National Academies Press.

Sugarman, J. (1991). *Building early childhood systems*. Washington, DC: Child Welfare League of America.

Tucker, M. (2016). *9 building blocks for a world-class education system*. Washington, DC: National Center on Education and the Economy.

UN General Assembly. (2015). *Transforming our world: The 2030 agenda for sustainable development*. New York, NY: United Nations.

UNESCO. (2006). *Strong foundations: Early childhood care and education* [EFA Global Monitoring Report, 2007]. Paris, France: Author.

Urban, M., Vandenbroeck, M., Van Laere, K., Lazzari, A., & Peeters, J. (2012). Towards competent systems in early childhood education and care: Implications for policy and practice. *European Journal of Education, 47*(4), 508–526.

Vargas-Barón, E. (2013). Building and strengthening national systems for early childhood development. In P. Britto, P. Engle, & C. Super (Eds.), *Handbook of early childhood development research and its impact on global policy* (pp. 443–466). Oxford, England: Oxford University Press.

CHAPTER 2

Maintaining the Reform Momentum in Australia

Collette Tayler, Tom Peachey, and Bridget Healey

The large and magnificent country of Australia offers a revealing story of enormous growth, enhanced by rich population diversity. It simultaneously exposes both cautionary tales and exemplary models for those interested in early childhood care and education (ECEC).

HISTORY, VALUES, AND VISION

Diversity characterizes the Australian landscape, with the Aboriginal and Torres Strait Islander people—Australia's original inhabitants and the traditional owners of its land and waters—having established roots on the continent over 50,000 years ago. Joined by successive waves of immigration that began with the British in the late 18th century, Australia now boasts immigrants from over 200 countries, with approximately 28% of the total population born outside Australia (Australian Bureau of Statistics [ABS], 2017a). Together, the experiences of the Indigenous and immigrant populations have framed the nation's values, albeit in different ways and at different times.

The immigrant experience ushered in many of Australia's posited values of trust in and appreciation for diversity. Australians aspire to live an egalitarian way of life, focusing on "a fair go" and placing significant value on individual freedoms. Indeed, the Commonwealth of Australia, formed in 1901, memorialized these values through the Australian Constitution by prioritizing democracy and freedom of religion as bedrock principles. Not fully representing the experience of Indigenous peoples, however, these values have been more recently accompanied by a growing understanding of social injustices and inequities. Consequently, value commitments to more authentically egalitarian rights are being manifest in rhetoric and policies

For factual details on early childhood in Australia, see Appendix A

that honor the heritage and culture of Indigenous populations, so that the "fair go" value has a better chance of becoming a reality for all.

The Constitution distributes power between the Commonwealth Government (referred to as the "Australian Government") and the six state governments and two main territories (the Northern Territory and the Australian Capital Territory). Considerable authority is assured to the states and territories, which hold the power to make their own laws over matters not controlled by the Australian Government under the Constitution. The Constitution grants most revenue-raising power to the Australian Government, however, which provides it a lever with which to influence state/territory policy in areas including ECEC. Moreover, even a century after federation, the assertion of states' rights continues to be a theme in Commonwealth–state relations.

Given Australia's egalitarian values, it is not surprising that the Australian Government is committed to the well-being of its citizenry; given its structural divide, it is also not surprising that primary human service responsibilities are distributed between the Commonwealth and the states/territories. For example, the Australian Government, in addition to having responsibility for defense, immigration, foreign affairs, trade, postal services, and taxation, has broad national powers in welfare, health, and employment policies and provisions. These welfare and social programs have a long history, expanding in the early 1970s to include the establishment of Australia's universal health care system and the provision of national funding for child care through the Australian Child Care Act of 1972. Meanwhile, the states and territories play a major role in designing and delivering early childhood education services, such as pre-primary and preschool programs. To promote policy collaboration between the Commonwealth and states/territories, the Council of Australian Governments (COAG) was established in 1992 and addresses matters such as ECEC policy reform. A series of COAG-brokered national agreements identifies roles and responsibilities and facilitates Australian Government funding to the states/territories, which in turn deliver services in key sectors.

Despite efforts to resolve ambiguities in federal roles, the Commonwealth-state/territory division foreshadows an enduring split in ECEC provision between child care and education. Moreover, it illustrates the transcendent influence of the Australian political, social, geographic, and economic context on the evolution of services for young children. Stated differently, Australian ECEC does not stand alone; like a mirror, it reflects both inherent geographic conditions and the broader social pulse. With regard to geography, Australia—with its estimated population of 24 million (ABS, 2016) spread across a vast continent—has low population density on average (ABS, 2017b). Furthermore, the population is unevenly dispersed, with 89% of the population living in urban areas concentrated on the coastlines (World Bank, 2017). Meanwhile, a declining population in rural and remote

Australia is beset by higher-than-average levels of unemployment, poverty, and disadvantage. This places additional pressure on educational and social services in a context where distance and delivery already make access difficult. The divide between remote/rural and urban Australia creates equity challenges in a range of policy contexts.

The sociopolitical and economic contexts have also heavily influenced the evolution of Australian ECEC. In the 1970s, under the aegis of a socially activist federal government, Australia saw notable increases in public social service expenditure, which were fueled in part by a desire to uphold the rights of women and Indigenous Australians. Short-lived, this era of expansion gave rise to concerns over government spending and government's role in social programs, leading successive governments from the 1990s on to pursue the marketization and privatization of social services. Within ECEC, child care expanded, abetted by burgeoning investments by the private, for-profit sector. This, in turn, has generated considerable debate about the appropriate level of governmental regulation needed for the increasingly privatized sector.

Shifts in economic policies, like the press toward privatization, are often accompanied by shifts in social trends. Two major social shifts precipitated significant growth of Australian ECEC. First, in the 2000s, the country became increasingly concerned about future workforce productivity and thus began a series of reforms concerning human capital development. This was manifest in the implementation of the National Reform Agenda (2007), which focused on educational and economic participation and productivity. Early childhood development was one of the four targeted areas of education, thereby fostering a renewed interest in, and a period of considerable change for, Australian ECEC.

Second, Australian ECEC was given a boost as social interest in young children's development (particularly that of more vulnerable children) took hold. Irrefutable data regarding the potency of ECEC as an elixir of both positive individual gains for children and vast societal savings fueled interest in investment. Moreover, the advent of Labor governments at the Commonwealth, state, and territory levels and the surge in for-profit provision solidified interest in both ECEC accessibility and quality enhancements.

To help address these concerns, Australian governments, through COAG, agreed to a partnership to establish a National Quality Framework for Early Childhood Education and Care (National Quality Framework, or NQF) in 2009. Intended to streamline regulations and improve the quality and consistency of ECEC services throughout the country, the NQF not only replaced diverse state and territory licensing and quality assurance processes, but also assured that a common regulatory framework would adhere across both child care (e.g., long day care, family day care, and outside school hours care) and education (e.g., preschool programs). Furthermore, the NQF adopted the first national "early learning" framework and, through the National Quality Standard, set national benchmarks for ECEC services. The national ECEC vision laid out by the NQF thus reflects the country's deeply embedded values, holding the rights and best interests of all children as paramount. It also underscores that: (a) children are successful, competent, and capable learners; (b) equity, inclusion, and diversity underpin ECEC; (c) Australia's Indigenous cultures are valued; (d) the role of parents and families is respected and supported; and (e) best practice is expected in the provision of ECEC services.

Though remarkable in scope and application, the NQF sits upon historically embedded structures that distinguish between care and education. Characterized by distinct planning and different organizational bodies, funding formulae, service expectations, and staff wages and industrial conditions, these entrenched structures continue to perpetuate the split in Australian ECEC between child care and education.

SERVICES PROVIDED

Health Services

Predicated on its commitment to citizen well-being, Australia has high-quality and universally available primary and hospital health care, which are publicly funded via Medicare. Covering all Australians, Medicare funds free or subsidized treatment by health professionals (e.g., doctors, specialists, optometrists), as well as hospital treatment. Usage of and satisfaction with Australian health care is high (Steering Committee for the Review of Government Service Provision [SCRGSP], 2017), although rurality and population dispersal complicate service delivery and have given rise to telehealth services that aim to provide Australians with access to 24-hour health-related telephone or videoconference advice and symptom triage (St. George, Cullen, Gardiner, & Karabatsos, 2008). Notably, the Australian Government also funds the Indigenous Australians' Health Program, supporting 140 Aboriginal community-controlled organizations, mainly in rural and remote areas, to provide health services.

With regard to supports for pregnant and new mothers and their partners, health screening for pregnant women is provided based on the *Australian Antenatal Guidelines* (Australian Health Ministers' Advisory Council [AHMAC], 2012) and is widely used. Almost all women (99.9%) who gave birth in 2014 had at least one prenatal visit, 87% had seven or more visits, and 57% had 10 or more visits. Women living in very remote and low-socioeconomic-status areas were marginally less likely to attend five or more prenatal visits. Indigenous women were less likely to attend a prenatal visit in the first trimester or to attend five or more visits. However, the proportion of Indigenous mothers attending an antenatal visit in the first trimester has been increasing in recent years (Australian Institute of Health and Welfare [AIHW], 2016a). Prenatal parenting education resources and supports such as birthing or early parenting classes are also provided. Moreover, guided by the *National Framework for Universal Child and Family Health Services,* screenings for developmental milestones and early identification of children with special needs and maternal health checks are routinely provided. Australia also has universal neonatal hearing screening, providing free screenings to all newborns to ensure early detection and intervention for hearing loss. Notably, Victoria's universal Maternal and Child Health program provides 10 free nursing consultations from birth to age 3.5 on maternal and infant health, as well as child learning and development.

Parental leave is an important component of comprehensive family policies. In 2011, Australia introduced government-funded paid parental leave of 18 weeks for eligible employees who are primary caregivers of children and two weeks for eligible partners (including same-sex partners). Payments are in line with the national minimum wage and are made directly to the employee. Eligibility for the payments requires that the recipient has worked 10 of the past 13 months, with income of up to $117,554 (AUD $150,000) in the previous financial year. In addition, all employees are entitled to 12 months of unpaid parental leave providing they have worked for their employer for at least 12 months (Department of Social Services [DSS], 2017).

Almost all births in Australia (98%) occur in conventional hospital labor wards (AIHW, 2016a). Early breastfeeding is prevalent, with exclusive breastfeeding initiated for 90% of babies. This tapers off, however, as only 39% of infants are exclusively breastfed to 4 months, and 15% to around 6 months. Indigenous babies are half as likely to be exclusively breastfed to around 4 months as non-Indigenous babies (AIHW, 2011). Inoculation rates are also quite high. Overall, 93.4% of 1-year-olds and 91.4% of 2-year-olds were fully immunized in 2016, with slightly lower rates for Indigenous children (91% and 89%, respectively) (Department of Health, 2017).

Australia's health and well-being services are overseen by different levels of government and provided through a range of organizing frameworks. The Australian Government leads primary health services policy and the provision of subsidies. Primary health care is provided through a regulated market in which health practitioners set up medical and allied health practices in their communities. The states and territories license private hospitals (typically serving patients with medical insurance, who are thus ensured their own choice of medical practitioner/specialist) and operate public hospitals (where those same medical practitioners/specialists also provide services). States and territories also oversee services for vulnerable children and families. Support services, such as Joint Investigation Response teams (consisting of community service and health service practitioners), mental health therapeutic interventions, sexual abuse counseling, and specialist support to families or caregivers where ongoing intervention is required, are generally provided by nongovernmental organizations.

Child Protection Services

Child protection services are designed for children and young people aged 0–17 years who are at risk of abuse and neglect, or whose families do not have the capacity to protect them. Statutory child protection services are the responsibility of state and territory governments. Services include investigation, intervention when it is in the best interest of the child (according to state/territory legislation), and monitoring of care and protection orders.

Two additional types of services exist. *Intensive family support services* aim to prevent the imminent separation of children from their family due to child protection concerns, and to reunify families where separation has already occurred. Such services often include mental health supports, particularly due to increasing recognition of the impact of infant mental health on subsequent development. A second kind of care, *out-of-home care*, provides short-, medium-, or long-term care for children away from their parents or home, for reasons of safety or family crisis. In 2014–2015, some 11,600 children entered out-of-home care and over 11,100 children were discharged (AIHW, 2016b). Subsidized by the government through payments to providers or caregivers, out-of-home care is regarded as a necessary element in a repertoire of protective services.

In 2014–2015, approximately 152,000 children received child protection services, with Indigenous children overrepresented compared to non-Indigenous children. Rates of entry to child protection continue to grow, with the number of children known to protective services expanding. There is pressure on available services to meet individual needs and demand for support.

Care and Education Services

Despite continued accessibility challenges, participation in care and education services has risen in recent years, with children aged 3–5 enrolled at proportionately higher rates than their younger counterparts. Notably, there is rising interest in the universal provision of preschool education for both 3- and 4-year-old children. Further, there is growing recognition of successful efforts to link services that are run under different auspices, largely as a result of the NQF and its allied regulatory and pedagogical requirements. Despite these advances, however, immense geographic and economic variation means that these ECEC services, like the population itself, are not evenly distributed.

ECEC programs vary in their structure and funding patterns based on the historical schism between education (e.g., preschool) and care (e.g., long day care, family day care, outside school hours care), despite being united under the Education and Care Services National Law. Complicating matters, a wide array of care and education services are available for young children that take quite different forms and are carried out in different kinds of settings. Additionally, special services are made available for remote areas and/or areas where ECEC market gaps are greatest. Each form of ECEC is discussed in the following subsections.

Center-Based ECEC Services. Center-based services are the most common in Australia, accounting for 93% of the sector in 2016, and include long day care, occasional care, and preschool programs (Australian Children's Education and Care Quality Authority [ACECQA], 2016). *Long day care* (LDC) services provide regular care and education for children from birth to school age, and can include before- and after-school care. LDCs must be open for at least 8 hours a day, Monday to Friday, for a minimum of 48 weeks each year (Department of Education, 2012). They are part of the NQF and must use the Early Years Learning Framework (EYLF) or an equivalent state/territory learning framework and have a qualified teacher.

Occasional care settings provide child care on a casual basis (i.e., when a family does not need regular care but needs services that are flexible, seasonal, or of limited duration). The National Occasional Care Program is not part of the NQF. Funding for these services (which do not meet eligibility requirements for regular child care subsidies) is provided through a capped program, with limited funded places available (Department of Education, 2012).

Preschool is offered for 4-year-olds (i.e., children in the year before entry to school), and is universally available for 15 hours per week, or 600 hours across the year. Attendance is not mandatory, and while parents are charged (usually small) fees, participation is very high (>95%). Some states also fund a year of preschool for "at-risk" 3-year-olds (SCRGSP, 2016). Preschool programs are taught by a qualified teacher and may be delivered in LDC centers, schools, or dedicated stand-alone preschool facilities. These stand-alone preschools typically operate for school hours (approximately 9 a.m.–3 p.m.), with children attending the 15-hour (or greater)–per-week program on a sessional basis Monday through Friday. Stand-alone preschools may offer wrap-around care in addition to the preschool program; however, this care is not eligible for government child care subsidies. Like LDCs, preschools must adhere to the NQF and use the EYLF (or equivalent state/territory learning framework).

Family Day Care (FDC) and In-Home Care. FDC is the most common form of home-based care provision, accounting for 7% of the overall ECEC market in 2016. It is delivered by a qualified educator, typically within their own residence, though in limited circumstances it may also be provided in an approved nonresidential venue. FDC is available for children up to age 12, consisting of small groups of four or five (depending on the state/territory) under-school-aged children and two school-aged children. It is regulated under the NQF and is eligible for child care subsidies. There are no restrictions on the overall number of subsidy-eligible child care services or places in FDC. Providers of FDC are called "educators" under the NQF legislation and are organized into local family day care coordination units; the units have trained staff who provide regular support to the educators as they work to meet the requirements of the NQF and implement the EYLF.

In-home care, as distinguished from FDC, operates in circumstances where it would otherwise be difficult for the family to access care (e.g., disability, illness, rurality, or having three or more children under school age). In-home care is not regulated under the NQF, but it is subject to interim standards in anticipation of this occurring.

Outside School Hours Care (OSHC). OSHC services are provided for school-aged children (primarily 5- to 12-year-olds) before and/or after school and during school vacations. OSHC is considered part of the ECEC system, and it is subject to the NQF. Instead of the EYLF, OSHC providers are required to apply the learning framework *My Time Our Place: Framework for School Age Care* (Department of Education, Employment and Workplace Relations [DEEWR], 2011), which contains the same broad child outcomes as the EYLF, customized to school-aged children.

Budget Based Funding (BBF) Services. BBF services are predominantly located in regional, remote, and Indigenous communities where the market would otherwise fail to deliver services to meet the needs of children and their families (Department of Education and Training [DET], 2017). BBF services receive government funding to directly support the operational costs of service provisions, which differs from market-based funding. They generally include a mix of center-based services, long day care, outside-school-hours care, multifunctional Aboriginal children's services, mobile early childhood services, playgroups, and flexible services (e.g., toy libraries, nutrition programs). BBF services are not yet a part of the NQF.

Parenting Education. Parenting education is a minor component of the ECEC landscape, with targeted programs offered in Indigenous and disadvantaged communities. Delivered in playgroup settings (e.g., rooms, playgrounds, or landmarks such as shady trees), parenting education can stand alone or be combined with the ECEC efforts discussed above. In general, parenting education reflects a commitment to family capacity-building as part of a dual-generation approach. Programs include children from birth, and they typically focus on children's emerging literacy and numeracy foundations, leading toward a transition into preschool programs.

Enrollment in ECEC

Several key factors impact enrollment in care and education services. Foremost among these is the age of the child. In 2014, 22% of children under age 2 attended child care settings, with participation rising to 54% for 2- and 3-year-olds, then declining to 42% for 4-year-olds, when some children move to stand-alone preschool settings. When combined with preschool, it is estimated that two-thirds (66%) of 3-year-olds attend some form of ECEC nationally. The percentage of 4-year-old children who are enrolled in ECEC in the year before school is 95.1% (SCRGSP, 2016). Other child and family factors impact enrollment rates as well. For instance, children with disabilities are underrepresented in ECEC. Children who are from families deemed "at risk" are also less likely to be enrolled, while Indigenous children participate at about half the rate of their representation in the community. Extensive government efforts aim to better engage these families. Moreover (and discussed later), the ways in which child care and preschool are governed, financed, and regulated complicate their delivery and often delimit access and quality.

ECEC Services for Aboriginal Families and Communities

Barriers to Aboriginal and Torres Strait Islander ECEC participation are not limited to a lack of available services, but also relate to unmet cultural or support needs of families, remoteness, and/or lack of transport; negative associations with institutions and government services; and lack of culturally competent staff. Aboriginal and Torres Strait Islander families often do not have confidence in the cultural competency of mainstream Australian ECEC services, finding that the generic support available does not offer a holistic educational experience for their children.

Services that are owned and run by Aboriginal communities can develop strong understandings of and relationships with communities. These understandings enable effective and responsive programs that build on community and cultural strengths and deliver better outcomes for children and families. Research suggests that Aboriginal leadership and self-determination: (a) enable services to address community-specific issues; (b) prioritize access for the most disadvantaged members of a community; and (c) through features such as community management, overcome many of the barriers Aboriginal families experience in accessing ECEC. Despite significant challenges in funding, infrastructure, and workforce development, these services continue to be a vital resource for Aboriginal and Torres Strait Islander families across Australia.

GOVERNING AND FUNDING ECEC

Governance

Responsibility for ECEC policies, practices, and funding is split along two dimensions. First, there is a split between the Australian Government and the state/territory governments. Second, and closely aligned with the former, there is a split in how ECEC services are conceptualized and delivered. Services funded at the Australian Government level are primarily seen as part of workforce policy and thus are driven by the desire to assure adequate availability and affordability of child care for working parents. The Australian Government Department of Education and Training leads federal funding and policy for child care and administers subsidies for these services to families. Conversely, ECEC preschool programs, including their organization and availability, are the primary responsibility of the states/territories and are closely aligned with education.

Nonetheless, there is an overarching order to the Australian governance system. COAG provides a forum to promote cooperative action on policy reforms among governments. Comprising representatives from the Australian Government and the states/territories, including education ministers, COAG was established to untangle jurisdictional responsibilities, making them more transparent and consistent. COAG spans issues that pertain to key sectors, serving as a coordinating entity for a series of national partnership agreements. It also works to facilitate Australian Government funding to states and territories.

COAG has established a dedicated Education Council to ensure that integrated Australian education systems seamlessly promote high achievement for all students, from birth to higher education, regardless of circumstances. The COAG Education Council is supported by the Australian Education Senior Officials Committee, which provides policy advice to the council and implements decisions. Because ECEC is fundamentally regarded as a part of education, the COAG Education Council has been heavily involved in efforts to enhance the quality of services for young children. It led the development of the NQF, and it now leads the overall implementation effort, which includes monitoring overseen by the Australian Children's Education and Care Quality Authority (ACECQA). As a result of this cooperation, the NQF has been institutionalized across the Australian and state/territory governments. Importantly, the NQF is likely to be sustained because changes to it must be agreed on by all governments; in this sense, the COAG Education Council provides ballast to an essentially divided ECEC system, one that is increasingly characterized by change and market forces.

Within the COAG Education Council, the Australian Education Senior Officials Committee provides policy advice, some of it advanced by an early childhood policy group. There is some concern that these efforts are hampered by a lack of data and data-sharing among those who seek to coordinate and improve ECEC services. Furthermore, efforts at service integration and collaboration are impeded by diverse financing strategies that render collaboration across service sectors challenging. Because major improvements take a long time to implement, there is concern that the energy expended to develop the NQF will be challenging to maintain. Sustaining momentum to provide more integrated ECEC services and better-linked governance is regarded as a key challenge for the Australian Government and states/territories.

Finance

The continuing split between "care" and "early childhood education" in Australia is further institutionalized by disparate government funding arrangements. The Australian Government allocates public funding for the care component of the ECEC system, and the states and territories provide the majority of public funding for education (preschool) programs. In 2014–2015, approximately 83% of total government funding for ECEC was Australian Government funding for child care, whereas preschool funding (contributed by both the Australian and state/territory governments) constituted approximately 17%.

Key public supply-side funding streams channel dollars directly to the provider. This approach predominates in education, underscored by the principle that supply-side funding is necessary to ensure an educated population and advance the learning of diverse students. As such, it is the primary method of funding universal preschool programs for 4-year-olds. The Australian Government provides a block grant to the states and territories that covers only about 30–35% of the total government funding for preschool; the states and territories, therefore, make up the predominant government funding. Supply-side funding is also used to finance services in areas where they would otherwise be sparse, notably rural and remote areas of the country. Further, supply-side subsidies have been used to support child care providers as they develop property, secure equipment, and procure training for staff.

In contrast, demand-side funding, calculated on a per-child basis, helps families select and access programs from a wide repertoire of services. Demand-side funding is the predominant mode of funding for child care in Australia (about 90%). Because the Commonwealth Government takes the lead on child care, it pays about two-thirds of the cost of approved care, and families pay the residual costs. Most families received subsidies of 50–90% of their child care fees in 2011–2012, with low-income families receiving the highest subsidies (Productivity Commission, Vol. 1, 2014). The prevailing view in Australia is that some level of co-payment—through an out-of-pocket cost—is generally desirable in social service systems.

There are two core demand-side subsidies. The Child Care Benefit (CCB)—a means-tested benefit targeted toward low- and middle-income families—covers up to 24 hours of ECEC per week, or 50 hours of ECEC per child per week when meeting a work/activity threshold. Support is tapered based on income levels. The second form of subsidy is the Child Care Rebate (CCR)—a non-means-tested payment providing additional assistance to families in which both parents meet a work/training/study test and are using approved care. CCR provides up to 50% of a family's out-of-pocket child care costs after any CCB is deducted, up to a maximum of $5,878 (AUD $7,500) per child per year. These subsidies can be used by parents to access services provided by public (state, local), nongovernment (charities, community-owned), and private for-profit providers (ranging in size from small to corporations).

Though subsidies address affordability in the short term, as a funding strategy they do little to address positive systemic outcomes, such as infrastructure development, equitable service distribution, or even longer-term affordability. Thus, though several reform attempts in Australia have sought to address affordability through increased subsidies, out-of-pocket costs continue to grow much faster than the Consumer Price Index. This partially negates the impact of the subsidy and demands more systemic approaches to reform. A further example of reform can be seen in the recently legislated national reform package, the Jobs for Families Package. This will combine the two main subsidies (CCB and CCR), introduce a maximum hourly subsidy rate, and seek to create a more flexible system to enhance competition. There is concern, however, that this package will reduce subsidies for nonworking and vulnerable families. Moreover, concern has mounted over a proposal to move BBF services to the CCB, imposing new requirements incompatible with the principles and orientation of services in Indigenous communities. For instance, a recent Commonwealth policy initiative includes a "caregiver activity test" to determine child care subsidy eligibility (Australian Government, 2016). Raising and charging fees and requiring services to sustain higher numbers of enrollments do not support the BBF focus on supporting the most vulnerable members of communities. Further, these services are extremely vulnerable to fluctuating enrollments (Secretariat of National Aboriginal and Islander Child Care [SNAICC], 2012).

Clearly, Australia's financing of ECEC reflects a market orientation, which has engendered considerable debate. The approach promotes an increasingly large and concentrated private provider market, with a substantial for-profit presence. Moreover, a range of other profit-driven sectors have a strong financial interest in ECEC, including training and property enterprises that engage in long-term commercial property leases. Reliance on subsidies and parental choice can work well when parents have the means, knowledge, and options to freely select appropriate child care for their children. Unfortunately, in a nation as vast and diverse as Australia, such resources and options are not always available, limiting opportunity for those who can least afford the services and who are often most likely to benefit from them. Heavy reliance on demand-side strategies may instantiate extant social and economic inequities because young children who are at risk may not be able to participate in the life-changing opportunities associated with quality ECEC. Moreover, the demand-side strategy fails to address elements of the infrastructure (e.g., professional development, data systems) that are necessary to support long-term systemic ECEC advancement.

TEACHING YOUNG CHILDREN

Guiding Framework

Working with young children so that they are engaged, active learners demands attention to pedagogy (i.e., how to teach) and content (i.e., what to teach). Continuing its long history of philosophically grounded, child-centered ECEC, Australia has experienced a paradigm shift in the way it articulates, regulates, and evokes quality pedagogy and content. Comprehensive and groundbreaking, the NQF was introduced in 2009 with the goal of raising quality, driving continuous improvement, and fostering consistency among ECEC services nationwide. Strategic and prescient, the focus on these three goals was essential to addressing increased ECEC service provision, changing demographics, and the previous lack of any cohering curriculum or regulatory apparatus that bridged the care-education chasm. To that end, the NQF incorporated the development of the Early Years Learning Framework (EYLF), which guides curriculum planning and decisionmaking for all care and education services for children from birth to age 5. The NQF also set forth corresponding regulatory authorities to monitor the implementation of the EYLF in all delivery systems or programs, irrespective of funding source or jurisdiction. Given its importance, it is appropriate that: (a) the EYLF was developed over time through collaboration between the Australian and state/territory governments; and (b) it included extensive public feedback. Representing an unprecedented collaborative effort between the Australian Government and the state/territory governments, the NQF and EYLF have revolutionized Australian ECEC.

Comprehensive in design, the EYLF encourages a contextual view of knowledge, in which teaching is a facilitative process, rather than mere transmission. It encourages teachers to: (a) work together with families and children to "construct curriculum and learning experiences relevant to children in their local context"; (b) be aware of the influence of their own beliefs and values on their practice; and (c) draw on a range of perspectives and beliefs to continually challenge and refine their practice (DEEWR, 2009, p. 11). Teachers are encouraged to apply eight practice elements: holistic approaches, responsiveness to children, learning through play, intentional teaching, learning environments, cultural competence, continuity of learning and transitions, and assessment for learning. It expresses five broad and interconnected learning outcomes for children: (a) children have a strong sense of identity; (b) children are connected with and contribute to their world; (c) children have a strong sense of well-being; (d) children are confident and involved learners; and (e) children are effective communicators. In short, the EYLF identifies both holistic learning goals and a cyclical decision-making process in which educators draw on their professional knowledge, including their in-depth knowledge of each child.

Although the EYLF is the generally accepted curriculum framework, in recognition of the diversity of the country, five jurisdiction-specific frameworks that customize the EYLF to local conditions and priorities have been approved. Teachers are required to base their educational program on the EYLF or the jurisdictionally approved learning framework, but they have flexibility in its implementation, as long as their pedagogy and content reflect the framework's intentions.

Monitoring Children and Programs

Prior to entry to formal school at age 5, Australia does not conduct formal assessments of children's learning. Rather, educators are expected to use ongoing (formative) informal assessments of each child to monitor their development and to plan relevant learning experiences in accordance with the approved guiding framework. To accomplish this, educators use ongoing observation, often coupled with individual child learning portfolios that document progress. These data are not reported to authorities, but they are often shared with parents to apprise them of their children's progress. Every three years, the Australian Early Development Census (AEDC) takes a national population-level assessment of children's development as they enter primary school.

Rather than using formal child data, Australia relies heavily on program monitoring to assure quality service provision. The vast majority of ECEC services in Australia are regulated under the NQF using its seven National Quality Standards (NQS): (a) educational program and practice; (b) children's health and safety; (c) physical environment; (d) staffing arrangements; (e) relationships with children; (f) collaborative partnerships with families and communities; and (g) leadership and service management (ACECQA, 2012). After being assessed by trained officers, programs are given a rating for each of the seven areas and an overall rating, ranging from "working towards the NQS" to "exceeding the NQS." In some circumstances, programs may receive a rating of "Excellent," if they apply for and are granted this status. All ratings are made available online to the public. As part of the assessment and rating process, services are obliged to develop and implement a quality improvement plan, which is taken into account during their assessment and rating.

Workforce

The ECEC workforce is large, consisting of more than 150,000 employees, about 90% of whom are female. Under the Australian Education and Care Services National Law Act 2010, the workforce has four distinct positions: nominated supervisor, educational leader, early childhood teacher, and educator. Typically a center or program director, the *nominated supervisor* manages a preschool, long day care, or family day care service; the individual must have management, leadership, and governance skills to implement the NQF. A newly added role, the *educational leader,* guides and mentors other educators in planning, implementing, and reflecting on their learning program. Possessing knowledge of child development and the skills to guide the pedagogy of others, an educational leader must be available in each center. *Early childhood teachers* (bachelor qualified) deliver specific early learning programs (preschool) in a dedicated preschool or long day care center, and *educators* (Certificate III or Diploma-qualified) generally support teachers and provide education and care to a group of children. Diploma-qualified educators generally take an active role, under the guidance of an educational leader, in developing, planning, and implementing a program for a group of children.

Within the context of these roles, states and territories set the requirements for working with children, which include, at a minimum, criminal records checks. Beyond this baseline, the NQF established higher qualification mandates (noted above), and concomitant expectations for curriculum and pedagogical skills. Despite these mandates, levels of educational attainment vary tremendously within and between care and education (see Table 2.1).

Table 2.1. Distribution of ECEC-Related Educational Attainment for Contact Staff Who Work in Child Care Services in Australia

Staff Categories That Serve Children in ECEC	DISTRIBUTION OF EDUCATIONAL ATTAINMENT (%)			
	Below Certificate III	Certificate III/IV	Advanced Diploma/ Diploma	Bachelor's Degree or Higher
Long Day Care	1.2	40.1	35.4	11.5
Family Day Care	1.5	53.3	24.3	3.9
In-Home Care	3.4	32.1	21.7	6.9
Occasional Care	2	38.6	42	7.5
Preschool	1.6	30.5	19.4	38.8

Source: DET, 2014

Prospective educators have a number of options to achieve established requirements. Australian universities, which are generally considered to be of high quality, provide preservice preparation, as do vocational education and training (VET) entities. Recent workforce growth and the NQF requirements for minimum qualifications have greatly increased demand in the VET sector, leading to a proliferation of private registered training organizations of variable quality. To that end, the Australian Skills Quality Authority (ASQA) regards the ongoing regulation of training organizations offering ECEC courses as a priority (Australian Skills Quality Authority [ASQA], 2015).

Professional development has been regarded as a complement to preservice training, but many promising efforts have now been curtailed. For example, professional development for most ECEC workers was, until mid-2016, delivered through the Australian Government's Inclusion and Professional Support Program, which funded professional support coordinators to organize, advise, and train ECEC professionals on a variety of topics. However, the closure of this program placed responsibility for professional development back on employers. Further, the NQF had provided professional development funding, with scholarships or studentships for staff upgrading their qualifications to the new required minimum; this too ended in 2016. Despite these national-level changes, efforts to maintain attention to preservice training exist in some states/territories, where registered teachers must complete specified hours of professional development each year. Professional agencies, such as the Early Learning Association of Australia and Gowrie Australia, provide professional development opportunities, particularly to community (nonprofit) providers, although staff from across service management categories take part.

ECEC compensation is generally low. Salaries for child care professionals range from about $28,963 (AUD $36,000) (just higher than the national minimum wage) to $50,940 (AUD $65,000) per annum (Fair Work Ombudsman, 2017), and staff report, in submissions to a national review, that they could earn more in retail (Productivity Commission, 2011). Moreover, in the 2013 National ECEC Workforce Census, only 49% were satisfied with their pay and conditions (DET, 2014). In an attempt to systematize compensation, the Fair Work Commission (Australia's workplace relations tribunal) sets the minimum wages and conditions for preschool and child care professionals; it also establishes the pay rates and conditions of employment such as leave entitlements, overtime, and shift work. Organizations, including governments, also negotiate enterprise agreements with employees that supersede the award conditions. Workers unions are active in negotiating enterprise agreements on behalf of their members.

In general, with the advent of the NQF reforms, there has been a cultural change toward the professionalization of ECEC. The extant double challenges of variability in professional development and depressed compensation, however, suggest that Australia must prioritize workforce issues with alacrity. This is particularly the case given that the quality of the ECEC system rests on the quality of its workforce.

Transitions

Because continuity is critically important to the developing child, ECEC systems are placing increasing emphasis on transitions—those that take place as children leave their homes for the first time and enter care, those that they make daily, and those that take place as they transition into primary school. Recognizing the importance of these transitions, the EYLF espouses a continuous philosophy and orientation for children from birth to age 5; it also emphasizes the importance of a smooth transition to school and sets the expectations that early childhood professionals will actively engage both children and families in transitions and that they will work collaboratively with the children's new school educators and other professionals to ensure a successful transition to school.

A variety of strategies support children's transition to school, organized at the state/territory level. Typically, jurisdictions require a transition policy outlining a range of activities that may take place, such as sharing documents ("transition statements") that describe each child's strengths and interests with receiving schools (mandated in the three largest states), or visits by children to the new setting. In some areas, such as Western Australia and the Northern Territory, preschool is offered within the school setting, creating linkages within the site itself. Notably, Tasmania's Launching into Learning program facilitates family relationships with schools. Designed for children before they start preschool and offered through all Tasmanian government schools, it involves parents, teachers, and children in joint activities such as playgroup, music, or water awareness (Tasmanian Department of Education, 2016). Another innovation, the Victorian Early Years Learning and Development Framework (DET Victoria, 2016), guides practitioners working with children from birth to 8, providing continuity between settings and a common language for professionals.

INFLUENCING ECEC POLICY AND PRACTICE

As a democracy, Australia relies on numerous inputs to achieve social change. In ECEC, families have traditionally been heavily engaged at the program level, working to advance community-governed services. In this role, parents and families served on parent committees and advocated for their own children and for the services that were designed and implemented for them. So central is this to effective ECEC that collaborative partnerships with families and communities is one of the seven quality areas forming the NQS,

affirming the value of families as partners with the right to actively participate in ECEC service provision. This standard (Quality Area 6) emphasizes:
(a) the importance of respectful and supportive relationships with families;
(b) support for families in their parenting roles, values, and beliefs; and (c)
the need to engage families in collaborations with other organizations and
service providers. Monitoring data reveal that 91% of ECEC service providers meet this standard (ACECQA, 2017). Having noted this, however,
there is variability in the extent to which family engagement and support
are effective in diverse demographic settings. Services are seen to be more
effective when the service providers are aware of and respond to the cultural
practices of the engaged families. In Indigenous communities, this has been
achieved by engaging employees who share the cultural and linguistic traditions of the families being served.

Despite these efforts, a shift in the nature and structure of Australian
ECEC service provision has altered parents' roles. Specifically, changes in
funding strategies have rendered parents and families as players in a system
that is governed by national legislation and implemented via cooperation
across federal, state, and territory governments. In this context, parents and
families are largely cast as clients and consumers of services, whose influence lies in exercising their choice of service provider, aided by the routinely
published NQF service quality ratings. As such, the formal advocacy role
for families and communities to engage in the ECEC policymaking process is underdeveloped (Fenech, 2013). There is no coordinated parent body
working collaboratively to influence policy, although efforts to address this
are beginning taking hold. For instance, The ParentHood, a not-for-profit
digital campaign organization, has become Australia's largest collection of
parent voices. There is room for continuing expansion of such a role to
inform policymaking.

Nonetheless, there are opportunities for the public to become involved
in policy. Indeed, Australia's legislative development process mandates in-
vitation to public comment on proposals so that individuals and advocacy
groups have opportunities to guide and legitimate policy efforts. Given the
wide range of stakeholders affected by the system, consultative groups representing different constituencies (e.g., for-profit providers, teachers) provide policy input nationally and in the states/territories. Advocacy related to
curriculum, access, and/or quality is led by professionals in groups such as
Early Childhood Australia. The media also draws attention to critical ECEC
issues, often focusing on child care access and affordability.

Reflecting global trends, Australia draws on diverse kinds of research
and data to inform its policymaking processes and content. Governments
often commission specific research, including sector reviews, empirical studies, or evaluation studies, that are immediately germane to emergent policy
issues. In addition, governments may sponsor inquiries to consider important and transcendent policy issues. The Australian Government, through

competitive grant rounds, also funds research efforts that sometimes engage university researchers and government groups. Despite these efforts, three caveats permeate the Australian ECEC research enterprise. First, priority is often given to health and medical research that impacts children, with educational research on youngsters often taking a slight backseat. Second, much of the education-related ECEC research is produced overseas, so that the Productivity Commission has encouraged Australia to conduct more of its own trials and studies, with the goal of using a combination of international and domestic data to inform policy. Third, although administrative data collected by the government are helpful to policymakers, there are limitations on their use, and often pertinent data are not systematically accessible.

REFLECTIONS ON THE AUSTRALIAN ECEC SYSTEM

Australia, like many Western democracies, finds itself wrestling with considerable change amid social, environmental, demographic, and economic turmoil. Globalization has accelerated the movement of people across borders, stirring debates about values, cultures, and the nature of societal obligations to an increasingly diverse population. Corollaries to globalization, increased international trade, and technological advances are altering workforce practices, roles, and expectations. Changes in the environment alter relationships with the planet at large and with national land. Although these developments are not all new, there has been a marked and continuing acceleration in the pace of change, which demands more nuanced understandings of the implications of these shifts for contemporary life. Many countries, including Australia, increasingly regard education as a key elixir and, more specifically, are turning to early education as a means of addressing social cohesion and economic productivity. In the service of these goals, Australia has made considerable strides in advancing the quantity and quality of ECEC. Political shifts, however, have slowed the process down somewhat, raising concerns regarding the best approach to maintain momentum and propel Australian ECEC forward for the future. Five themes warrant reflection.

Acknowledging Gains

Historically, Australia has been an exemplar of health and social services provision. Comprehensive services have been and continue to be made available to support pregnant women and new families. Similarly, the country has enjoyed notable commitment to the earliest years of life through its care and education services. Indeed, since the 1970s, considerable progress has been made in both the quantity and quality of services provided to young children. Rooted in the Australian social fabric is a twofold historical rationale for its strong commitment to young children. First, early care was regarded as an essential support to families and the economy in that it enabled women to join the workforce. Second, early education was regarded as a key to advancing learning and development, particularly for at-risk populations. This focus on dual outcomes has remained consistent today, fostering two lines of support: care and education.

The late 1980s and early 1990s saw the rapid expansion of services. Consistent with broader governmental reforms, a market-driven strategy was adopted to skirt the intense fiscal involvement of governments that characterizes many Nordic and Western European countries. Attesting to the strengths of this approach, ECEC and child care expanded rapidly in diverse sectors—public and private, for-profit and nonprofit. With the market handling the bulk of ECEC provision, the Australian and state/territory governments saw their roles as regulators, service and subsidy monitors, and information producers, most notably so that parents could make informed consumer choices.

Such engagement begot critical issues of quality and equity, which mushroomed as provision grew, and ultimately led to the launch of the NQF in 2009. Encompassing both child care and preschool services, the NQF fostered a renewed focus on quality pedagogy, a new curriculum, new standards, and new approaches to quality acceleration. Moreover, it has built in important consistencies for young children, notably through its common pedagogy and regulatory apparatuses that transcend the traditionally split sectors of care and education. It has acquainted policymakers and researchers with the strengths and challenges associated with ECEC, and it has drawn much-needed attention to the sector. In addition, it has provided a platform for collaboration among the Australian Government and the states/territories. Indeed, the NQF represents the crown jewel in Australian ECEC services, as evidenced by the large support it enjoys even years after its development.

Fostering Equity

Despite these notable accomplishments, serious inequities in access and quality persist in the Australian ECEC system, most notably in urban, regional, and remote Australia. Indigenous people are the most disadvantaged population group in Australia, as manifest on numerous social, educational, and health indicators. With the goal of uplifting the social conditions and building on the rich cultural traditions of Indigenous people, the Australian Government has advanced a range of policies and strategies, including targeted resources, enhanced subsidies, and an array of social, education, and health programs.

Yet the strategies used to advance some of these efforts, and ECEC efforts in particular, cannot begin to ameliorate inequities. Within the ECEC sector, a market strategy is ill-suited to advancing equity. First, it assumes that an array of services exists from which parents can choose, which is not always the case, particularly in rural and remote regions. Second, market strategies raise challenges regarding the engagement of marginalized populations whose cultural backgrounds or program preferences (e.g., hours of operation, programmatic offerings) may not match operators' profit motives or preferences. Third, market strategies do not provide for robust, durable, and differentiated funding. Moreover, such strategies do not build in resource certainty, sustained service provision, self-determination, or durable control, all fundamental for Indigenous communities. In short, the need to produce more equitably available services is not likely to be addressed by market strategies alone. This equity challenge is thus among the greatest challenges facing the Australian ECEC system.

Overcoming Implementation Barriers to Teaching and Learning

As noted above, Australia has made remarkable progress with its durable quality framework, the NQF, and its EYLF. Acting as bedrocks for reform, these initiatives have propelled Australian ECEC far. Unfortunately, significant barriers persist, requiring strategic work in areas that cannot be reached by the NQF and the EYLF alone. Namely, there is a need for a far more systemic orientation and for far more attention to the workforce.

Market strategies presume, rather than foster, the existence of a system infrastructure. In fields where system infrastructure is embryonic, as it is in Australian ECEC, market strategies falter. Though they enhance the supply of direct services, they give only limited regard to the nature of that supply—they are not designed to boost quality or provide well-trained and compensated personnel. In the face of Australia's heavy reliance on market strategies, the NQF and the EYLF are limited in the change they can elicit. Continued momentum is needed to establish a diversified system infrastructure and buttress capacity-building efforts.

Arguably the single most potent area for investment in any organization or field is its workforce. Here, Australia has made some strides, but in light of the heavy market orientation, progress is somewhat stalled. The market approach, by design, keeps costs to families low so as to remain affordable. It also encourages providers, particularly in the for-profit sector, to yield a profitable return on capital investment. Given these motivations, savings will generally come in two ways: on one hand, through improved business practices and economies of scale; on the other, through lowering investment in staff in areas such as salaries, training, qualifications, staff-to-child ratios, and professional development.

As such, the Australian ECEC workforce is structurally and operationally compromised by low wages. When compared to primary school teachers, ECEC educators—even with the same qualifications—often earn less.

Even within the ECEC field, significant disparities in wages exist; teachers in stand-alone and government-provided preschools are often on an enterprise agreement that is typically more beneficial than the national award under which long day care teachers frequently operate. Addressing these wage differentials is essential to implementing high-quality ECEC services.

The Australian workforce is also compromised by the quality of preservice education. Efforts have been made to enhance the quality of preservice preparation, but though Australian universities are generally considered to be of high quality, there has been great variability in training provision among the technical and further education and VET providers. In response, new minimum training standards were implemented in 2015, but given the importance of educator preparation, there is a continuing need for attention to quality in the training system. Such training must have content alignment with the NQF and EYLF, and it must pay special attention to the needs of Indigenous and at-risk populations. It must also focus on the need to balance process and structural quality, and on implementation of intentional teaching within a play-based context.

However important such content is, it must be provided in supported and sustained ways. Workforce productivity is compromised when service providers themselves must resource the professional learning and development of their staff. Indeed, poor staff conditions may undermine the investments governments are making, thus necessitating further national discussion regarding the role and function of ECEC professionals in the market-driven context. Investing in the workforce is essential to high-quality service provision.

Engaging Parents

As noted earlier, there has been a gradual shift in the perceived role of parents in Australia's ECEC system, from drivers of local ECEC service provision to consumers concerned primarily with their own children's learning. Although parental choice is an important aspect of the Australian ECEC system, it has benefits and limitations. The benefits include honoring parents' preferences in the nature, locus, and number of services desired. Liabilities exist, however, when markets fail and parents do not have the knowledge to make choices, or when they do not have an array of quality services from which to select.

Moreover, ECEC would benefit from parents' collective advocacy and involvement in policy development. This could foster their understanding of the broader field and engender a cadre of supporters for future ECEC legislation. Groups of parent advocates for schooling education may provide a model for ECEC parents to develop a more organized perspective that contributes to state and federal governments, education departments, and the media. In short, parents need to be seen not simply as consumers of ECEC, but as fundamental and primary partners.

Advancing Second-Stage National Reform

Achieving national reform is not new to Australia. It has been done before and it can be done again. The question at hand is how best to frame second-stage national reforms in light of those reforms already achieved and in light of the country context. Throughout this review, the split between care and education has been apparent, as have concerns with an overreliance on market strategies to address issues of quality, equity, and sustainability. Second-stage reform efforts, in addition to the above four points, must take a systemic stance and build comprehensive governance and finance approaches that harness resources and develop long-term, data-driven plans for incremental policy advancement.

Coordinated ECEC planning between the Australian Government and the states/territories to develop a unified vision and approach to policy and practice should be considered. Building off experiences in other countries, such planning could be handled simply by establishing a planning framework that would allow for better mediation of the key divisions that currently characterize ECEC. Alternatively, a more durable mechanism could be created, for example, through the development of an entity that links data-driven planning for care and education services supply at the national level, with corresponding entities in the states/territories. Clearly, such efforts, irrespective of the form they take, might encounter areas of resistance among the range of stakeholders. Eschewing entrenched positions, fostering creative problem solving, and instantiating effective negotiating processes can advance the system while also resolving problems as they emerge. Given the unprecedented cooperation that existed in the development of the NQF, it is anticipated that such an effort could be marshaled again.

Above all, Australia should adopt systems thinking as it goes about its next wave of reforms. Systems thinking is rooted in shared values and vision for childhood in Australia. It is buttressed by a coherent, planned strategy that honors and respects historical traditions but is not held hostage to them. It means moving from a focus on service provision to one that pedestals quality and equity as key goals and that regards a focus on the infrastructure as a viable and requisite means of achieving durable reform. Systemic thinking means embracing the role of families in meaningful ways. History and policy have created various constructions of ECEC across Australia, but it is now time to consolidate the gains and plan for systemic reform that firmly lodges the child and the family as the central reference point. Such efforts will have merit to the degree that they balance benefits for the "children of today" with Australia's system for tomorrow.

REFERENCES

Australian Bureau of Statistics. (2016). *Australian Demographic Statistics, June Quarter 2016* (Catalogue No. 3101.0). Canberra, Australia: Author.

Australian Bureau of Statistics. (2017a). Migration Australia, 2015–2016 (Catalogue No. 3412). Canberra, Australia: Author. Retrieved from abs.gov.au/ausstats/abs@.nsf/lookup/3412.0Media%20Release12015-16

Australian Bureau of Statistics. (2017b). Regional Population Growth Australia 2016. Population Density (Catalogue No. 3218.0). Retrieved from abs.gov.au/AUSSTATS/abs@.nsf/Latestproducts/3218.0Main%20Features752016

Australian Children's Education and Care Quality Authority. (2012). National Quality Standard. Sydney, Australia: Author. Retrieved from acecqa.gov.au/national-quality-framework/the-national-quality-standard

Australian Children's Education and Care Quality Authority. (2016). NQF snapshot. Q3, 2016. A quarterly report from the Australian Children's Education and Care Quality Authority, November. Sydney, Australia: Author. Retrieved from docs.education.gov.au/documents/child-care-service-handbook

Australian Children's Education and Care Quality Authority. (2017). NQF snapshot. Q4, 2016. A quarterly report from the Australian Children's Education and Care Quality Authority, February. Sydney, Australia: Author.

Australian Government. (2016). Family Assistance Legislation Amendment (Jobs for Families Child Care Package) Bill 2016, September. Canberra, Australia: Author. Retrieved from legislation.gov.au/Details/C2016B00102

Australian Health Ministers' Advisory Council. (2012). Clinical Practice Guidelines: Antenatal Care—Module 1. Canberra, Australia: Australian Government Department of Health and Ageing. Retrieved from consultations.health.gov.au/phd-tobacco/clinical-practice-guidelines-antenatal-care-module/

Australian Institute of Health and Welfare. (2011). *2010 Australian National Infant Feeding Survey: Indicator results*. Canberra, Australia: Author.

Australian Institute of Health and Welfare. (2016a). *Australia's mothers and babies 2014: In brief* (Perinatal statistics series no. 32. Catalogue No. PER 87). Canberra, Australia: Author.

Australian Institute of Health and Welfare. (2016b). *Child protection Australia 2014–15.* (Child welfare series no. 63. Catalogue No. CWS 57). Canberra, Australia: Author.

Australian Skills Quality Authority. (2015). *Report: Training for early childhood education and care in Australia.* Canberra, Australia: Commonwealth of Australia.

Department of Education. (2012). *Child care service handbook.* Canberra, Australia: Commonwealth of Australia.

Department of Education and Training. (2014). 2013 NWC State Tables. Retrieved from docs.education.gov.au/node/35839

Department of Education and Training. (2017). Budget Based Funding program. Canberra, Australia: Author. Retrieved from education.gov.au/budget-based-funded-program-1

Department of Education, Employment and Workplace Relations. (2009). *Belonging, being & becoming: The early years learning framework for Australia.* Canberra, Australia: Commonwealth of Australia.

Department of Education, Employment and Workplace Relations. (2011). *My time our place: Framework for school age care.* Sydney, Australia: Author.

Department of Health. (2017). Vaccination data hub. Canberra, Australia: Author. Retrieved from immunise.health.gov.au/internet/immunise/publishing.nsf/Content/vaccination-data

Department of Social Services. (2017). Paid parental leave scheme. Retrieved from dss.gov.au/our-responsibilities/families-and-children/programmes-services/paid-parental-leave-scheme

Fair Work Ombudsman. (2017). Pay Guide. Children's Services Award 2010 [MA000120]. Retrieved from fairwork.gov.au/ArticleDocuments/872/childrens-services-award-ma000120-pay-guide.docx.aspx

Fenech, M. (2013). Quality early childhood education for my child or for all children? Parents as activists for equitable, high-quality early childhood education in Australia. *Australasian Journal of Early Childhood, 38*(4), 92–98.

Productivity Commission. (2011). Early Childhood Development Workforce, Research Report, Melbourne, Australia. Retrieved from pc.gov.au/inquiries/completed/education-workforce-early-childhood/report/early-childhood-report.pdf

Productivity Commission. (2014). *Child care and early childhood learning* (Inquiry Report No. 73, Vol. 1–2). Canberra, Australia: Author.

Secretariat of National Aboriginal and Islander Child Care. (2012). SNAICC submission to the Department of Education, Employment and Workplace Training: Quality early childhood education and care for children in regional, remote and Indigenous communities review of the Budget Based Funding program. Fitzroy North, Australia: Author. Retrieved from snaicc.org.au/wp-content/uploads/2015/12/02897.pdf

St. George, I., Cullen, M., Gardiner, L., & Karabatsos, G. (2008). Universal tele-nursing triage in Australia and New Zealand: A new primary health service. *Australian Family Physician, 37*(6) 476–479.

Steering Committee for the Review of Government Service Provision. (2016). *Report on government services 2016* (Vol. B & Vol. E). Canberra, Australia: Productivity Commission.

Steering Committee for the Review of Government Service Provision. (2017). Report on government services 2017 (Vol. E). Canberra, Australia: Productivity Commission. Retrieved from pc.gov.au/research/ongoing/report-on-government-services/2017/health

Tasmanian Department of Education. (2016). Launching into learning. Retrieved from education.tas.gov.au/About_us/publications/school-brochures/Pages/Launching-Into-Learning/

World Bank. (2017). World Bank open data. Retrieved from data.worldbank.org/

Victorian Department of Education and Training (DET Victoria). (2016). *Victorian Early Years Learning and Development Framework* (Rev. Ed.). Melbourne, Australia: Victorian Curriculum and Assessment Authority.

CHAPTER 3

Laying the Foundation for Lifelong Skills

Universal and Integrated Early Childhood Services in England

Kathy Sylva, Grace Murkett, and Lily Fritz

England, the largest country of the United Kingdom, has enjoyed a long and remarkable history of political stability, having had no experience of successful invasion or occupation since 1066. As a result, "reform not revolution" has been the watchword that has led to successive policies for children and families (Marr, 2007). Since the turn of this century, English governments have had two main aims: a thriving economy, and social cohesion based on equity (Eisenstadt, 2011). The care and education of young children, delivered through integrated and free services, is one major means of educating a skilled workforce and fostering cohesive communities with shared values.

VALUES AND VISION

There are approximately 3.3 million children under 5 in England, with 70.7% classified by the national census as White British (Office for National Statistics [ONS], 2013). Many ethnicities and cultures coexist, however, due to encouraged immigration from ex-colonies of the British Empire and relaxed migration control in the 1970s, '80s, and '90s. Today, 94% of the population age 3–15 speak English as their main language. England is a highly industrialized country, with 92.4% of the population living in urban areas. This industrialization accentuates stark inequalities between socioeconomic statuses, although social welfare policies have been forged in an attempt to address them, including universal free health care and targeted

---

For factual details on early childhood in England, see Appendix B

cash benefits for the poor. A universal early childhood education and care (ECEC) system has also been created as one major plank in successive governments' aim to reduce the effects of economic inequalities on children's life chances.

Universal ECEC—a free "entitlement" for children over 3—is guaranteed by parliamentary law and constitutes part of the welfare state, which, following some important precursors, came into existence after World War II. In 1946, a war-weary population that was hungry for change elected the left-wing Labour Party to govern with a mandate to provide services for all segments of society, especially returning soldiers and the citizens who had so heroically supported the war effort. The immediate postwar period thus saw the dawn of the "welfare state": key industries (e.g., steel, coal, and railway) were nationalized, and the National Health Service was introduced ("Free health care from cradle to grave"). Five decades later, at the turn of the 21st century, a new Labour government was elected, one that promised increased social welfare and a special focus on the disadvantaged segments of the population, especially families with young children.

Between 1997 and 2007, the Labour government increased spending on ECEC threefold to $3.2 billion[1] (£2.5 billion) (Gambaro, Stewart, & Waldfogel, 2014; Stewart, 2013). By establishing ECEC as the foundational stage of a citizen's educational trajectory, policy attention and increased funding led to a transformation of the architecture of the ECEC system (Sylva & Pugh, 2005). Although education before school had historically been seen as the family's responsibility (or in the case of poor working parents, the "care" responsibility of urban municipalities), early education became the responsibility of central government and was viewed as a tool to combat social inequalities. Today, early childhood services continue to be seen as a powerful means to enhance child development and increase parental employment in disadvantaged families, thus reducing inequalities between the rich and the poor.

Centralized Services and a Mixed Economy of Provision

Despite the consolidation of services under a single ministry (the Department for Education, or DfE) and the development of a national curriculum in the late 1990s, there has always been a mixed economy of public and private provision in England. In other words, there is a single model of governance but a hybrid model of provision.

After World War II, ECEC was offered for free in the public sector, but it remained fee-based and paid by parents in the private sector, with fees ranging from modest to quite expensive. All this changed in the early 2000s, when a free child care entitlement for children over 3 was established, at first for 12.5 hours per week, then increased to 15, and in 2017 to 30 hours, providing virtually full-time education and care. For each child over 3, the government pays the ECEC provider, whether public or private—the money follows the child. The high value placed on a seamless and centralized education system at the top governance level thus complements the high value placed on parental choice of provider on the ground.

Using Data for Quality Improvement

Between 1997 and 2010, the Labour government invested heavily in ECEC research, with a particular focus on provision in disadvantaged communities (Eisenstadt, 2011). Successive governments have continued to embrace the use of research data to guide policy, meaning that the entire ECEC system is subject to continuous improvement, with new policies and services brought on stream in response to routinely collected data on children's development and the services that support it. In general, the DfE funds large-scale research studies monitoring educational outcomes and effectiveness, whereas government-funded research councils and private grant-awarding bodies fund more theoretical research on pedagogy and children's learning. The financial crisis in 2008, coupled with the election of a new coalition government in 2010, changed the research focus in England from promoting equity to increasing school readiness. Although accompanying funding cuts have led to research programs being scaled down, research continues to impact policy development.

Since the 1990s, the government has been committed to collecting diverse kinds of information, notably about the developmental status of all pupils in statutory schooling. The first two national assessments, at ages 2 and 5, do not consist of formal tests but are a combination of observed tasks and interview data from parents and ECEC providers. The 5-year-old developmental "profile" is included in the national pupil database, which contains children's scores on the subsequent national tests taken at ages 7, 11, 16, and 18. From this database, anonymized datasets of children's 5-year-old profiles allow local municipalities to target resources to those settings or neighborhoods where children's scores are lowest. In addition, an annual national census of all ECEC providers monitors numbers of each type of provision, staffing levels and qualifications, and enrollment of children by age and demographic status. This information is used to identify groups that might not take advantage of free ECEC and encourage enrollment, especially of vulnerable groups.

Another hallmark of the English system is its common inspection/ monitoring framework, delivered through the same agency responsible for inspecting primary and secondary schools. The Office for Standards in Education (Ofsted) is respected by government and parents alike, adding to the credibility of the entire ECEC system and guiding efforts at improvement.

A Centralized System

The vision of an ECEC system that fuels a skilled workforce and national co-hesion requires a strong, coherent, and integrated system of governance. For several centuries, England has had a highly centralized government, initially through a monarchy that reigned over a unified country. Today, England's integrated approach means that policy decisions are made by Parliament, after discussion in the Cabinet led by the prime minister. Ministries are then charged with operationalizing these policies through structures, regulatory practices, and funding streams. Centralization is manifest in a single lead ministry for the learning and development of children from birth to the end of schooling (the DfE) and a single policy document for each age range (e.g., the Early Years Foundation Stage for children 0–5). There is also a single agency for inspection and monitoring of each educational stage (Ofsted). Thus, the single ECEC system supports efficient and sustainable services under one of the most centralized governments in Europe.

RANGE OF SERVICES

Health Services

The National Health Service (NHS), established in 1946, is governed at a national level by the Department of Health. It provides free health care in hospitals and community health centers for all residents of England. Each child receives a unique NHS number at birth that entitles him or her to all NHS services, including services for physical and mental health, and preventive services such as inoculations and dentistry. There is almost universal take-up of NHS services because they are offered for free in the local community, without stigma.

Many health services are provided for pregnant mothers and young children, as well as 39 weeks of statutory pay for expectant parents and parents with newborns, and a further 13 weeks of statutory employment leave that guarantees the job remains available. Unemployed parents receive equivalent funding through another government stream called "family benefit." These services are highly regulated to ensure that all individuals receive the same entitlements regardless of their geographic location or employment status. All services for pregnant women and those in the perinatal period are free at the point of delivery, with government funding provided by the NHS. Mothers can attend antenatal classes (National Health Service [NHS], 2015a), which cover topics including health during and after pregnancy, feeding and caring for babies, and relaxation techniques. Mothers expecting their first child may also attend up to 10 antenatal appointments with their midwife or doctor (NHS, 2015b), whereas mothers expecting a second or subsequent child attend around seven. These appointments include antenatal screening tests for abnormalities or health problems.

Within 72 hours of giving birth, parents are offered a physical examination for their baby, called the Newborn Physical Examination (Babycentre, 2014). This examination checks for signs of disability and includes a screening test to check the baby's eyes and hearing. When the child is 8 weeks old, a five-in-one vaccine (which protects against diphtheria, tetanus, whooping cough, polio, and Haemophilus influenzae type b), a pneumococcal vaccine, a rotavirus vaccine, and a meningitis B vaccine are offered (NHS, 2016). At 12 weeks old, second doses of the five-in-one and rotavirus vaccines are administered by a general practitioner.

Around the time of their baby's birth, parents are given a personal child health record (popularly called "the red book"). This is used by health professionals to record the child's weight, height, vaccinations, and other important health information. The book also contains a section on developmental milestones for the parents to update and questionnaires to be filled in before the child's health and development review. These free reviews are carried out by health professionals when children are 10–14 days old, 6–8 weeks old, 9–12 months old, and 2–2.5 years old. They cover general development (e.g., movement, speech, social skills, hearing and vision), growth, healthy eating and keeping active, behavior and sleeping habits, tooth-brushing, child safety, and vaccinations. Reviews may be carried out in the home, community health center, or children's center; once the child begins school, health and development support is taken over by the school nursing team and school staff. Routine health care is offered to all families for free through their local NHS health center, and though not mandatory, there is almost universal take-up. Hospital care for serious illness is also free and run by the NHS.

Child Protection Services

Child protection and social services are governed at a local level, although local municipalities must follow central government statutory guidance. All municipalities use the Common Assessment Framework to identify children who are "in need" of additional support to assure healthy development, such as those with history of family abuse or dysfunction (children with a disability also fall under this definition but receive separate support). As part of the municipality's assessment, a social worker must decide whether there is reasonable cause to suspect that the child is suffering, or likely to suffer, "significant harm" (Her Majesty's Government, 2015a). If it is decided that the child is in need of additional services but is not in harm, the family and other professionals will agree to a *child in need plan* to ensure the child's future welfare. If it is decided that the child might be at risk of harm, an interagency child protection conference is convened to draw up a *child protection plan*, which is subject to ongoing review and revision.

Children whose parents or caregivers no longer have legal responsibility for them are "looked after" by the local municipality. The majority of looked-after children are placed in foster family care, whereas others may be placed in secure units, children's homes, or residential schools, or are placed for adoption. The goal is for looked-after children to live in as homelike a setting as possible.

There is also legislation to assure a safe and secure family environment. Domestic abuse, including both physical violence and coercive control, is a recognized offense (Her Majesty's Government, 2015b). Domestic violence protection orders are issued to prevent ongoing risk of violence to victims, especially mothers and children. Integrated protection services are provided by "child-centered teams," and typically include policing, social work, health, education, housing, and welfare.

Education and Care Services

Education and care services for children between birth and Year 1 of formal schooling are characterized by integration and centralization, as they fall under a single ministry and common legislation. All formal ECEC providers in England must follow the Early Years Foundation Stage (EYFS) curriculum and health and safety requirements, and they must be registered with Ofsted (the monitoring and inspection agency). All are inspected by Ofsted at least once every four years, but more frequently if there is cause for concern. The government is committed to providing 30 hours of funded child care per week for working parents of 3- and 4-year-olds, and 15 hours for 3- and 4-year-olds whose parents are not employed and for 40% of the most disadvantaged 2-year-olds. These government-funded hours can be taken in any ECEC setting, public or private, that parents choose. Table 3.1 presents the different kinds of ECEC provision available in England.

The only form of formal in-home child care in England is *childminding*. As a formal provider of child care, childminders' homes, like centers, are inspected at least once every four years. Childminders can take children from birth upward and typically provide ECEC services for the whole working day, with a maximum of three children under the age of five. The vast majority of childminders are self-employed and make individual contracts with families determining their working hours and hourly rates. Similar to all ECEC services, childminders must follow the EYFS curriculum: children are encouraged to play and participate in cognitively stimulating activities, such as woodwork or cooking.

In the private or charitable sector there are several types of center-based provision, all of which follow the EYFS. Private *day nurseries*, which can take children who are a few months old up to the age of compulsory

Table 3.1. A Comparison of the Different Forms of ECEC Provision in England

Sector	Type	Hours of Operation	Age Range	Funded by?	Governed by?	Inspected by?
Private	Childminders in their own homes	Per individual arrangement	Birth–4+ years*	National Early Years 30-hour entitlement for children over 3; under 3s paid for by parents with mutually agreed hourly rates	Childminders themselves	Ofsted
	Day nurseries	Usually 8:30–5:30	Birth–4+ years	National Early Years 30-hour entitlement for children over 3; parents pay for younger children or for hours outside the entitlement	Owners	
Voluntary/ charitable	Preschools	9:00–11:30, 12:30–3:00	2 years–4+ years	National Early Years 30-hour entitlement for children over 3; parents pay for younger children	Parent body	
	Charitable centers	8:00–6:00	Birth–4+ years	National Early Years 30-hour entitlement	Committee of charitable foundation	Ofsted
Public	Nursery schools	9:00–12:00, 1:00–3:00 (some stay for lunch)	2.5 years–4+ years	National Early Years 30-hour entitlement	Nursery school governors	
	Nursery classes within a primary school	9:00–11:30, 12:30–3:00 (some stay for extended hours)	2.5 years–4+ years	National Early Years 30-hour entitlement + funding from primary school budget	Primary school governors	Ofsted
	Reception classes within a primary school	9:00–3:00	4+ years–5+ years	Funding from primary school budget	Primary school governors	
	Children's centers	8:30–5:30	Birth–4+ years	Usually from the "high needs" block of local municipality education funding	Center governors	

*Because most children enter Reception class in September, their age at entry will vary from 4 to 5 years, depending on month of birth. 4+ is therefore used to describe children at the age of 4 who are not yet attending Reception in a statutory capacity.

schooling, are the most common form of provision for children under the age of 3 (Department for Education [DfE], 2014). They may be run by employers, private companies, or private schools. Charitable *preschools* (sometimes called "playgroups") are often run by parents and cater for children aged 2–4+ years in part-time sessions of up to four hours a day. Not-for-profit organizations also run *charitable centers* with professional social work support in addition to full-day ECEC.

State-run ECEC services in England are all school-based. *Nursery schools* are local municipality schools in their own right, but like primary schools, they have a well-paid head teacher and highly trained teachers on their staff. Though referred to as "schools" and led by teachers, they follow the play-based curriculum of the EYFS. Historically, nursery schools have been located in neighborhoods of high disadvantage to serve the most vulnerable children. Despite providing higher-quality ECEC than other providers (Office for Standards in Education [Ofsted], 2015b), budget cuts have led to reductions in the overall number of nursery schools, down to only 400 in 2016 (DfE, 2016a).

About a quarter of primary schools include a *nursery class* whose provision is very similar to nursery schools; they are usually housed in a separate unit on the site of a primary school with protected outdoor space. The integrated education and care is always led by a teacher with Qualified Teacher Status (the highest qualification among early years staff and equal to that of primary school teachers). Nursery classes may have up to 26 children, led by two members of staff. Nursery classes have not increased in number in this century; rather, the greatest expansion has been in the (cheaper) private sector despite reports indicating that quality is higher in school-based provision (Ofsted, 2015b).

Reception class is both a form of ECEC and an important feature of primary schools in England. Free for all who attend, Reception classes provide full-time early childhood education during normal school hours for children aged 4–5+ years. There is some discrepancy among reports on English ECEC as to whether Reception classes are included in ECEC or as part of primary education. Some reports, especially those published before the 2008 EYFS, classify them as the first year of formal schooling owing to their location in a primary school and their full-day (i.e., 6 hours) provision. However, Reception class is compulsory only for children over 5 and it follows the EYFS curriculum, rather than the Primary curriculum beginning in Year 1. Throughout the United Kingdom, all children must begin education at the start of the term after their fifth birthday. Thus, some children attending Reception classes are fulfilling a statutory requirement, because they have turned 5, whereas others are not.

Most ECEC provision for children under the age of 3 is run by private or charitable organizations and is paid for by parents; after children turn 3 there is a balance between private and public provision, with all children entitled to public ECEC in the Reception class. It is estimated that only 1–3.5% of young children do not attend any ECEC provision before Reception (DfE, 2010). Enrollment data show that higher-income parents are more likely to enroll their children in formal ECEC services at an earlier age, in part owing to a greater capacity to pay for them (DfE, 2014). However, the enrollment of poorer children has been increasing steadily since 1997, with free ECEC provided from age 3 (and age 2 for children from the 40% most disadvantaged families).

Integrated Service Provision—Children's Centers

The vast majority of local municipalities in England run *children's centers* in disadvantaged neighborhoods, with the aim of providing a single place where parents and children can access health, education, and welfare services. Many services are "mainstream" and offered to all children and families, such as breastfeeding support from midwives, whereas others are "specialized," such as speech therapy or budgeting advice for families in debt. While the 2,500 children's centers offer open-access services for all families, they increasingly and successfully target outreach and home-based services for at-risk families, offering support and encouragement and thereby enhancing the home learning environment and reducing parental stress (Sammons, Hall, Smees, & Goff, 2015). Children's centers are funded through the local municipalities, with all services free to families. They have suffered under austerity cuts since the financial crisis of 2008; although their number has not decreased dramatically, the range of services has narrowed through "hollowing out," with increasing focus on specialized, rather than mainstream, services.

SYSTEMIC/STRUCTURAL COMPONENTS

Structural Components

Governance. National policy is set centrally by the prime minister and his or her Cabinet, which is composed of elected members of parliament (MPs) and appointed by the prime minister. Government departments (e.g., defense, health, education, environment) are staffed by a professional civil service that implements, not decides, policy. On-the-ground delivery of educational policy is delegated to local municipalities, which receive central funding to provide education and care (and welfare) for children and families. Each municipality has a locally elected council that oversees provision of services and tailors them to local needs. For example, local councils decide where to locate public provision, such as children's centers, and offer professional support to centers with poor Ofsted inspection results.

The English ECEC system is characterized by strong centralization, with one ministry in charge of all ECEC services, including social welfare. When two ministries have overlapping responsibilities (as is the case with the national developmental assessment of 2-year-olds), temporary interministerial task forces are set up to ensure joined-up regulations. Thus, cross-department work occurs at a high level in central government. One example of a task force is the Child Care Implementation Task Force, established to "drive delivery of a coherent and effective government-wide child care entitlement to support parents to work" (Cabinet Office, 2016); this task force has been responsible for the delivery of the new extension from 15 to 30 government-funded ECEC hours for children of working parents.

When central government promises a children's service, local government has the legal duty to provide it. Local municipalities are run by elected councilors, who have decisionmaking powers within broad outlines laid down by the central government. Although funding and guidance for services comes from the central government, local municipalities are responsible for deciding how the funding they receive will be spent on services, and in times of economic austerity, they must strategize to "make do" with the budget they are given. Thus, although ECEC provision can be ensured via municipalities' legal obligation, the standards of quality cannot.

Finance. Revenue for public spending on education comes from national taxation. For 2017–2018, the DfE's total expenditure limit is set to $78 billion (£60.1 billion), $4.4 billion (£3.4 billion) of which is to finance ECEC (Her Majesty's Treasury, 2017). A large part of these funds is transferred to local municipalities through the Dedicated Schools Grant (GOV.UK, 2017), which is the principal source of public supply-side funding for all education, including public and private ECEC settings. The Dedicated Schools Grant also includes funding for Ofsted regulation, teacher training, educational research, and national assessment. The total amount allocated to each municipality is based on a funding formula that takes account of numbers and needs (e.g., disability, poverty, or children who speak English as an additional language) of children in the area. The grant is split into three notional blocks: 80% is suggested for the Schools block (Reception class, primary, and secondary), 7% for the Early Years block, and 13% for the High Needs Children block. Local municipalities are ultimately responsible for deciding how to divide central government funding, and they may divert money from one block to another.

To promote equity across regions and sectors, the central government sets a standard allocation rate per child care hour that municipalities must pay to all providers in their area. Set at $6.33 per hour (£4.88) for children aged 3 and 4, and $6.87 per hour (£5.30) for children under 3 in 2017, this "hourly rate" must cover staffing, materials, and premises costs and derives from the Early Years component of the Dedicated Schools Grant given to municipalities. Municipalities are allowed to use a small portion of the grant to provide professional development or to support centers with low Ofsted inspection grades.

On the demand side of funding, families with lower incomes (falling in the bottom 40%) are entitled to tax relief on child care expenses that fall outside of the free entitlement. This includes care for children under the age of 3 (outside of the 15 funded hours entitlement for disadvantaged 2-year-olds) and also child care outside normal working hours, such as weekends. A new "tax-free child care" scheme was rolled out nationally in 2017, requiring the government to pay 20% of working parents' ECEC costs if they fall outside the national entitlement.

Regulation and Inspection. The central government sets standards (e.g., early learning goals) and regulations (e.g., staff-to-child ratios at each age) for education, health, and social welfare services. Regularly monitored, these standards lead to common practices across the country (although lapses do sometimes occur). All formal providers of ECEC must register with Ofsted and meet all EYFS curriculum framework and staffing requirements. All new regulatory requirements are developed on the basis of national consultation, with input from parents, providers and teachers, and experts.

Ofsted inspectors must have relevant experience within the education sector and undergo rigorous and continuous training. ECEC settings are inspected on their provision in support of the 17 early learning goals specified by the EYFS framework. Following the *Early Years Inspection Handbook* (Ofsted, 2015a), inspectors rely on observations, interviews with staff and parents, and document review to ensure that practice supports child development in all key curriculum areas. In addition to curriculum, the inspection framework outlines safeguarding and welfare requirements, employee regulations, staff qualifications, staff-to-child ratios, health (e.g., providing healthy food or giving medicine to children), environmental safety (e.g., fire safety and hygiene requirements), and risk assessments. Thus, a single inspection framework specifies standards relating to the national curriculum, pedagogy, safeguarding, and health requirements along with requirements for teacher qualifications, ratios, and reporting to parents. Nationally set, these criteria are comprehensive and guide regular inspection.

Following inspection, settings are awarded a grade for overall effectiveness, as well as subgrades for "effectiveness of leadership and management," "quality of teaching, learning, and assessment," "personal development, behavior, and welfare," and "outcomes for children." These grades are assigned on a scale from 1 (outstanding) to 4 (inadequate). Settings that receive an overall inspection grade of 3 (requires improvement) are inspected again within a year and receive support for improvement from the local municipality. Those that get a grade of 4 are either closed or receive immediate intervention from the municipality. Immediate feedback is given to centers about strengths and challenges, with full reports subsequently published on-line. Inspection reports are avidly read by parents, and centers use them for self-improvement. As of March 2015, 85% of early years–registered providers (including center-based, school-based, and childminder provision) were rated "good" or "outstanding" (Ofsted, 2015b).

Parliament does not provide detailed legal specifications regarding how centers should operate. However, the "teeth" in the system is Ofsted, the regulatory agency, whose inspectors use the *Inspection Handbook* to determine quality of ECEC provision across centers. Although there are no laws about the amount of time spent on adult-initiated and child-initiated play, for example, Ofsted looks for a balance that suits the needs of the enrolled children based on the inspectors' judgments. Therefore, the government does not need to create legislation specifying how ECEC providers should provide high-quality service; rather, all providers must meet the requirements set forth in Ofsted's inspection framework, which can be updated more easily than laws. Regulation thus plays an important role in maintaining the quality and accountability of ECEC providers in England.

Instructional Components

Curriculum and Pedagogy. In 2008, the Department for Education published its first continuous curriculum for birth to school entry, referred to as the Early Years Foundation Stage, or EYFS (Department for Children, Schools and Families, 2008). This cohesive, statutory framework for early childhood education and care is a legal requirement for all early years settings in England (DfE, 2017). Therefore, all children enrolled in ECEC services receive care and education in accordance with this curriculum, wherever they live and whatever type of formal service caters to them.

The EYFS is made up of the Statutory Framework, which contains the purpose and aim of ECEC, the learning requirements, and the assessment processes, and the Practice Guidance, which details how the EYFS should be implemented. In 2012, the original 2008 curriculum was "slimmed down" to increase flexibility of practice (DfE, 2012). The current framework includes early learning goals distributed across seven areas of learning and development:

1. Communication and language
2. Physical development
3. Personal, social, and emotional development
4. Literacy
5. Mathematics
6. Understanding the world
7. Expressive arts and design

The first three areas are "core" and pertain to development from birth to entry into Year 1, the first year of formal schooling. The next four areas are "specific" and pertain to children's learning from age 3 to entry into Year 1. A focus on diversity and cultural representation underpins the content of the EYFS curriculum; when planning activities, practitioners are encouraged to take into account the cultural backgrounds of the children and choose activities and experiences to which they can relate.

The EYFS does not prescribe a single pedagogical approach. Instead, it encourages practitioners to employ a variety of pedagogical approaches and practice flexibly, in accordance with the current developmental stages of individual children. Broadly, the EYFS promotes play and a balance between child-initiated and adult-led activities. Certain other pedagogical practices are also recommended, such as "scaffolding" and "sustained-shared thinking," which both promote high-quality interactions between adults and children, but it is left to the practitioner to identify suitable situations and adapt the practice to suit the child. The curriculum is thus designed to provide appropriate pedagogy for all children, regardless of developmental stage or background. Although the EYFS has been widely approved by families and the workforce, some critics argue that the pedagogy implemented to achieve the early learning goals is too formal, especially for younger children. That said, Ofsted reports refute this, with annual increases in centers achieving "good" or "outstanding" judgments for curricular implementation and pedagogy across the age range from birth to 5+ (Ofsted, 2015b).

Monitoring Child Development. Children's development is monitored in a variety of ways. At age 2–2.5, municipality-employed health visitors—funded from the national health care budget—conduct a developmental assessment (the "2-year-old check"). This check assesses the physical development of the child, as well as his or her cognitive and socioemotional development, with the cooperation of the parents, as well as the early years practitioner if the child is already in ECEC provision. Any child found to have developmental delays or special educational needs is offered free, specialized ECEC provision to address these needs. This developmental assessment contributes to the national database on all 2-year-olds in the country, which is maintained by the Department of Health but shared with local municipalities and the Department for Education. This provides comparative data that are used to improve service quality and efficiency, allowing the government to adjust funding to reduce inequalities and provide extra funds to areas with concentrations of high-needs children.

The 5-year-old EYFS profile is the second national assessment of children's development. Conducted by the DfE, it takes place in Reception classes shortly before children start Year 1. Each child's EYFS profile is based on practitioners' knowledge of the pupil, garnered predominantly through observation and interaction in a range of daily activities, but also includes examples of the child's work and discussion with her family. This profile is used to compare the child's current level of development to the 17 early learning goals set out in the curriculum. For each goal, children are marked as: (a) not yet at the level of development expected at the end of the EYFS (emerging); (b) at the level of development expected (expected); or (c) beyond the level of development expected (exceeding). In addition to this, practitioners must include a brief paragraph explaining how the pupil engages in play and exploration, active learning, creating, and thinking critically—the characteristics of effective learning outlined in the EYFS curriculum. In contrast to the early learning goals, these focus on processes rather than outcomes.

Ongoing formal child assessment is not recommended through the EYFS, but practitioners are encouraged to create informal developmental portfolios that document developmental progress. Practitioners often create a "working profile" using anecdotal evidence from everyday activities; they may also include copies of formative observations, photographs or videos of the child, or comments from the child or their parents about the child's development and interests.

Transitions. The transition from the EYFS to Year 1 is accorded considerable attention through a variety of strategies. It is greatly aided by the fact that the final year of preschool is spent in a Reception class in primary school, which allows children to have daily contact with older peers and become familiar with school facilities. The transition from ECEC to primary education is further aided by the precise alignment between three of the four "specific areas" of learning and development outlined in the EYFS (Literacy, Mathematics, and Understanding the World) and the three "core subjects" of the National Curriculum for Primary and Secondary Education (English, Mathematics, and Science).

The EYFS profile created by the Reception teacher is also important in informing a professional discussion between the Reception and Year 1 teachers, and helping Year 1 teachers plan an appropriate curriculum that will meet the needs of all children in their class (DfE, 2017). The profiles and discussions are particularly important for pupils with special educational needs or disabilities (SEND), as the EYFS practitioner completes the profile with the understanding that a child with SEND may demonstrate learning and development in a different way. Hand-over discussions are also crucial for children whose home language is not English so that the ECEC practitioner can communicate whether the child's language development in her home language is at the expected level (which may not be reflected in their EYFS profile). The EYFS practitioner should also convey the cultural background of the child to help the Year 1 teacher understand the values held by the child that help explain her responses to social situations.

Workforce. Just as England has a "mixed economy" of provision in the public as well as private sector, it has a "mixed economy" of educators and caregivers whose qualifications range from none to higher degrees. This mixed economy is fueled by the fact that ECEC providers operate in diverse settings that often contour their work. A large divide exists between public and private centers, with public-sector provision located in schools under local municipality control and charitable and private provision usually in stand-alone centers. This leads to differences in ethos, with school-based ECEC staff gaining the benefits of working alongside highly qualified colleagues and having access to opportunities for professional development, whereas staff in the private sector tend to be younger, receive lower salaries, and have fewer opportunities for professional and personal growth.

Staff qualifications are detailed in a national framework for all qualifications across diverse occupations in England, ranging from Level 1 (lowest) to Level 8 (highest). In order to work with children in ECEC settings in England, an individual must hold one of the "statutory" ECEC levels as described in Table 3.2. These are defined and regulated by the National College for Teaching and Leadership, an executive agency of the DfE that sets the content and standards for teacher training courses. Staff in ECEC settings are distinguished by these qualifications, which determine the type of work they can do and the number of children for whom they can be responsible. Only three levels of staff qualification are used in the ratios or job specifications of the ECEC workforce: Level 2, Level 3, and Level 6. Table 3.2 provides an insight into how these levels relate to the kinds of work that members of staff can undertake across different ECEC settings.

A major difference between public and private provision is the balance of staff at the different levels. Approximately half of ECEC staff in the public sector are at Level 6 (because school classrooms must be led by a degree-level teacher) and half are at Levels 2 and 3. In the private sector, there is usually at least one Level 6 staff member to lead/manage the setting, but the majority of staff members are at Levels 2 and 3. In the charitable centers, many settings do not have a Level 6 staff member, but most have at least one Level 3 staff member.

Wages are usually higher for staff in public-sector settings (nursery schools and nursery and Reception classes) than in private or charitable ones (day nurseries and preschools). On average, staff in private day nurseries earn $10.90 per hour (£8.40), compared to $18.30 per hour (£14.10) in public nursery schools (DfE, 2014). This reflects the "educational" rather than "care" tradition of the public sector, and the different characteristics of children served. For example, there are typically more children with special educational needs and disabilities in public provision, as public providers of ECEC have higher ratios of degree-level staff and better facilities to support these children. Level 6 teachers in school-based provision are paid on

Table 3.2. An Overview of the Different Levels of Staff and Their Responsibilities in a Variety of Settings

Qualifications	Job Categories	
	Center-Based Settings (day nurseries, preschools, charitable centers)	*School-Based Settings* (nursery schools, nursery class, or Reception class in a primary school)
Level 2		
General vocational qualifications obtained in secondary education at age 16–18	*Paid child care staff* Not qualified to look after groups of children on their own	*Early years support staff* Not qualified to look after groups of children on their own
Level 3		
Specific, ECEC-related qualifications obtained through Further Education at age 16–18; may include advanced vocational training	*Supervisory staff* Qualified to look after groups of children on their own	*Nursery nurses* Not qualified teachers but are qualified to look after groups of children on their own
Level 6		
Degree-level qualifications (either through bachelor's degrees or postgraduate teacher training courses); these grant Early Years Teacher Status (for teaching the EYFS) or Qualified Teacher Status (for teaching children in early years and primary school)	*Senior managers* Have overall responsibility for running the setting	*Teachers* Have Early Years Teacher Status or Qualified Teacher Status and supervise and lead classes

the same salary scales as primary school teachers, and for this reason, their hourly pay is usually double that of supervisory staff in private provision.

Therefore, although two individuals working in the public and private sectors may possess equivalent qualifications, individuals working in public provision are likely to be paid more than those employed in a private setting. Public-sector employees also have better conditions of employment (e.g., working hours, holiday entitlement, professional development), all leading to lower rates of turnover in the public sector and overall higher quality.

The EYFS states that all providers must support staff to undertake appropriate professional development to ensure they offer quality learning and development experiences for all children. Moreover, during inspection, evidence of inservice training or professional development is expected and contributes to the overall judgment. The content of training requirements is outlined in the EYFS (e.g., curriculum, pedagogy, safeguarding, work with parents and the community), but the details are left up to the individual trainers, with no centrally defined criteria. ECEC providers are often expected to organize and fund their own professional development training from private trainers; since the financial crisis of 2008, few local municipalities have sufficient budget to offer inservice training for free.

Engagement Components

Families and Communities. Parental choice is a key feature of English ECEC, and parents have complete choice over which setting their child attends. In general, parents are satisfied with the quality (64%) and flexibility (80%) of child care in their area (DfE, 2016b). Of parents who do not use child care for children under 3, only 2% cited reasons relating to quality or availability of child care providers, with the highest proportion (73%) saying they would rather look after their child themselves.

Parent engagement is considered key to supporting consistent learning approaches at home and school. ECEC provision in public schools has strong links with parents and communities through the school's mandated board of governors, which must contain parent representatives. In contrast, parent participation in governance for private ECEC settings is not mandated through legislation. Nonetheless, evidence of frequent parental engagement in all ECEC settings is expected by Ofsted inspectors, who typically ask to speak with parents to hear their view of the provision in order to inform their judgment. Parent engagement is a good example of the way that Ofsted promotes good practice; although there is no statutory mandate for private centers to include parents on their governing body, in reality most do because they know that inspectors will "mark" them on this.

Other Influences (Research, Advocacy, Foundations, Media). The government funds several large-scale studies evaluating the effectiveness of different approaches to early childhood. A well-known example of this was the Effective Pre-school, Primary and Secondary Education (EPPSE) study, which followed more than 3,000 children from age 3 through the school system until post-16 education, training, or employment, in order to identify the effectiveness of ECEC provision (Sylva, Melhuish, Sammons, Siraj-Blatchford, & Taggart, 2010; Sylva, Melhuish, Sammons, Siraj, & Taggart, 2014). The study, which predated the free entitlement, found that ECEC attendance increased children's academic and socioemotional development throughout the education system, compared to those who did not attend. These findings helped to justify the ECEC free entitlement in 2002 and subsequent public funding for a more qualified workforce (see Mathers et al., 2011). An update to the EPPSE study, the ongoing (2013–2020) Study of Early Education and Development (SEED) aims to evaluate the effectiveness of early education on children's outcomes. SEED will also investigate the "value for money" of providing different kinds of funded early years experiences from age 2 (Speight et al., 2015).

The government also funds large-scale evaluations of specific, innovative programs. These evaluations are used to identify areas of change, cancel specific programs altogether, or justify public spending. For instance, the National Evaluation of Sure Start (2012)—a community-based intervention—found no consistent benefits on the development of children living in poor neighborhoods (Belsky, Barnes, & Melhuish, 2007; Eisenstadt, 2011), which prompted the government to initiate massive changes in more than 3,000 neighborhoods with a new focus on center-based services in place of less-focused community services.

In addition to being shaped by data collected by the government and researchers, policy is influenced by professional organizations and public consultations. Some professional organizations have great influence; for example, the National Day Nursery Association, which is a membership organization mainly for providers in the private sector, has been instrumental in securing a nationally mandated hourly rate for child care. Their high-profile public campaign in 2015 put an end to local municipalities allocating more funds to the public sector than the private.

SYSTEMIC INSIGHTS

Universal and Consolidated Services

Structural Consolidation. The English ECEC system was transformed in the late 1990s and early years of the 21st century through increased funding and the integration of virtually all elements of the system at national and local levels (Sylva & Pugh, 2005). By establishing ECEC as a foundational part of each citizen's educational trajectory, policy attention intensified and focused on the best ways to educate young children so that all had a "fair chance" in society. The transformation began with the integration of care services into educational ones. Previously, while early education in nursery classes in primary schools fell under the Department for Education, voluntary/charitable preschools and private day nurseries were considered "care" and fell under the Department of Health. In the late 1990s, all ECEC services became the sole responsibility of the DfE, where they were viewed as the first phase of lifelong education and, importantly, were brought together under a single inspection agency. Locating all ECEC inspection within Ofsted demonstrates how seriously the country takes early education.

Curricular Continuity. With early childhood so firmly established under the education ministry, the next step for the new century was the development of a continuous early years national curriculum. Prior to consolidation, an "education" curriculum for children aged 3 to school entry had centered on "academic" domains of development (especially literacy, numeracy, and the environment), with some additional attention accorded to socioemotional development and creativity. A separate "care" curriculum for younger children (aged 0–3) put at its heart socioemotional development and relationships between children, staff, and families. Finally and happily, the two documents were merged in 2008 into a single and continuous curriculum from birth to Year 1 (age 5+/6): the EYFS. This education *and* care curriculum combined the best of the two previously separate documents, with a dual focus on "relationships" alongside "academic subjects" such as literacy and numeracy.

Universal Entitlement through Diverse Providers. Despite the existence of a single curriculum under a single ministry, there has always been a hybrid system of public and private provision in England. In the 1990s, ECEC was free in the public sector but costly in the private sector. In 2002, the free, supply-side entitlement was legislated, and since then each enrolled child has been paid for by the government, no matter whether provision is located in the public or private sector. Taxpayers are willing to pay for this system because it is universal: Every family benefits. Moreover, it is thought to contribute to equity, as an entitlement to free early education should help ameliorate social inequalities. Thus, important hallmarks of the English system include: (a) the free entitlement with ongoing, durable funding for both public and private settings; (b) a common curriculum and common inspection framework; and (c) the use of data to drive improvement.

Effectiveness of the System

Three powerful forces contribute to the effectiveness of the system: *strong legislation* guaranteeing every child the right to high-quality early education, a *statutory funding system* with equity at its core, and the routine collection of *objective data* on children's development and provision quality.

Quality Is Built into the Infrastructure. England's ECEC system has high levels of structural quality (e.g., facilities and resources) and moderate levels of process quality (i.e., children's experiences that support their development). In terms of structural quality, the EYFS specifies very generous staff-to-child ratios, allowing individual attention to children's interests and needs. There are also stringent requirements for staff training, though these differ between public and private settings.

With regard to process quality, the latest version of the EYFS curriculum outlines the experiences that children should have to support learning and development (DfE, 2017). This was developed over many years in consultation with child development experts, practitioners, and parents; many experts from teacher training or the academic community believe that the popularity of the EYFS is the result of this careful and thorough approach. The curriculum framework provides goals for children's development at the end of the preschool period, and a companion document, *Development Matters*, outlines the temporal pattern of development within each domain. In addition to informing practice, the EYFS is the backbone of process quality in the inspection service, which has reported continuing increases in assessed quality. Overall, assessed quality remains highest in nursery schools (Ofsted, 2015b).

The EYFS policy document is seen as the "jewel in the crown" of the English ECEC system. An extensive consultation with professionals and the public showed widespread praise for the EYFS and agreement with its principles (Tickell, 2011). Respondents pointed to the advantage of a single document that lays forth the goals, governmental structures, and regulations that underpin England's ECEC system, all of which rest on a solid body of research. Many praised that a single document for children from birth through Year 1 entitles them to the same learning experiences, the same monitoring of progress, and the same criteria for inspection, wherever they attend ECEC or live. Because structural quality components (e.g., staff-to-child ratios, staff qualifications, and health and safety procedures) are mandated for all settings, children and staff can expect similar standards even as they may move across the system. The clear alignment between the EYFS curriculum and the common monitoring framework for all providers contributes to the continuing high standards of overall ECEC provision in England, as demonstrated by the gradual improvement in inspection judgments year on year (Ofsted, 2015b).

Equity Is a Central Motivator of English ECEC. The ECEC system is firmly embedded as the foundational stage of an education system that aims to provide a "fair start" to all children in Year 1 and beyond. However, PISA scores continue to show a very wide gap in performance of 15-year-old students in England. This gap between disadvantaged children and their more advantaged peers is present at age 3 but narrows over the preschool years (Sylva et al., 2010), suggesting that while ECEC cannot eradicate all differences in attainment, it does go some way toward alleviating disadvantage by cultivating skills needed to tackle the school curriculum. Indeed, scores on national assessments ("profiles") of 5-year-old children at the end of their

Reception year have been steadily increasing, with a slight narrowing of the gap between rich and poor.

Equality in attainment is not the only measure of equity; there remains the issue of access. The annual Early Years Census collects data on ECEC staff numbers and qualifications, salaries, premises, and numbers and demographics of children served. This allows the government to detect challenges in equity and coverage and so initiate remediation. There are also annual studies of samples of parents with children in ECEC that inquire into their experience of ECEC provision, reason for choice of provision, and uptake of government-funded hours. These datasets are used to monitor the quality, equity, and sustainability of the ECEC system and to provide feedback on the implementation of certain policies—for example, by analyzing the use of government-funded hours by socioeconomic status to see if disadvantaged children are taking up ECEC provision. Moreover, national data from Ofsted inspections are used by the government to ensure equitable provision—that is, that disadvantaged children are as likely as their more affluent peers to be in high-quality provision.

Finally, the funding formula for the Dedicated Schools Grant allocated to municipalities from the central government is adjusted to reflect the relative poverty of each municipality. Some of these funds go toward an "early years premium" through which each provider receives a supplement of $778 per annum (£600) for each disadvantaged child over the age of 3 in their care. Ofsted inspectors routinely check whether the Early Years Pupil Premium has been spent on effective, evidence-based interventions. ECEC providers are therefore incentivized to use efficient and effective strategies to enhance the development of disadvantaged children.

A Data-Driven ECEC System for Improvement, Accountability, and Sustainability. The ECEC system in England is based on objective evidence, much of it collected or funded by the government. This includes child data (e.g., through national assessments at ages 2 and 5), program data (e.g., through Ofsted scores), and data on the effectiveness of the system in providing access (e.g., through the Annual Census of Providers/Early Years Census) and supporting children to achieve the early learning goals laid out in the EYFS.

All public services in England are guided by continuous monitoring and review at central and local levels. For example, at the national level, the "2-year-old check" by the Department of Health guides the allocation of services to communities in need. At the local level, it allows the health professional carrying out the check to refer children with atypical development to appropriate services. Similarly, the 5-year-old EYFS profile carried out in Reception classes can be shared with health professionals—for example, in cases of language delay. In both instances, national monitoring leads to appropriate and targeted service provision.

Ofsted provides information to the government about institutional quality across regions, and to individual settings about their own quality. To supplement this, the government commissions large-scale research to explore the effects of different factors—for example, the presence of a graduate teacher, or different levels of process quality. Although the government also collects administrative data such as child profiles and Ofsted scores, there is still a need for focused research on why some children thrive and others do not. The official datasets provide the bare bones for answers to such a question, but they are not fine-grained enough to measure the details of pedagogy, for example. The government should build on its extant research capacity by conducting future research into, for instance, different pedagogical approaches for different children, or the impact of the Early Years Pupil Premium on narrowing the attainment gap.

It should be noted that the data-driven system is not universally admired. One complaint is that the rigorous Ofsted inspections drive the system through a "tick-box mentality," diminishing creativity. The regulatory system is also expensive; however, the government believes it is worth the cost because it incentivizes and increases quality through the power to close providers and to publicize reports on (named) weak and strong centers. Despite mixed opinions about the use of data to drive services, the commitment to collecting data on children and providers means that gaps or weaknesses in the system can at very least be identified, and improvements can be made to guarantee a moderate degree of quality.

Challenges, Implications, and Recommendations

Although the architecture of the system is sound, with ECEC firmly established as the first phase in lifelong education, there are serious tensions. These stem primarily from shifting governmental priorities and persistent failure to develop and retain a high-quality workforce.

Attracting, Developing, and Retaining the Workforce. The Achilles heel in the English ECEC system is the workforce. A drive to up-skill the workforce stalled in the wake of the global financial crisis in 2008–2009, and although the government is committed to steadily increasing professionalization, staff members with degrees are still the exception rather than the norm in the private sector (Mathers et al., 2011). This is largely due to insufficiently competitive salaries, which cannot attract the caliber of teachers found in the school sector. Overall, the costly requirement for generous ratios drives the system, suggesting that the government has chosen structural quality (generous ratios) over a well-paid workforce able to deliver process quality in all settings.

With regard to attracting a quality workforce, grave disparities exist between the public and private sectors, even for staff with equivalent qualifications. Prior to 2017, the government allocated more funds per child in the public sector, leading to better resources and richer pedagogical quality (Sylva et al., 2010). This differential is now eroding with the establishment of a common funding formula across sectors. As funds migrate from the more expensive public sector into the private and charitable one, quality in state-run nursery schools and classes will be threatened, as they will struggle to continue paying equivalent wages to nursery teachers as are paid to primary teachers. What will remain, however, will be university-trained teachers in the Reception year; because many children in Reception classes are of statutory school age (i.e., 5 years old), their teachers are funded as part of the school budget, and not on the hourly rate of provision for younger children. It will therefore remain easier to recruit highly qualified staff into this final year of the EYFS compared to the private or charitable sectors.

The government's extension of the free child care entitlement from 15 to 30 hours per week, effective since September 2017, will test its capacity to recruit sufficient numbers of new staff. Because of low pay, especially in the private and charitable sectors, child care is not an attractive career for well-educated young people. Finding more money for better salaries would require fundamental change to the financing of the system (e.g., transferring funds from primary or secondary education to ECEC), which seems unlikely. Another option is to generate new funds by raising taxes—another unlikely scenario. The last option is to require wealthier parents to pay for their children's ECEC whereas poorer parents would receive free services from better paid teachers. However, convincing voting parents and grandparents to relinquish their free child care entitlement would be political suicide for any politician. Given the unlikeliness of these scenarios, the workforce will continue to be poorly paid in the private sector, and recruitment of highly qualified staff will remain a challenge.

With regard to developing the extant workforce, recent research across Europe demonstrated the capacity of effective continuing professional development (CPD) to lift practice quality (Sylva, Ereky-Stevens, Pastori, Slot, & Lerkkanen, 2016). England would benefit from developing new ways to carry out CPD efficiently and economically, perhaps based on distance learning, which is cheap but requires further evaluation to test its effectiveness. Additionally, Ofsted has responsibility for ensuring that all settings participate in "effective" CPD, but the government does not provide or monitor this. Unfortunately, this is one of the weaknesses of the English ECEC system: preservice training is highly regulated and monitored for quality, whereas inservice training is unregulated and largely not evaluated.

Forced Choices: A Changing Focus from Child Development to Parental Employment. In times of prosperity, the ECEC system can simultaneously serve the goals of child development (early education) and parental employment (day care). However, times of austerity demand hard choices, and in 2017, the

Conservative government's main policy goal shifted from the enhancement of *child development* for all children to the goal of *making child care more affordable* so that parents can work. This is exemplified by the government's decision to use precious "extra" funding to extend the free ECEC entitlement from 15 to 30 hours per week for working families, rather than to improve the quality of the experience provided for young children.

In another move to encourage parental employment, the government has mandated that any new primary schools must be built with space for ECEC provision. The government has also made new funds available to existing primary schools so that they can extend their physical space to accommodate ECEC children outside the free entitlement hours ("wrap-around care"). The shift in priority from child development to care for working parents may be a response to the economic uncertainties brought about by the U.K. leaving the European Union, with concern about filling jobs left by exiting Europeans. Although expanding hours and space for ECEC shows an enduring commitment, these efforts increase the amount of time children can spend in ECEC but do not improve its quality. Improved pay for the workforce, yet to be achieved, would be one way of doing that.

The Need for New Research. There is an urgent need for research on up-skilling the workforce, and on ways to fund higher wages. Research on CPD has been previously discussed, but there is a critical need for research on innovative ways to enhance the workforce, including pay and conditions. Increasing the generous staff-to-child ratios, which drive up costs, could free funds for staff salaries and so attract more qualified teachers. However, government proposals to do so have been met with enormous resistance by parents and staff alike (DfE, 2013). Pilot programs that increase ratios while maintaining quality might be one way forward. Until wages are improved and the workforce transformed, process quality in England will continue to fall short of "outstanding." Unfortunately, an austerity economy suggests that salaries will remain low and that inexpensive, distance CPD may be the only practical solution to up-skilling the workforce. Research on innovative ways to do this is needed.

CONCLUDING REMARKS

The English system has strong policy foundations that stem from a national commitment to a welfare state that provides free educational and health services to support the development of all children, regardless of social background or ability. At the heart of ECEC is a focus on three critical prongs that adhere across sectors and regions: (a) the Early Years Foundation Stage curriculum to which each child is entitled (for free) from age 3 or from age 2 in poor families; (b) centralized monitoring of child development and service provision; and (c) a dedicated ECEC funding mechanism that supports parental choice.

ECEC is part of a range of integrated comprehensive early development services that are led nationally through two main ministries, with the Department for Education taking the lead on education and welfare and the Department of Health leading on physical and mental health of children and families. There is sufficient funding for baseline services, as well as for targeted services for children with special/additional needs. The hybrid system of universal entitlement to ECEC, delivered through a mixed economy of public and private provision, works well, although private centers often have lower quality than their public counterparts.

Still, the English early childhood system is highly susceptible to the economy. Although early childhood services are seen as a powerful means to promote child development, increase parental employment, and reduce inequalities, in England they are still considered less important than primary or secondary education. With a booming economy in the first decade of this century, investment increased threefold and the integrated system of education, health, and welfare was put in place. In the second decade, ECEC has been operating on more stringent budgets, with "hollowing out" of services and the closure of many public sector nursery schools (the highest-quality provision). Still, the important legacy of the expansion period is that the free entitlement remains, as do the generous ratios, the inspection agency, and the buildings that house ECEC services, such as children's centers. Just as important, there remains the expectation of parents and voters that ECEC is a national priority for both children's development and for equity. If the institutional architecture combined with brick and mortar remains, then the system legislated by Parliament will be ready for new investments in more prosperous times.

Helping to sustain the overall ECEC system is the complex system of data collected routinely as part of administrative monitoring, along with specialized research intended to answer specific questions about subgroups or about possible changes to the system. These nationally collected data enable continuous monitoring and improvement of the ECEC system in achieving the curricular goals of early childhood through well-functioning, self-improving centers, and through effective administrative structures that support and fund them. Published comparative attainment data on different groups of young children bring inequality to the fore and lead to public calls for greater investment in ECEC services. ECEC services used to be called the "Cinderella" of English education, whose older sisters Primary and Secondary went to the ball. This has now changed, thanks to newfound public commitment to universal, high-quality, and demand-led ECEC provision. Although many services, such as children's centers in poor neighborhoods, have been scaled down, the architecture of the system is still in place, guaranteed by legal entitlement and ready for new expansion in more favorable economic times. What is important is a shared aspirational vision for every child, whatever their family circumstances, to thrive from birth onward as part of a well-educated workforce and a tolerant, multicultural society.

NOTE

1. Dollar amounts reported in this chapter are in *U.S. dollars*, with British pounds bracketed for British readers. The conversion followed the U.S. Bureau of Fiscal Service Treasury Department protocols, using the current quarterly conversion rate of exchange as of June 2017. On this exchange rate £0.77 is equivalent to $1.00 (U.S. Bureau of Fiscal Service, 2017).

REFERENCES

Babycentre. (2014). Newborn baby tests and checks. Retrieved from babycentre.co.uk/a569381/newborn-baby-tests-and-checks

Belsky, J., Barnes, J., & Melhuish, E. (Eds.). (2007). *The National Evaluation of Sure Start: Does area-based early intervention work?* London, England: Policy Press.

Cabinet Office. (2016). List of Cabinet committees. Retrieved from gov.uk/government/uploads/system/uploads/attachment_data/file/560912/cabinet_committees_list_18_10_2016.pdf [this webpage is now unavailable as it was updated in 2018]

Department for Children, Schools and Families. (2008). Statutory Framework for the Early Years Foundation Stage. Retrieved from lse.ac.uk/intranet/LSEServices/nursery/pdf/statutoryframework.pdf

Department for Education. (2010). Month of birth and education: Schools analysis and research division. Retrieved from gov.uk/government/uploads/system/uploads/attachment_data/file/182664/DFE-RR017.pdf

Department for Education. (2012). Statutory Framework for the Early Years Foundation Stage. Retrieved from educationengland.org.uk/documents/pdfs/2012-eyfs-statutory-framework.pdf

Department for Education (2013). More great child care: Raising quality and giving parents more choice. Retrieved from gov.uk/government/uploads/system/uploads/attachment_data/file/219660/More_20Great_20Child care_20v2.pdf

Department for Education. (2014). Child care and Early Years Provider Survey 2013. Retrieved from gov.uk/government/uploads/system/uploads/attachment_data/file/355075/SFR33_2014_Main_report.pdf

Department for Education. (2016a). Child care and Early Years Providers Survey: 2016. Retrieved from gov.uk/government/statistics/child care-and-early-years-providers-survey-2016

Department for Education. (2016b). Child care and Early Years Survey of Parents 2014 to 2015. Retrieved from gov.uk/government/uploads/system/uploads/attachment_data/file/516924/SFR09-2016_Childcare_and_Early_Years_Parents_Survey_2014-15_report.pdf.pdf

Department for Education. (2017). Statutory Framework for the Early Years Foundation Stage. Retrieved from gov.uk/government/publications/early-years-foundation-stage-framework--2

Eisenstadt, N. (2011). *Providing a Sure Start: How government discovered early childhood.* London, England: Policy Press.

Gambaro, L., Stewart, K., & Waldfogel, J. (2014). *An Equal Start?: Providing Quality Early Education and Care for Disadvantaged Children.* Bristol, UK: Policy Press.

GOV.UK. (2017). Dedicated schools grant (DSG): 2017 to 2018. Retrieved from gov.uk/government/publications/dedicated-schools-grant-dsg-2017-to-2018

Her Majesty's Government. (2015a). Working together to safeguard children. Retrieved from gov.uk/government/uploads/system/uploads/attachment_data/file/419595/Working_Together_to_Safeguard_Children.pdf

Her Majesty's Government. (2015b). A Call to End Violence against Women and Girls: Progress Report 2010–15. Retrieved from gov.uk/government/uploads/system/uploads/attachment_data/file/409510/VAWG_Progress_Report_2010-2015.pdf

Her Majesty's Treasury. (2017). Public Expenditure: Statistical Analyses 2017. Retrieved from gov.uk/government/uploads/system/uploads/attachment_data/file/630570/60243_PESA_Accessible.pdf

Marr, A. (2007). *A history of modern Britain.* London, England: Macmillan.

Mathers, S., Ranns, H., Karemaker, A., Moody, A., Sylva, K., Graham, J., & Siraj-Blatchford, I. (2011). Evaluation of the graduate leader fund: Factors relating to quality: Findings from the baseline study. *Report to the UK Department for Education, 28.*

National Evaluation of Sure Start. (2012). The impact of Sure Start Local Programmes on seven year olds and their families. Retrieved from gov.uk/government/uploads/system/uploads/attachment_data/file/495329/The_impact_of_Sure_Start_local_programmes_on_7-year-olds_and_their_families.pdf

National Health Service. (2015a). Antenatal classes. Retrieved from nhs.uk/Conditions/pregnancy-and-baby/Pages/antenatal-classes-pregnant.aspx

National Health Service. (2015b). Screening tests in pregnancy. Retrieved from nhs.uk/Conditions/pregnancy-and-baby/pages/screening-tests-abnormality-pregnant.aspx

National Health Service. (2016). Vaccinations. Retrieved from nhs.uk/conditions/vaccinations/pages/vaccination-schedule-age-checklist.aspx

Office for National Statistics. (2013). DC2101EW—Ethnic group by sex by age. Retrieved from nomisweb.co.uk/census/2011/dc2101ew

Office for Standards in Education. (2015a). Early Years Inspection Handbook. Retrieved from gov.uk/government/publications/inspecting-registered-early-years-providers-guidance-for-inspectors

Office for Standards in Education. (2015b). Early Years annual report. Retrieved from gov.uk/government/uploads/system/uploads/attachment_data/file/445730/Early_years_report_2015.pdf

Sammons, P., Hall, J., Smees, R., & Goff, J. (2015). The impact of children's centres: Studying the effects of children's centres in promoting better outcomes for young children and their families. Retrieved from gov.uk/government/

uploads/system/uploads/attachment_data/file/485346/DFE-RR495_Evaluation_of_children_s_centres_in_England__the_impact_of_children_s_centres.pdf

Speight, S., Maisey, R., Chanfreau, J., Haywood, S., Lord, C., & Hussey, D. (2015). Study of early education and development. Retrieved from seed.natcen.ac.uk/media/5645/Study_of_early_education_and_development_survey_of_families.pdf

Stewart, K. (2013). Labour's record on the under fives: Policy, spending and outcomes 1997–2010. CASE paper, CASE/176. Centre for Analysis of Social Exclusion, The London School of Economics and Political Science, London, England.

Sylva, K., Ereky-Stevens, K., Pastori, G., Slot, P. L., & Lerkkanen, M. K. (2016). Integrative report on a culture-sensitive quality & curriculum framework. Retrieved from ecec-care.org/fileadmin/careproject/Publications/reports/D2_4_Integrative_Report_wp2_FINAL.pdf

Sylva, K., Melhuish, E., Sammons, P., Siraj-Blatchford, I., & Taggart, B. (Eds.). (2010). *Early childhood matters: Evidence from the effective pre-school and primary education project*. London, England: Routledge.

Sylva, K., Melhuish, E., Sammons, P., Siraj, I., & Taggart, B. (2014). Students' educational and developmental outcomes at age 16. Retrieved from gov.uk/government/uploads/system/uploads/attachment_data/file/351496/RR354_-_Students__educational_and_developmental_outcomes_at_age_16.pdf

Sylva, K., & Pugh, G. (2005). Transforming the early years in England. *Oxford Review of Education, 31*(1), 11–27.

Tickell, C. (2011). The Early Years Foundation Stage (EYFS) review: Report on the evidence. Retrieved from gov.uk/government/uploads/system/uploads/attachment_data/file/516537/The_early_years_foundation_stage_review_report_on_the_evidence.pdf

U.S. Bureau of Fiscal Service, Department of the Treasury. (2017). Treasury reporting rates of exchange as of June 30, 2017. Retrieved from fiscal.treasury.gov/fsreports/rpt/treasRptRateExch/itin-06-30-2017.pdf

CHAPTER 4

A Principled, Personalized, Trusting, and Child-Centric ECEC System in Finland

Kristiina Kumpulainen

Finland's early childhood education and care (ECEC) system is rooted in a historic social welfare model that values universalism and social rights while advancing a fervent commitment to equality and equity. At its core, the Finnish ECEC system reflects a powerful narrative predicated on principled, personalized, and child-centric services.

VALUES AND VISION

The legacy of the Finnish welfare model—a value proposition and strategy that developed over three key periods in the nation's history—is central to the conceptualization and design of the nation's present ECEC system. From the Middle Ages to the early 19th century, Finland was part of the kingdom of Sweden, which led to Swedish legal and social systems taking root. This era ended in 1809 when Finland was ceded to Russia, becoming an autonomous grand duchy wherein Finnish language, culture, and economy continued to develop. By the early 20th century, however, Russian restrictions on Finnish autonomy sparked the emergence of a budding nationalist movement. Finland ultimately secured independence during the final phases of World War I, when, on December 6, 1917, the nascent nation's declaration of independence was formally approved by the Parliament of Finland.

Today, Finland is a parliamentary republic of just over 5.5 million people, about 20% of whom are under the age of 18 (Vipunen Education Statistics Finland, 2017). Although 2016 marked the sixth consecutive year of declining birth rates, the country's population is on the rise due to migration (Official Statistics of Finland, 2017a). The majority of the population (about 89%) speak Finnish as their mother tongue; Swedish and Sami, the

For factual details on early childhood in Finland, see Appendix C

other two official languages, are spoken by 5.3% and 0.1% of the population, respectively. Foreign languages spoken in the country include Russian, Estonian, Arabic, Somali, and English (Official Statistics of Finland, 2017b). The largest religious community is the Evangelical Lutheran Church of Finland, with membership covering 72% of the population. About a quarter of Finns (1.3 million people) are not registered with any religious group (Ketola, Hytönen, Salminen, Sohlberg, & Sorsa, 2016).

Broadly, Finnish society and policies are based on three core principles associated with the Nordic welfare model: universalism (i.e., social welfare programs for all citizens), social rights (i.e., citizenship as a basis of entitlement), and equality (i.e., equal access to services) (Miettinen, 2013). Despite Finland's market-based economy, the state plays an important role in developing and managing welfare policies and services. The government's responsibility to provide education, health, welfare, and security is written into the Finnish Constitution so that citizens are guaranteed the right to income and care.

These values are also reflected in the nation's embrace of a collective responsibility for young children, manifest in diverse comprehensive early development (CED) policies that have emerged over time. For instance, legislation passed as early as 1938 provided dedicated maternity boxes to every Finnish newborn; eight years later, a formal child benefit scheme was put in place. In 1973, local authorities were given a statutory obligation to provide day care for children under school age, with child care leave policies (1989), day care and home care allowances (1990), and private day care allowances (1997) following soon thereafter. Sustaining this policy commitment, the 21st century has witnessed the emergence of free preschool education provided for all 6-year-olds (2001) and paternal leave raised to 54 working days (2013). Today, universal and integrated ECEC services ensure that children and their families, wherever they live and whatever their social, economic, ethnic, or cultural background, have access to an array of nationally defined, universally offered ECEC services.

RANGE OF SERVICES

General Services

In Finland, several types of universal CED services and allowances are provided to all children under age 18 and their families.

Prenatal and Perinatal Services

Prenatal and perinatal services for children, mothers, and families are publicly available and free of charge throughout the country. During pregnancy, health clinics monitor and promote the health and well-being of women through a range of services, including ultrasounds and amniotic fluid fetal chromosome tests. Deliveries are generally managed by hospitals, which have facilities and resources for enhanced supervision of mothers and babies, including the capacity to perform emergency C-sections. After a child is born, the child's development and mother's and family's well-being are monitored at a health clinic via regular checkups. Parenting and family counseling services covering topics such as breastfeeding, nutrition, and child development are universally available.

Child Health Services

Regular checkups at health clinics are provided by qualified clinical staff who monitor and document children's physical, physiological, mental, and social development based on nationally defined standards. During these health and well-being checks, parents are given information on vitamins and nutrition, and they are advised how to promote children's healthy development at home. Printed and digital materials on parenting and child development and well-being are also widely available. Dental care and a national vaccination program are offered to all children.

Typically, a child's health and development will be monitored weekly in their first month of life, with monthly monitoring continuing for the remaining 11 months of their first year. Thereafter, health and development checks are conducted annually until the age of 6. When a child enters primary school, in-house nurses and doctors continue to monitor his or her healthy development and well-being on an annual basis.

Parental Leave

Various types of publicly funded parental leave are available in Finland. Pregnant women have the right to 105 paid working days (i.e., Monday to Saturday) of maternity leave. Additionally, fathers can take 54 working days of paternity leave after their child's birth, 18 of which may be used while the mother is on maternity leave. Following this, either the mother or father can take a further parental leave of 158 working days after the maternity leave period ends, with an extension of 60 working days for each child in the case of multiple births (i.e., twins, triplets). Parental leave allowance is taxable, means-tested, and based on parents' income, with a minimum payment of about $28[1] (€23.73) per working day covered by the Social Insurance Institution of Finland (KELA) for those with no or little income. This can rise significantly; for instance, for a parent with an annual income of $71,000 (€60,000), the payment is about $136 (€115.66) per working day.

Home Care Allowance

After the parental leave period ends, parents have the right to take unpaid leave from work until the child reaches the age of 3; during this time, they are supported by KELA through a taxable home care allowance. For one child under the age of 3, or one newly adopted child over the age of 3, the allowance is about $401 (€342.53) per month. For each additional child under the age of 3, the allowance is approximately $120 (€102.55), and for each additional child under school age, the allowance is about an additional $77 (€65.89). Low-income families may also apply for an income-based child care supplement, which has a maximum value of about $215 (€183.31) per month.

Child-Benefit Scheme (Child Allowance)

Finland's monthly tax-free child benefit scheme was established in 1948 as part of the Nordic welfare model. Also called a child allowance, it is provided by KELA to parents of all children under 17, regardless of income (KELA, 2017a). In 2017, the benefit for the first child was $112 (€95.75) per month, the second about $124 (€105.80), the third about $158 (€135.01), the fourth about $181 (€154.64), and the fifth or any additional child about $204 (€174.27). For example, a family consisting of two adults and three children would altogether receive about $394 (€336.56) per month, tax-free. In addition, single parents receive a supplement of about $53 (€45.30) per month per child (KELA, 2017b).

Services for Children with Special Needs

Children diagnosed with special needs and/or a disability based on the judgment of ECEC and health care professionals are entitled to special services and assistance free of charge. Depending on a child's particular needs, these services may include transportation or access to a personal assistant or facilities/devices to help the child engage more fully in day-to-day life. Generally, children with special needs and/or disabilities are placed with typically developing children in mainstream ECEC groups and provided with additional support, although ECEC services can also be arranged in special groups consisting of only children with disabilities. Children with severe disabilities are also entitled to medical rehabilitation funded by KELA.

To coordinate services and assistance mechanisms for a child with disabilities, relevant authorities from KELA, health, welfare, and/or education, in conjunction with parents, create an individualized support plan that covers the child's needs. Typically, children are also assigned a contact person who will liaise between the family and various authorities, fostering coordination among them. In addition, not-for-profit nongovernmental organizations (NGOs) and the municipal ombudsman for social services are available to help support these children and their families. Parents of children with special needs are also eligible for financial benefits from KELA, including a disability allowance for children under the age of 16 and a special care allowance.

ECEC Services

All children between the ages of 0 and 6 have a universal right to ECEC services, which may take the form of center-based, family-based, or open services. Importantly, only the final year (pre-primary) is compulsory, followed by primary education beginning the year children turn 7. Though both are compulsory, pre-primary education is considered part of ECEC, whereas primary education is part of basic education, which extends through secondary education. As pre-primary education is only half-day, most 6-year-olds in Finland also use other ECEC services in their pre-primary year. A key principle framing Finnish ECEC services is parental choice, which is actualized by the availability of a wide variety of ECEC options, as discussed in the following subsections.

Center-Based ECEC

The most common form of ECEC provision in Finland is center-based ECEC. These centers typically operate from 6:15 a.m. to 5:30 p.m. on weekdays, although some centers provide evening, 24-hour, and/or 7-day care (known as round-the-clock care). In center-based ECEC, children are generally organized into age groups of 0–3 years old and 3–5 years old. Six-year-olds form a separate group, as they attend a pre-primary education program.

Center-based ECEC is offered by municipalities, municipality-outsourced ECEC providers, and private ECEC providers. Private ECEC service providers can be either for-profit or not-for-profit and may specialize in particular activities (e.g., languages, arts, sports) or advance a specific pedagogical approach (e.g., Montessori, Reggio Emilia). Regardless of these differences, all ECEC providers must meet Finnish legal requirements for the provision of ECEC. Namely, they must adhere to quality measures, such as the national core curriculum, staff-to-child ratios, professional qualifications, and staffing patterns and structures. The municipality and Regional Administrative State Agencies (AVIs) are jointly responsible for overseeing the provision of all ECEC programs in their area.

Family-Based ECEC

Family-based ECEC, another publicly available service, provides care and education to small groups of children aged 0–6 years old in a homelike environment. Such care is typically organized at the ECEC caregiver's home or at a child's home; it is offered by municipalities, municipality-outsourced ECEC providers, or private for-profit ECEC providers. Requirements for family-based ECEC services are the same as for center-based services. Operating hours are generally defined by the needs of participating children and families, although the total length of daily service is usually eight to nine hours. Despite the advantage of flexibility that family-based ECEC offers, the past decade has seen a gradual decrease in the number of such offerings. In 2013, family-based ECEC accounted for only 15% of the total market, compared to 74% for center-based ECEC (Kumpulainen, 2015).

Open ECEC Services

Various types of open ECEC services are offered by municipalities, municipality-outsourced ECEC providers, or private ECEC providers (both for-profit and not-for-profit). Although these vary among municipalities, they might include a combination of playground clubs, family houses, and/or "park auntie" activities. Playground clubs, the most popular modality, can be found throughout the country in nearly all municipalities.

Playground Club Activities. Playgroup club activities, which operate in municipality-run playgrounds or on the premises of ECEC centers, are intended for children in home care from age 2 to the beginning of pre-primary education. Activities are free of charge and operate for about three hours per day, usually from 9 a.m. to 12 p.m., up to four days a week. Supervised by city-employed ECEC caregivers, activities often include play, singing, and physical exercise. There may also be mother/father and child activities, language courses for migrant parents, sleep guidance, baby massages, infant family activities, and outdoor recreational and sports activities. Some cities may outsource playgroup club activities; Helsinki, for instance, provides service vouchers worth about $117 (€100) per month that families can use to pay for activities organized by private service providers.

Family Houses. Municipality-organized family houses (i.e., community centers) offer many services for families with small children, including drop-in, temporary child care services; resident-oriented activities; and various courses and group meetings for parents and ECEC professionals. Family houses also distribute information on child care and child development. Both parks and family houses offer families the opportunity to meet other families and share experiences of everyday life.

Park Auntie Activities. Park auntie programs offer short-term care in the mornings for children under the age of 6. Activities may include singing, playing, and physical exercise, supervised by playground supervisors or "park aunties" (i.e., ECEC caregivers) employed by the city. Parents may choose to take part in the activities or simply drop off their child with the caregiver for a few hours. In the park, children are free to play as they wish, although the park auntie may assist or participate.

Other ECEC Activities. In addition to municipality-organized ECEC services, local churches, NGOs, and cultural institutions (e.g., libraries, museums, science centers, community groups, religious communities) provide open ECEC services for young children and their families. Municipalities and private bodies also offer various forms of physical and sports activities. Some of the activities, such as many sports clubs, are fee-based, although there are also supervised activities free of charge.

Participation in ECEC Services for Children Aged 0–5

Although Finland provides extensive access to free ECEC services, there are significant differences in the participation rates among children of different ages. Children become more likely to participate in center-based ECEC as they grow older, with rates rising from 0.8% for those under the age of 1, to 29% for 1-year-olds, 52% for 2-year-olds, 59% for 3-year-olds, and 75% for 4- to 6-year-olds (Kumpulainen, 2015). These statistics reflect the robust support mechanisms and incentives that are available to enable parents to take care of their child at home in the child's first three years (Sipilä, Rantalaiho, Repo, & Rissanen, 2012). The home care allowance is particularly popular among parents with low levels of education and income, as well as immigrant families (Pölkki & Vornanen, 2016; Repo, 2009, 2010). Emergent policy proposals, however, aim to alter ECEC fees, the child home care allowance, and the child care leave length in order to increase under-3-year-olds' participation in ECEC (Karila, Kosonen, & Järvenkallas, 2017). These potential changes challenge the basic principle of parental choice and potentially signal that the children of unemployed, low-income, and/or immigrant families are "at risk" and require institutional ECEC services.

Pre-Primary Education

Pre-primary education, which typically begins in the autumn of the year a child turns 6, is designed to support children's learning, development, well-being, and smooth transition to school. Although pre-primary was made compulsory in 2015, attendance rates prior to this change were already high, hovering above 98% (Kumpulainen, 2015). Today, compulsory pre-primary education is organized for 700 hours per academic year, or about 4 hours per day. With costs fully covered by the state, it is provided free of charge to children, including all materials and meals. In addition, children who live over five kilometers from their pre-primary education provider, or who live where the route is dangerous, are entitled to free transport (OPH, 2017a).

All Finnish pre-primary education follows both the national core curriculum and a local curriculum; individualized education plans are also created for each child. Approximately 80% of pre-primary students are enrolled in services organized by ECEC centers, with the remaining 20% participating in pre-primary education on the premises of primary schools (Kumpulainen, 2015). About 6–8% of children attend pre-primary education offered by private, for-profit ECEC providers, situated either in schools or ECEC centers (T. Kumpulainen, personal communication, November 2, 2017). Privately organized pre-primary education, whether for-profit or not-for-profit, must follow the national core curriculum and meet all Finnish legal requirements and standards.

Recent Trends and Changes in ECEC Provision

Increasing For-Profit ECEC Provision. Traditionally, ECEC services have been provided as part of the array of universal services organized by municipalities and funded by a combination of public support from the state and municipalities and parent fees. This is changing, however, as more for-profit providers emerge, particularly in urban areas, with the goal of promoting diversity, parent choice, and cost reduction (Ruutiainen, 2016). Nonetheless, the Finnish for-profit ECEC sector is still small (about 10%) and primarily dominated by three main providers, which are able to benefit from economies of scale and reduced overhead costs (J. Lahtinen, personal communication, August 11, 2017). There are persistent criticisms regarding the involvement of for-profit ECEC providers, particularly regarding the possible creation of inequalities between children (Ruutiainen, 2016).

Legal Change. Spurred by economic challenges, the ECEC law that came into effect in August 2016 has, for the first time in national history, removed children's right to equal access to ECEC regardless of their family's economic position or engagement in the labor market. Now, children whose parents are not students or full-time workers have only a 20-hour per week entitlement to ECEC, and have no right to part-time ECEC beyond their compulsory participation in pre-primary education. Previously, no such restrictions existed, allowing all children to participate in full-time ECEC. Moreover, this law increased the adult-child ratio in 3-year-old ECEC groups to one adult for every eight children (from 1 to 7). Driven by the need to reduce public expenditures, these changes have heightened public concern because they contradict research evidence and Finland's historic commitment to social equity. Indeed, the law appears to weaken children's equal rights to ECEC, particularly for children who come from more vulnerable families (Karila et al., 2017).

Primary Education

All children in Finland must attend primary school starting in the year they turn 7, through age 12. As part of the Finnish basic education system, primary education is free of charge, with no cost for materials, meals, or, when applicable, transport. It is typically provided in municipality-run schools and follows the national core curriculum for basic education, meeting minimum requirements for the organization of time and delivery of the curriculum. For example, every child attending grades 1 (age 7) and 2 (age 8) has the right to receive at least 19 hours of primary education a week, with school days no longer than five hours. As school days typically end earlier than parents' working hours, many children who attend grades 1 and 2 also participate in after-school clubs (Kuntaliitto, 2017).

There are only a small number of private primary schools in Finland, serving less than 2% of children. Private primaries must acquire a license from the Finnish National Agency for Education; if granted, the school receives government funding but, unlike private ECEC services, cannot make a profit (OPH, 2017b).

SYSTEMIC/STRUCTURAL COMPONENTS

Structural Components

Governance

The Finnish Ministry of Education and Culture and the Ministry of Social Affairs and Health share responsibility for services for young children and their families, with the former responsible for ECEC and the latter responsible for services that deal with children's health and welfare. This dynamic was established in 2013, when, to emphasize the educational role of ECEC, purview was transferred from the Ministry of Social Affairs and Health to the Ministry of Education and Culture. Although no formal interministerial coordination agency exists, the ministries and their officials collaborate, exchange knowledge, and form working groups when needed.

The governance of ECEC in Finland is also divided between national and municipal levels. Governance by the Ministry of Education and Culture involves national policymaking, financing, minimum standard-setting, curriculum framework development, and national monitoring, whereas municipal-level governance covers local financing, curriculum specification, and local monitoring of ECEC services. In 2017, there were 311 self-governing municipalities in Finland that collect municipal taxes and hold legal responsibility for organizing public services, such as ECEC, for residents. In addition, there are six Regional State Administrative Agencies (AVIs). These agencies work in close collaboration with municipalities in order to ensure regional equality, such as universal access to basic public services including ECEC and health care. This is realized by AVIs carrying out executive, steering, and supervisory tasks laid down in the law.

Finance

The share of GDP dedicated to ECEC services in Finland is higher than the OECD average (1.3% compared to 0.8%). Annual ECEC expenditure per child for children under 3 is also above the OECD average (about $12,092, compared to $8,070). The same applies to children over 3 years, where the expenditure per child is about $10,477, compared to the OECD average of about $8,704 (OECD, 2016b).

Generally, ECEC services for children aged 0-6 years old are funded jointly by the central government, municipality, and parents. Notably, state funding to municipalities is not earmarked to ECEC but rather covers all public services that municipalities are legally required to deliver, allowing flexibility in the way they expend state funds. Funding to municipalities is allocated according to a means-tested formula that takes into account the number and age of residents, employment rates, and immigration rates and patterns. Municipalities then co-finance and administer the state's funding for public services, including ECEC, while taking parental contributions into consideration. Though there is some local variation in parent fees for ECEC services, national law stipulates the maximum amount that may be charged to parents, which, in 2017, was about $339 (€290) per month for full-day provision (Kuntaliitto, 2017). Parent fees are typically means-tested depending on the size and income of the family, and generally cover around 13% of total municipal ECEC budgets, with the rest coming from the state and municipality (J. Lahtinen, personal communication, August 11, 2017).

In the private sector (both for-profit and not-for-profit), ECEC fees are set by providers, and are typically higher than in the public sector, as they are unregulated. To lessen the burden on parents, KELA offers both private day care allowances and income-adjusted care supplements to families who choose to place their children in private ECEC provision. In addition, some municipalities or cities, such as Helsinki, may pay for additional private care support to parents (City of Helsinki, 2017) due to a shortage of municipality-run ECEC centers in the face of growing demand.

Though part of municipal basic services, pre-primary and basic education receive full public funding from the state. Finland's public expenditure on education (excluding ECEC) is 6.8% of GDP, which is the second only to Sweden (7.1%) among EU member states (Eurostat, 2017).

Instructional Components

Curricula Overview

Finland's national ECEC curriculum framework covers children between the ages of 0 and 5. Though separate curricula exist for pre-primary and primary education, all three curricula are designed to ensure quality, equity, and effectiveness, and are thematically linked to support children's continuous learning. The curricula are the responsibility of the Finnish National Agency for Education and are developed in partnership with a range of stakeholders, experts, and citizens, including educational policymakers, teachers and other ECEC professionals, families, trade unions, professional organizations, and research communities.

The Finnish ECEC curriculum and pre-primary curriculum are pedagogically underpinned by a recognition of the intrinsic value of childhood and an emphasis on the importance of play for development and learning. Drawing on socioconstructivist and sociocultural theories of learning and development, they incorporate children's own cultures, previous experience, knowledge, skills, and personal interests as important building blocks (OPH, 2016a, 2016b). Learning is considered a holistic process in which actions, emotions, sensory perceptions, and bodily experiences interact. As a result, the ECEC curriculum does not set specified learning or performance targets for children under age 6; instead, it promotes child-centered pedagogy and humanistic values inspired by the Froebelian approach (Froebel, 1887), which fosters children's agency and autonomy. Simultaneously, there is an emphasis on encouraging social interactions and relationships and creating a sense of community among children, ECEC staff, families, and the local community (OPH, 2016a, 2016b).

The content of the Finnish ECEC curricula, including pre-primary education, is organized into five core entities (OPH, 2016a). These cover: (a) *diverse forms of expression*, including music, visual arts, crafts, and physical and verbal expression; (b) *rich world of language*, including linguistic skills and competencies, and language as a tool for thinking, expression, and interaction; (c) *me and our community*, aiming to help children understand themselves and others while appreciating diversity in society; (d) *exploring and interacting with my environment*, addressing the development of children's science, technology, engineering, and mathematics (STEM) skills; and (e) *I grow and develop*, addressing physical activity, food and nutrition, and consumer skills, as well as health and safety issues.

Each of these five areas is framed by the concept of transversal competence—knowledge, skills, values, attitudes, and will—that support personal growth, lifelong learning, working life, and civic activity in the 21st century. Importantly, many transversal competencies are promoted in the Finnish education system across the age spectrum, from ECEC to the end of compulsory schooling, thereby providing crucial learning continuity. These include: (a) thinking and learning skills; (b) cultural competence, interaction, and self-expression; (c) skills to take care of oneself and manage daily life; (d) multiliteracy and participation and involvement in civil society; and (e) from preschool onward, information and communication technology skills.

Curricular Adaptations

Local Adaptations. Each municipality is responsible for developing a modified local curriculum for each level of education, beginning with ECEC, that adheres to the provisions of the national core curriculum (OPH, 2016a, 2016b, 2017b). When preparing this local curriculum, the municipality and local ECEC program service providers (both public and private) specify: (a) the language(s) of instruction; (b) structure, topics, form, and evaluation; (c) strategies for family and community participation and communication; and (d) plans to promote equity and equality. They also strategize for cooperation with other partners and stakeholders in the community, including ECEC providers, basic education teachers, and professionals in the health care and social welfare sectors.

Adaptations for Individual Children. Every child attending ECEC (including pre-primary education) has the right to an individual education plan (IEP) (OPH, 2016a, 2016b), which tailors the national and local curriculum to support his or her personal learning, development, and well-being in culturally and contextually sensitive ways. IEPs state goals and means for ECEC for each child and list any additional support required. Each plan is co-constructed by the ECEC teachers, parents, the child, and sometimes other social welfare professionals, who meet at the beginning of every year. It is then revisited with the parents and child at least twice a year.

Transitions

Under the Finnish national core curriculum, much attention is accorded to helping children transition smoothly from pre-primary into school. Pre-primary providers are required to collaborate with children's former or future education providers to share relevant information about each child (OPH, 2016a, 2016b). A number of transition efforts—which are planned and evaluated by teachers, parents, and the child—may take place throughout the pre-primary year (Kumpulainen et al., 2015). They may include: (a) school visits by children; (b) parent-child-teacher meetings; (c) parents' evenings; (d) specific targets for each child's school readiness in their IEPs; (e) the transfer of child-created portfolios between pre-primary and primary education; and (f) the nomination of an older "sibling" to help the transitioning child with orientation and schoolwork. As children in Finland typically attend the local primary school nearest their home, pre-primary school students often know in advance which school they will be attending. Furthermore, as has been discussed previously, children experience a continuity of curriculum and pedagogy, which facilitates and eases their transition. In these diverse ways, Finland creates structural continuity for children and recognizes the importance of transitions through purposeful activities and planning.

Assessment of Learning and Development

Although there are no early learning performance requirements or outcome specifications for children's learning and development in ECEC, teachers are required to systematically observe and document how their pedagogical work fosters each child's learning; moreover, they are required to factor these observations into planning future activities. This formative assessment needs to take account of the general objectives established by the ECEC curriculum, along with individual objectives outlined in children's IEPs. Throughout the year, teachers provide parents with regular feedback on their child's progress. Moreover, as an indication of the trust accorded children, providers are required to promote children's own capabilities for evaluating their learning; the ability to self-assess by children is considered a core competency for the 21st century (OPH, 2016a).

Furthermore, all children's development and well-being is monitored and supported by health clinics and school health care teams during annual medical examinations. Other services, such as immunizations, are also provided free of charge and enjoy wide public support and uptake (Wiss, Frantsi-Lankia, Pelkonen, Saaristo, & Stahl, 2014).

Program Quality

The national policy definitions (i.e., Act on Early Childhood Education and Care 36/1973) and Curriculum Guidelines on Early Childhood Education and Care (OPH, 2016a, 2016b), as well as local policy definitions and plans, provide the basis for program quality in ECEC. The minimum regulatory standards cover areas including maximum permitted group sizes (e.g., 20 pre-primary children if two adults are present, or 13 if one is present) and staff qualifications (e.g., one third of staff in ECEC centers must have a higher education degree in ECEC). Staff-to-child ratios are also strictly regulated. For instance, in center-based ECEC, one adult must be present for every four children aged 0–3, and for every eight children aged 3–5. Furthermore, all ECEC providers are required to use their local curriculum and develop an IEP for each child.

The responsibility of monitoring ECEC program quality rests with municipalities and AVIs. Because monitoring takes place at the local level, there are no shared national criteria for program quality in ECEC in Finland (Karila, 2016). This lack of a national quality framework, along with limited training on monitoring program quality, poses a challenge. It is anticipated, however, that program evaluations of ECEC services will become increasingly systematized, as in 2015 the National Evaluation Center (FINEEC) was made responsible for formulating four-year plans for the execution of national evaluations on program quality in Finnish ECEC.

Professional Preparation and Development

ECEC Workforce Requirements. Compared to other OECD countries, Finland's preservice training requirements for ECEC staff are relatively rigorous (OECD, 2016b). For example, at least one third of staff working with children aged 0–6 in center-based ECEC must have a bachelor's degree or equivalent in early childhood education (i.e., they must be ECEC teachers). Generally, center-based ECEC teams consist of at least three different types of ECEC staff: *educational staff* (ECEC teachers and special needs ECEC teachers), who are qualified at a tertiary level (typically bachelor's or master's level in ECEC) (International Standard Classification of Education [ISCED] 6–7); *care staff*, with a minimum qualification at a postsecondary non-tertiary level in health and welfare (ISCED 4–5); and *auxiliary staff*, who usually have a minimum qualification at the upper secondary level (ISCED 3) (UNESCO Institute for Statistics, 2012).

Officially, ECEC teachers have primary responsibility for pedagogy and curriculum delivery in center-based ECEC, with assistance provided by other members of the staff. In reality, however, the comparative roles and responsibilities of ECEC teachers and the rest of ECEC workforce are blurred, which has led to calls for clarification on job descriptions and management/leadership structures in the workplace (Karila & Kinos, 2010; Karila & Kupila, 2010; Onnismaa, Tahkokallio, & Kalliala, 2015). Initiatives are also under way to increase the number of ECEC teachers with pedagogical expertise, as the requirements of the new ECEC curriculum cannot be met by the current care-focused professional structure (Karila et al., 2017). Qualification requirements in family-based ECEC and open day care services are lower than for center-based ECEC, as they do not require any ECEC staff to have a tertiary-level education in ECEC. The minimum requirement is a postsecondary, non-tertiary level education in health and/or welfare.

Directors of ECEC centers, or directors of ECEC services who work at the municipal level managing all ECEC services (both center-based and family-based), must have, at minimum, a tertiary level degree in health or welfare and extensive work experience in the field. ECEC directors increasingly have a bachelor's, master's, and/or a doctoral degree in ECEC.

Preservice Teacher Education. The preservice ECEC teacher education program typically lasts between 3 and 4 years, and consists of 180 European Credit Transfer System (ECTS) credits, with an additional 60 ECTS credits in special needs education required for those who wish to become special needs ECEC teachers. The aims of the ECEC teacher education program are ambitious and demanding, with an emphasis on both theory and practice in pedagogical studies. The education includes supervised field practice in different ECEC programs, including pre-primary classrooms, and an emphasis on the integration of research. This is aimed at teachers developing their own practical theory and adopting a research-oriented attitude toward their work. Typically, field practice accounts for 15 ECTS credits of the full program of 180 ECTS credits.

Entrance into ECEC teacher education programs is highly competitive, as the university-level degree and nature of the teaching profession attract many young people into the profession. Flexibility in pedagogical methods and materials also proves to be an attractive aspect of the work. Teachers are considered "co-designers" of children's learning, together with the child, family, and community. Interestingly, despite the profession's popularity, average salaries of ECEC teachers in Finland are below the OECD average (OECD, 2016a, 2016b).

Inservice Teacher Education. Continuing professional development (CPD) for the ECEC workforce is the responsibility of the municipality, though it is offered by diverse providers, including the municipality itself; private, for-profit providers; regional agencies; universities; and research institutions. With no existing national legislation governing CPD opportunities for ECEC, the nature and amount of CPD is left to the determination of the municipalities. Some estimates put the average amount at three to ten days annually per ECEC staff member, the cost of which may be met by the municipality or employer (Lastentarhanopettajanliitto, 2017).

Although municipalities have the major responsibility for CPD, the National Agency of Education coordinates a national network for developing ECEC, which includes a professional development ECEC task force operating within and across regions and municipalities. The national network provides opportunities for the sharing of information and ideas related to research, good practice, and networking.

Family and Community Engagement

The Finnish national core curricula for ECEC, pre-primary, and basic education stress cooperation between the child's home and ECEC setting staff. This perspective is predicated on the belief that a foundation for constructive dialogue between everyone involved in a child's life enhances the child's overall development and well-being (OPH, 2016a). For example, the co-construction of the IEP creates an important basis for parent-teacher partnerships, which are further strengthened by parent-staff conferences and parents' evenings.

Although the primary focus of parental engagement is supporting individual children's development, parents are also invited to participate in activities that contribute to the broader development of ECEC in the local context, through participation in parent/board associations, input into the local curriculum, and participation in its evaluation. In fact, the renewed law on early childhood education (Early Childhood Education and Care Act, 36/1973), which came into effect in 2015, reinforces the rights of both parents and children in the planning, execution, and evaluation of ECEC. Children's views are taken into account in a variety of ways (e.g., by asking children to share their experiences of the activities organized for them in multimodal ways) so as to simultaneously support self-expression and language skills (OPH, 2016a).

To foster community outreach, the core curricula of ECEC, pre-primary, and basic education require that providers collaborate with other organizations and stakeholders, such as libraries, science centers, museums, cultural centers, and sports facilities/programs. Municipalities and the National Agency for Education also encourage and support collaboration via development grants and professional development programs to ensure alignment with national policies and encourage links between cultural and educational institutions and communities (OPH, 2016a, 2016b). In 2016, the development projects funded by the National Agency of Education focused on, among other things: (a) developing learning environments and pedagogy for ECEC; (b) promoting children's digital literacies and creativity; (c) pedagogical leadership; (d) implementation of the new ECEC curriculum; and (e) using digital portfolios as tools for enhancing knowledge exchange between children, ECEC teachers, parents, and the community.

Research and Development

Finland's fairly well-established academic research apparatus is multidisciplinary in nature, encompassing the fields of psychology, education, sociology, social work, health and welfare, sport sciences, cultural studies, politics, and media studies. Research is conducted at universities, research institutions, and government-funded bodies and organizations, such as the Academy of Finland. In 2014, the Academy established a Strategic Research Council (SRC) to provide funding for long-term and program-based research aimed at finding solutions to some of the major challenges facing Finnish society. The SRC presently funds a national research consortium on ECEC focusing on potential sources of inequality in Finnish ECEC policies and strategies for overcoming them locally and nationally (Alasuutari, Repo, Karila, & Lammi-Taskula, 2017). Similarly, the Ministry of Education and Culture funds multiple research and development projects, such as recent work on strategies to promote young children's multiliteracies, in collaboration with university researchers, teacher educators, ECEC teachers, library and museum educators, and parents (Kumpulainen, 2017). The National Agency of Education also provides grants for development projects that aim to create scalable, applicable models, methods, and tools for early years education. In the international arena, Finland takes an active role in collaborative research, participating in projects such as the European CARE project on the effects of ECEC on child development (Melhuish et al., 2015).

PRINCIPLES AS SYSTEMIC INPUTS

Finland boasts a robust and unique approach to ECEC systems-building. Rather than a focus on individual systemic elements, Finland's core inputs are a set of transcendent values that permeate ECEC services and systems. Much like any system, these principles (i.e., systemic inputs) work together seamlessly, though they are teased apart in the following sections so as to make them transparent.

A Principled ECEC System

The ideological orientation of the Finnish system sets ECEC deeply within a social welfare context. Finnish society and public policies largely rest on a Nordic welfare model, with a national social contract serving as the basis for universally available public services that aim to provide high-quality education and care for children and their families on fair and equal grounds. That services are provided to all, and that they are grounded in the fundamental principles of society, fosters trust in both the services themselves and in the institutions that provide them. Fundamentally, then, Finland builds its services to young children and their families on the platform of a principled social contract.

To live up to these principles, Finland has strong legislative, funding, and regulatory structures in place to support high-quality, equitably distributed, sustainable, and efficient ECEC services. The national policy definitions and national curricula on ECEC, as well as local policy definitions and plans, provide the basis for quality in Finnish ECEC. They build in mechanisms for both structural quality (e.g., staff-to-child ratios, high professional competence of teachers) and process quality, most notably through the availability of a national core curriculum for ECEC based on holistic pedagogic goals, values, and approaches.

A Trusting ECEC System

The Finnish ECEC system's principles of equity and quality are swathed in a profound sense of trust: trust of and by government, and trust of and by families, teachers, and children. The citizenry assumes that the government will do its best to provide high-quality, equitable services. In turn, the government assumes that parents know and will do what is best for their children and consequently provides an array of diverse services and supports for young families so they will have plentiful choices. From the time of a child's birth, the family leave system fosters flexibility for parents as they adapt to their changing life situation. Subsequently, while many forms of government-supported ECEC service arrangements exist, parents can also make use of various allowances to stay at home with their child, or enroll their child in publicly or privately organized ECEC services. Across all ECEC settings, families and parents have respect for teachers as professionals, and reciprocally, teachers respect the privileged position of parents with regard to their children. Finally, there is ultimate and abundant respect for the feelings, voices, and expressions of young children. Manifest in the solicitation of children's opinions, the requirements that children participate in self-evaluation, and the premium placed on children valuing one another, the trust placed in young children echoes that placed in government, institutions, teachers, and parents.

A Personalized ECEC System

The Finnish ECEC system is designed to meet the diverse needs of children and their families in various ways. Above all, choice abounds, with parents accorded the trust to select among options for themselves and their children. But personalization does not stop with choice. Inherent in the national curriculum frameworks is an individualized approach to supporting children's development. Most notably, each child has an IEP, developed through collaboration and agreement among teachers, parents, and children. Inherent in the Finnish ECEC system is an array of commitments by the government to universal services, with an expectation that such services will be personalized to meet the tailored goals and desires of individual families and children.

A Child-Centric ECEC System

Beyond its historic and deep-seated commitment to education and ECEC and its principled, personalized, and trusting approach to delivery structure and policy frameworks, Finland is also noted for its adherence to child-centered pedagogy and practice. Finnish ECEC focuses on the intrinsic value of childhood and the positive development and well-being of children and families (Paananen, Kumpulainen, & Lipponen, 2015). Moreover, Finnish ECEC pedagogy stresses children's agency and the sociocultural nature of learning and development, with a focus on children's active interaction with peers, teachers, adults, community members, and the environment. This emphasis on children's agency also means that they are invited to participate in planning, creating, and evaluating their own activities and learning environments (Alasuutari, Karila, Alila, & Eskelinen, 2014; Hilppö, Lipponen, Kumpulainen, & Rainio, 2016; Sairanen & Kumpulainen, 2014). Enhancing children's trust in their own abilities and strengths as learners—through positive emotional experiences and opportunities for child-directed play, inquiry, and imagination—is regarded as an essential aspect of ECEC (Kumpulainen, Lipponen, Hilppö, & Mikkola, 2013).

ANALYSIS AND RECOMMENDATIONS

Framed by the above principles, overall, ECEC services and the condition of young children in Finland are excellent, as children are provided ample opportunities to live, learn, and develop. Despite this grounding, Finland, like all countries, faces significant 21st-century challenges as it seeks to adapt to global trends and conditions. In recent years, growing immigration has brought increased ethnic, cultural, and language diversity to the country (Official Statistics of Finland, 2017b). Compounding these demographic changes are troubling economic trends, including rising child poverty rates, growing inequalities between the rich and poor, regional differentiation, and national budget shortfalls (Official Statistics of Finland, 2016, 2017b). For the Finnish ECEC system, these shifting dynamics raise important questions, including how to best maintain and foster quality services across the country, how to attend to increasingly diverse family structures and needs, and how to promote the development and effective use of research and data. Each will be addressed below.

Fostering Quality Services

Addressing Regional Differences in ECEC Quality

Changes in the economic conditions, mobility patterns, and family demographics that characterize Finnish society challenge the provision of high-quality ECEC services across the country. Finland is experiencing a rapid decline in the number of people living in remote, rural regions, with the majority of people now concentrated in the south, particularly in the Helsinki capital area (OECD, 2016d). This decreasing population density across Finland's vast geography puts pressure on the state's ability to fund and support public services across the country on fair and equal grounds. With growing variation in the quality and availability of ECEC services between and within municipalities (Karila et al., 2017), the government will need to develop innovative strategies to ensure that children across the nation have equal access to high-quality services.

Defining a Quality Framework

Although municipalities monitor the quality of ECEC services, and teachers and children document ECEC practices and learning processes, Finland has no national criteria for ECEC program quality. The development of shared criteria will help promote strategic and systematic monitoring and development of ECEC program quality nationwide. Knowledge of areas of programmatic and geographic strengths and weaknesses would not only allow for resources to be targeted more effectively, but would help guide the implementation and further development of ECEC programs throughout the nation.

Preservice Education of ECEC Teachers

Increasing linguistic and cultural diversity, economic challenges and accompanying austerity measures, and digitization all challenge the competence of ECEC teachers and staff. Preservice ECEC teacher education programs and student admissions to these programs need to be responsive to these changes to ensure necessary 21st-century skill-building. One strategy to address these societal developments is to attract more males and culturally, ethnically, and linguistically diverse people into the ECEC field by altering entrance requirements for teacher preservice programs. Further, the curricula content of preservice ECEC teacher education programs should be enhanced to better equip ECEC teachers to respond to increasing linguistic and cultural diversity in their classrooms and to meet the needs of children and families in a digital and diverse society.

Retention

More dedicated attention is needed to retain and motivate the existing ECEC workforce, and help teachers and staff update their professional competencies regularly. One strategy to reach these goals would be to develop career and CPD pathways for all ECEC staff through the systematic use of personal professional development plans. Another strategy would be to increase the salaries of ECEC teachers to maintain and motivate a competent ECEC workforce.

Role Clarification

At present, there are concerns that the roles of Finnish ECEC staff are blurred and undefined and that, in particular, the pedagogical leadership and expertise of ECEC teachers is underused (Onnismaa et al., 2015). Although creating a balanced team of ECEC staff with different experiences and qualifications may be an effective and financially sustainable approach to producing quality in ECEC, more carefully organizing the use of those different skills, knowledge, and competencies would help promote the efficient deployment of human talent. Such role clarification requires particular attention at different policy, practice, and administrative levels, both locally and nationally.

Attending to Diverse Families and Family Needs

Reconciling Work and Family Life

Although Finland performs well in international rankings of women's participation in working life (75.9%, compared to the OECD average of 71.3%) (OECD, 2017), there is evidence that the Finnish approach to combining work and family still has a gender skew and remains inflexible (Kosonen, 2014). Therefore, CED policies and family benefits need to be further developed to underscore the importance of fatherhood, encourage women's participation in working life, and reconcile paid employment and family life so that there is an adequate level of income for families with children. Strategies may include creating more flexibility for working hours and remote work, as well as using media and public discourse to combat gendered thinking regarding parenting and working life.

Communication Strategy

Increasing cultural and ethnic diversity in Finland, as well as changes in family structures, draws attention to the need to support all parents' understanding and decisionmaking in the face of the wide array of CED service options available (Official Statistics of Finland, 2017b). For instance, Finland's growing immigrant community and population of single parents may require more targeted or culturally attuned information regarding the early years. The development of a dedicated national communication strategy designed to reach diverse parents across Finland and support their awareness of the various services available to them, nationally and locally, would be a key first step. This communication strategy should define the roles of various settings (e.g., ECEC centers, health care and welfare clinics, community centers) in disseminating knowledge on services, and it should create opportunities for diverse families to share their needs and concerns about

ECEC so as to enhance responsive policymaking and promote the delivery of services that meet the needs of all children and their families.

Effective Use of Research and Data

Enhancing Data-Driven Policy

Despite Finland's growing body of academic research on early childhood pedagogy and development, far less research has focused on systemic issues related to ECEC services. For instance, the effectiveness of various organizational schemes, funding mechanisms (such as the home care allowance system), and women's workforce promotion strategies have received comparatively little attention (Karila et al., 2017). Because this inattention may stem in part from a misalignment between university researchers' areas of interest and the policy aims of the state, a nationally defined research agenda, resourced and steered by the government, may encourage research projects with more direct relevance to policy objectives and practice in the field.

In the face of state budget constraints and an aging population (Official Statistics of Finland, 2017b), research on the efficient use of public funds for ECEC is increasingly necessary to inform social, education, and health service reforms. For instance, a national research agenda could promote program evaluations that examine how different types of ECEC services (e.g., in-home or family care options) and their financing mechanisms meet the government's aim of providing quality education and care to all children in Finland. A national research agenda or framework could also help streamline the process through which research is disseminated and translated into policy and practice. The wider, more systemic, and strategic publication of research findings could enhance the knowledge base of best practice in ECEC policy, service development, and delivery.

Understanding the Effects of Increased Privatization

Given the recent growth of the private ECEC sector in the face of the long tradition of public provision, more research is needed to understand privatization's effects on quality, equality, opportunity, and sustainability of ECEC services for children, their families, and society more generally. This need is particularly acute given the nation's shifting economic context. Despite decreasing poverty over the past 20 years, the child poverty rate is on the rise, and the gap between the rich and poor is now widening (Official Statistics of Finland, 2016), which may affect equity of access to private services. Findings from this case study will be critical for the future development and delivery of ECEC services that are attuned to Finnish values of providing care and education to every child, regardless of socioeconomic, cultural, ethnic, and/or linguistic background.

CONCLUSION

Finland performs well on many indicators of development, with high efficiency in education (OECD, 2016c), high levels of literacy (Miller & McCenna, 2016), and low mortality rates in childbirth (OECD, 2016b). A deeply shared commitment to democracy and equality has enabled Finland to develop a world-class welfare and education system (Castells & Himanen, 2002; Miettinen, 2013). Driven in part by a small population size, Finland's policymakers have shown a dedication to investment in human capital and development, and hence in mainstream education, health, and welfare services, which has been critical to ensuring the success of the information economy and the overall national survival and prosperity. The nation's commitment to early childhood—now shown by researchers to promote human capital, educational equity, social cohesion, and socioeconomic prosperity (Heckman, 2011; Heckman & Masterov, 2007; Heckman, Pinto, & Savelyev, 2013)—has been a core element of Finnish society for decades.

The principled, personalized, trusting, and child-centered Finnish ECEC system is characterized by comprehensive and adaptive ECEC services available to all children and families, backed by a professional ECEC workforce. A quality ECEC program, guided by national core curricula, promotes local adaptation so as to be responsive to each child's learning and development in culturally and contextually sensitive ways. The unique features of the Finnish education system, including the intrinsic value it places on childhood and play, its "whole child"–centered approach to ECEC, and the trust it places in teachers' and institutions' self-accountability instead of externally controlled, high-stakes testing and inspections, continue to attract international interest.

Nonetheless, Finland's ECEC policies and services are in a state of flux and face challenges that emanate from major societal, demographic, cultural, and economic changes. In parallel, global educational reform movements are introducing new trends and principles to the Finnish ECEC system, emphasizing increased accountability, standardization, and privatization (Paananen et al., 2015). It is unclear how these trends—which often contradict the fundamental beliefs that undergird the Finnish ECEC system—will unfold in the future. Consequently, the present story of a principled, personalized, trusting, and child-centric ECEC system of Finland must be read against the backdrop of a dynamic, continually evolving society.

NOTE

1. All currency rates of this case study are calculated according to the information provided by the Bank of Finland and European Central Bank, November 3, 2017,

retrieved from suomenpankki.fi/fi/Tilastot/valuuttakurssit/taulukot/valuuttakurssit_
taulukot_fi/valuuttakurssit_today_fi/

REFERENCES

Alasuutari, M., Karila, K., Alila, K., & Eskelinen, M. (2014). *Vaikuta varhais-kasvatukseen: Lasten ja vanhempien kuuleminen osana varhaiskasvatuksen lainsäädäntöprosessia.* Opetus- ja kulttuuriministeriön työryhmämuistioita ja -selvityksiä 2014:13. Helsinki: Opetus- ja kulttuuriministeriö.

Alasuutari, M., Repo, K., Karila, K., & Lammi-Taskula, J. (2017). Child care. Retrieved from jyu.fi/child care

Castells, M., & Himanen, P. (2002). *The information society and the welfare society: The Finnish model.* Oxford, UK: Oxford University Press.

City of Helsinki (2017). Private day care allowance. Retrieved from hel.fi/helsinki/en/day-care-education/day-care/private/allowance/

Eurostat (2017). Educational expenditure statistics. Retrieved from ec.europa.eu/eurostat/statistics-explained/index.php/Educational_expenditure_statistics #Public_expenditure

Froebel, F. (1887). *The education of man* (W. N. Hailmann, Trans.). New York, London: D. Appleton Century.

Heckman, J. (2011, Spring). The economics of inequality: The value of early childhood education. *American Educator, 25*(1), 31–35, 47.

Heckman, J., & Masterov, D. (2007). The productivity argument for investing in young children. *Applied Economic Perspectives and Policy, 29*(3), 446–493.

Heckman, J., Pinto, R., & Savelyev, P. (2013). Understanding the mechanism through which an influential early childhood program boosted adult outcomes. *American Economic Review, 103*(6), 2052–2086.

Hilppö, J., Lipponen, L., Kumpulainen, K., & Rainio, A. (2016). Children's sense of agency in preschool: A sociocultural investigation. *International Journal of Early Years Education.* DOI: dx.doi.org/10.1080/09669760.2016.1167676)

Karila, K. (2016). *Vaikuttava varhaiskasvatus. Tilannekatsaus 2016.* Raportit ja selvitykset 2016:6. Helsinki: Opetushallitus. Retrieved from oph.fi/download/176638_vaikuttava_varhaiskasvatus.pdf

Karila, K., Kosonen, T, & Järvenkallas, S. (2017). Roadmap on the development of early childhood education for 2017–2030: Guidelines for increasing the degree of participation in early childhood education, and for the development of the skills of daycare centre staff, personnel structure and training. Publications of the Ministry of Education and Culture, Finland 2017:30. Retrieved from urn.fi/URN:ISBN:978-952-263-487-0

Karila, K., & Kinos, J. (2010). Päivä lastentarhanopettajana—mistä varhaiskasvatuksen ammatillisuudessa oikein on kyse? In R. Korhonen, M-L. Rönkkö, and J-A. Aerila (Eds.), *Pienet oppimassa. Kasvatuksellisia näkökulmia varhaiskasvatukseen ja esiopetukseen* (pp. 284–295). Turku, Finland: Turun yliopiston opettajankoulutuslaitos, Rauman yksikkö.

Karila, K., & Kupila, P. (2010). Varhaiskasvatuksen työidentiteettien muotoutuminen eri ammattilaissukupolvien ja ammattiryhmien kohtaamisissa. Työsuojelurahaston hanke 108267 loppuraportti. Retrieved from tsr.fi/c/document_library/get_file?folderId=13109&name=DLFE-4301.pdf

KELA. (2017a). Quick guide for families with children. Retrieved from kela.fi/web/en/families

KELA. (2017b). Child benefit. Retrieved from kela.fi/web/en/child-benefit

Ketola, K., Hytönen, M., Salminen, V-M., Sohlberg, J., & Sorsa, L. (2016). *Osallistuva luterilaisuus. Suomen evankelis-luterilainen kirkko vuosina 2012-2015: Tutkimus kirkosta ja suomalaisista. Kirkon tutkimusseuran julkaisuja*, 125. Kuopio, Finland: Grano Oy.

Kosonen, T. (2014). To work or not to work? The effect of child care subsidies on the labor supply of parents. *The B.E. Journal of Economic Analysis & Policy, 14*(3), 817–848. DOI: doi.org/10.1515/bejeap-2013-0073

Kumpulainen, K. (2017). The joy of learning multiliteracies. Retrieved from monilukutaito.com/en

Kumpulainen, K., Lipponen, L., Hilppö, J., & Mikkola, A. (2013). Building on the positive in children's lives: A co-participatory study on the social construction of children's sense of agency. *Early Child Development and Care, 184*(2), 211–229. DOI: 10.1080/03004430.2013.778253

Kumpulainen, K., Theron, L., Kahl, C., Bezuidenhout, C., Mikkola, A., Salmi, S., Khumalo, T., & Malmivaara-Uusitalo, L. (2015). Children's positive adjustment to first grade in risk-filled communities: A case study of the role of school ecologies in South Africa and Finland. *School Psychology International, 37*(2), 121–139. DOI: 10.1177/0143034315614687

Kumpulainen, T. (Ed.) (2015). *Key figures on early childhood and basic education in Finland*. Publications 2015:4. Finnish National Board of Education. Tampere, Finland: Juvenis Print.

Kuntaliitto. (2017). *Varhaiskasvatuksen asiakasmaksut*. Retrieved from kuntaliitto. fi/asiantuntijapalvelut/varhaiskasvatuksen-asiakasmaksut

Lastentarhanopettajanliitto. (2017). *Täydennyskoulutus*. Retrieved from lastentarha.fi/cs/ltol/Täydennyskoulutus

Melhuish, E., Ereky-Stevens, K., Petrogiannis, K., Ariescu, A., Penderi, E., Rentzou, K., Tawell, A., Slot, P., Broekhuizen, M., & Leseman, P. (2015). *A review of research on the effects of early childhood Education and Care (ECEC) upon child development*. CARE project: Curriculum Quality Analysis and Impact Review of European Early Childhood Education and Care (ECEC). Retrieved from ecec-care.org/resources/publications

Miettinen, R. (2013). *Innovation, human capabilities and democracy: Towards an enabling welfare state*. Oxford, England: Oxford University Press.

Miller, J. W., & McCenna, M. C. (2016). *World literacy: How countries rank and why it matters*. London, England: Routledge.

Official Statistics of Finland (2016). Income distribution statistic: Income inequality (international comparison) 2015. Helsinki, Finland: Statistics Finland. Retrieved from stat.fi/til/tjt/2015/01/tjt_2015_01_2017-03-03_tie_001_en.html

Official Statistics of Finland. (2017a). Births. Helsinki, Finland: Statistics Finland. Retrieved from stat.fi/til/synt/index_en.html

Official Statistics of Finland. (2017b). Population structure. Helsinki, Finland: Statistics Finland. Retrieved from stat.fi/til/vaerak/2016/vaerak_2016_2017-03-29_kuv_002_en.html

Onnismaa, E-L., Tahkokallio, L., & Kalliala, M. (2015). From university to working life: An analysis of field based studies in early childhood teacher education and recently graduated kindergarten teachers' transition to work. *Early Years, 35*(2), 197–210.

OPH. (2016a). Varhaiskasvatussuunnitelman perusteet 2014. Määräykset ja ohjeet 2016:17. Tampere, Finland: Suomen yliopistopaino Oy. Retrieved from oph.fi/download/179349_varhaiskasvatussuunnitelman_perusteet_2016.pdf

OPH. (2016b). Esiopetuksen opetussuunniteman perusteet. Määräykset ja ohjeet 2016:1. Tampere: Suomen yliopistopaino Oy. Retrieved from oph.fi/download/163781_esiopetuksen_opetussuunnitelman_perusteet_2014.pdf

OPH. (2017a). Esiopetuksen järjestäminen. Retrieved from oph.fi/koulutus_ja_tutkinnot/esiopetus/esiopetuksen_jarjestaminen

OPH. (2017b). Perusopetus. Retrieved from oph.fi/koulutus_ja_tutkinnot/perusopetus

Organisation for Economic Co-operation and Development. (2016a). Starting Strong IV. Early childhood education and care. Data Country Note. Finland. Retrieved from oecd.org/edu/school/ECECDCN-Finland.pdf

Organisation for Economic Co-operation and Development. (2016b). Education at a glance 2016: OECD indicators. Paris, France: OECD Publishing. Retrieved from dx.doi.org/10.1787/eag-2016-en

Organisation for Economic Co-operation and Development. (2016c). Regional outlook 2016: Productive regions for inclusive societies. Retrieved from oecd.org/gov/regional-policy/regional-outlook-2016-finland.pdf

Organisation for Economic Co-operation and Development. (2016d). Regional outlook 2016: Productive regions for inclusive societies. Retrieved from oecd.org/gov/regional-policy/regional-outlook-2016-finland.pdf

Organisation for Economic Co-operation and Development. (2017). Labour force participation rate (indicator). DOI: 10.1787/8a801325-en

Paananen, M., Kumpulainen, K., & Lipponen, L. (2015). Quality drift within a narrative of investment in early childhood education. *European Childhood Education Research Journal, 23*(5), 690–705.

Pölkki, P., & Vornanen, R. (2016). Role and success of Finnish early childhood education and care in supporting child welfare clients: Perspectives from parents and professionals. *Early Childhood Education Journal, 44*(6), 581–594.

Repo, K. (2009). Pienten lasten kotihoito: Puolesta ja vastaan. In A. Anttonen, H. Valokivi, & M. Zechner (Eds.), *Hoiva: Tutkimus, politiikka ja arki* (pp. 189–206). Tampere, Finland: Vastapaino.

Repo, K. (2010). Finnish child home care allowance—User's perspective and perceptions. In J. Rissanen (Ed.), *Cash-for-child care: The consequences for caring mothers* (pp. 46–64). Northampton, MA: Edward Elgar.

Ruutiainen, V. (2016). Markkinoistuva varhaiskasvatus. Retrieved from blogs.uta.fi/childcare/2016/11/02/markkinoistuva-varhaiskasvatus/

Sairanen, H., & Kumpulainen, K. (2014). A visual narrative inquiry into children's sense of agency in preschool and first grade. *International Journal of Educational Psychology, 3*(2), 143–176. DOI: 10.4471/ijep.2014.09

Sipilä, J., Rantalaiho, M., Repo, K., & Rissanen, T. (Eds.). (2012). *Rakastettu ja vihattu lasten kotihoidon tuki.* Jyväskylä, Finland: Vastapaino.

UNESCO Institute for Statistics. (2012). International Standard Classification of Education ISCED 2011. Retrieved from uis.unesco.org/sites/default/files/

documents/international-standard-classification-of-education-isced-2011-en.
pdf

Vipunen Education Statistics Finland. (2017). Population. Retrieved from vipunen.
fi/en-gb/_layouts/15/xlviewer.aspx?id=/en-gb/Reports/Väestö%20-%20
ikäryhmä_EN.xlsb

Wiss, K., Frantsi-Lankia, M., Pelkonen, M., Saaristo, V., & Stahl, T. (2014). Maternity and child health clinics, school and student health care and oral health care
for children and young people 2014—Follow-up and monitoring of the implementation of the Decree (338/2011). National Institute for Health and Welfare.
Directions 21/2014. Retrieved from julkari.fi/bitstream/handle/10024/125349/
URN_ISBN_978-952-302-356-7.pdf?sequence=1

CHAPTER 5

Responsive Policymaking and Implementation

Enhancing ECEC System Quality and Equity in Hong Kong

Nirmala Rao and Carrie Lau

A dynamic society with deep roots in both Confucian tradition and British colonial influence, Hong Kong demonstrates a remarkable balance of continuity and change. The development of its early childhood education and care (ECEC) system reflects this careful interplay. Chinese heritage has conferred a strong emphasis on academic achievement through rote learning as a means of upward mobility, while a century and a half of British rule opened the education system to Western ideals of student-centered, active learning. These dual legacies have endured in the face of significant policymaking. In recent decades, prompted by demographic changes, civil society demands, and global trends in the field, the government has shifted away from its traditionally laissez-faire stance toward a more hands-on approach to ECEC. Hong Kong's ECEC system thus tells a story of both continuity and change, undergirded by responsive policymaking.

Such responsive policymaking is reflected in several important ways. First, the government has exerted considerable effort to ensure that stakeholders have numerous channels to provide feedback on proposed and ongoing programs. Second, policymaking has been especially responsive to Hong Kong's considerable income inequality, as demonstrated by the many financing initiatives designed to bridge gaps in access. The sections that follow illustrate how the government's responsive policymaking and enduring emphasis on quality and equity have influenced and enhanced the care and education of young children in Hong Kong.

The umbrella term comprehensive early development (CED) services is used in this chapter to denote holistic and converging services in health,

For factual details on early childhood in Hong Kong, see Appendix D

family care, education, and social protection for children from birth to 6 years of age; ECEC, a subset of these services, refers specifically to early care and education. In keeping with the terminology used by the Hong Kong government, the term *child care* is used to refer to services for children from birth to age 3, whereas the terms *kindergarten, preschool,* and *pre-primary education* (PPE) are used interchangeably to refer to educational services for children aged 3–6. Over the past few decades, Hong Kong's ECEC policy has focused squarely on children in this latter age range, resulting in dramatic changes in the governance and financing of PPE services. Attendant to these changes, as part of Hong Kong's preparation of its next generation of citizens, there has also been an increased emphasis on quality of services and their equitable distribution.

HISTORY AND CONTEXT

Historical Context

Hong Kong's unique historical and social context has contoured the territory's vision of young children, the services provided for them, and the evolving system of ECEC. A British Crown Colony since 1841, Hong Kong was ceded on July 1, 1997 to the People's Republic of China (PRC) and became the Hong Kong Special Administrative Region (HKSAR). Under the "One Country, Two Systems" model, the HKSAR is now permitted a high degree of autonomy from the PRC (Government of the HKSAR, 2015). It has continued to remain a free port, a separate customs territory, and an international financial center, and it can develop and implement independent agreements with foreign governments and international entities. The important implication of this governmental autonomy is that the Hong Kong government is allowed to formulate and implement ECEC policies distinct from those in the PRC.

The development of an ECEC system in Hong Kong was precipitated by an influx of refugees from the Chinese mainland in the 1940s and '50s. In response to this immigration, the British colonial government opened several child care centers as a welfare service for needy families (Opper, 1992). Continued population growth over the following decades fueled increases in kindergarten provision, with the number of kindergartens growing from 156 in 1953 to 801 in 1979 (Rao & Koong, 2000). This rapid expansion was accompanied by declines in structural quality, evidenced by increases in teacher-to-child ratios and decreases in the number of qualified teachers (Education Department 1959, 1972). Throughout this period, the British colonial government's laissez-faire attitude toward ECEC meant that it provided neither professional qualification requirements for kindergarten teachers nor curriculum guidelines (Rao & Li, 2009).

The 1980s and '90s brought a newfound focus on equality. Recognizing the need to address economic disparities in access, the government began providing PPE fee assistance for lower-income families (Lau & Rao, 2018), accompanied by funding to enhance teacher training. Yet there continued to be minimal regulation of pedagogical quality (Rao & Li, 2009). Broadly, ECEC policymaking in the 20th century took a distinctly hands-off approach, with limited value accorded to the early years.

In 2000, after Hong Kong's return to China, the post-handover government introduced a reform of the school education system. For the first time, PPE was recognized as an important element of this system, providing the foundation for lifelong learning (Education Commission, 2000). Since then, government policy has emphasized increasing service quality, and a concern with equality—first manifested in the 1980s—has become even more evident. Moreover, there has been a substantial increase in government funding for PPE since 2005.

Current ECEC Policy Context

In 2007, the government responded to continuing economic disparities by introducing the Preschool Education Voucher Scheme (PEVS), a non-means-tested, flat-rate, direct-fee subsidy to parents intended to defray kindergarten fees. This represented a significant reform, as prior PPE funding had been quite minimal. However, the scheme itself gave rise to inequities, as some middle-class parents enrolled their children in two kindergartens (one half-day using the voucher, and the other half-day paying fees).

The government's response to this situation was the implementation, from September 2017, of the Free Quality Kindergarten Education Policy (FQKEP), which replaced the PEVS (Education Bureau, 2016b). The objectives of this policy are to promote equal opportunities by providing high-quality and highly affordable PPE for all children aged 3–6, regardless of socioeconomic background. The FQKEP has changed the government's strategy from demand-side to supply-side, providing funding directly to kindergartens/child care centers instead of parents. The FQKEP is accompanied by more stringent service monitoring, intended to increase the overall quality of PPE.

All PPE institutions in Hong Kong are in the private sector, but they are regulated by the government. They must meet health, safety, and pedagogical quality benchmarks to be granted an operating license, with regular inspection visits determining whether these licenses will be renewed. Most (about 84%) receive financial subsidies from the government through the FQKEP (or previously under PEVS), and thus must meet additional criteria, such as following the government's curriculum guide and adhering to specified limits to fees that they can charge.

Private, independent kindergartens—those that do not participate in PEVS/FQKEP—typically charge higher fees and are better resourced, with higher-quality teachers. The difference in educational resources between government-subsidized and private, independent kindergartens evokes inequities. Responsive to this, the Hong Kong government's ECEC policy is specifically geared toward supporting less socially advantaged children, since children from families who are more capable of paying higher kindergarten fees are more likely to attend non-FQKEP kindergartens than those from poorer families.

Sociocultural Context: A Blend of Chinese and Western Cultures

As noted previously, Hong Kong's sociocultural context has uniquely contoured its ECEC system. Confucian philosophy, with its strong emphasis on education, is reflected in the commitment to ECEC at societal and classroom levels. Although PPE is not mandatory, there has been almost universal enrollment of 3- to 6-year-olds since the 1980s (Lau & Rao, 2018; Wong & Rao, 2015), largely because PPE is regarded as important preparation for primary school. Chinese cultural beliefs about the importance of effort, discipline, and obedience are also evident in the highly structured schedules and environments found in kindergartens (Rao, Ng, & Pearson, 2009).

At the same time, government policy has embraced Western pedagogical approaches that value child-centered, play-based learning and focus on the all-around, holistic development of young children. This is evident in the *Guide to the Pre-Primary Curriculum* (Curriculum Development Council, 2006), which Hong Kong kindergartens participating in FQKEP (and formerly PEVS) must follow. Hong Kong's British heritage has further contributed to an emphasis on English language teaching in kindergartens, despite the fact that Cantonese is the first language of the majority of the population. Both Putonghua (Mandarin) and English, the two languages of business in Hong Kong, are taught from the first year of kindergarten.

Governmental Context: Beliefs Contour Service Delivery

The Hong Kong government is committed to supporting children and families by providing universal, high-quality health care, adequate child welfare, and free kindergarten education to all young children. The structure and delivery of this CED service provision, however, is contoured by the belief that primary responsibility for the upbringing of young children lies with the family. One consequence of this is that the government does not provide universal subsidies for the care and/or educational of children under 3 years. If their mothers are employed, these youngest children are often instead looked after by grandparents or other relatives. Another consequence is the marketization of ECEC, with all education and care services for children younger than 6 outsourced to the private sector rather than provided by the government.

A belief in the importance of ECEC quality, emanating since the 1990s, has had a significant impact on recent policy, resulting in funds to upgrade the professional qualification of teachers and the establishment of curriculum guides. It is also reflected in the initiation of the PEVS in 2007, wherein encashment of the voucher was contingent on a kindergarten meeting quality benchmarks. The FQKEP enacted in 2017 expands this, with increased funding for teacher training, kindergarten-based educational research, and quality assurance monitoring. Taken together, the massive increases in public funding for PPE over the past two decades reflect the government's view that quality kindergarten education is an investment in the future welfare and productivity of society.

SERVICES FOR YOUNG CHILDREN AND FAMILIES

Health

The Hong Kong government provides free health services for the territory's population of 7.3 million people through its Department of Health (Census and Statistics Department, 2017). The Family Health Service of the Department provides family planning to all women of childbearing age; for pregnant women, free antenatal services include routine checkups, blood tests, and pregnancy health education offered at 32 Maternal and Child Health Centers (MCHCs) (Hong Kong Legislative Council, 2017a). All births take place with skilled attendants (World Health Organization, 2016) and the territory has one of the lowest infant mortality rates in the world (1.5 per 1,000 registered live births in 2015).

Hong Kong has a relatively short period of paid maternity leave compared to OECD countries, which precipitates a greater need for child care. Mothers are eligible for ten continuous weeks of paid maternity leave that can commence from up to four weeks before the expected date of confinement, whereas fathers are eligible for three days of paternity leave. To a certain extent, this brevity reflects the Chinese cultural expectation that women should return to work relatively soon after giving birth.

Children's health needs are serviced at MCHCs, which provide immunizations, health surveillance, and parenting programs (Department of Health, 2017). Of households in Hong Kong with children under age 6, a total of 95.2% have registered for child health services provided by MCHCs (Census and Statistics Department, 2013). Most children (over 95%) receive all their vaccinations in these centers (Department of Health, 2016). The centers' universal Health and Developmental Surveillance program is designed to identify problems in children's physical, cognitive, emotional, and social development in a timely manner. Moreover, an initial physical examination of newborns, followed by regular checkups, monitors each child's growth, hearing, and vision (Department of Health, 2011). These checkups constitute a partnership between parents, teachers, and other caregivers aimed at enabling them to observe children's development, to supplement more detailed assessments by doctors.

Parenting education, offered for free to all new mothers, covers topics such as nutrition and home safety, typically in the form of information leaflets. Workshops and individual counseling are also provided, but only in Cantonese. As a result, women from ethnic minority groups who are unable to speak Cantonese cannot receive the benefits of these free services. This type of preclusion is one of the equity issues being addressed by the government's policies to enhance Chinese learning, starting from kindergarten.

Hong Kong's mixed private-public health sector gives rise to other notable inequalities. Though the government operates a comprehensive public health care system that provides excellent health care at low cost, public services are accompanied by long waiting times. Another option is to use (often costly) private services, typically by taking out private health insurance. Therefore, those who can afford private insurance and the private system are able to have a wider choice of facilities and doctors and receive treatment more quickly (Localiiz, 2017).

Social Welfare

The Social Welfare Department (SWD), under the Labour and Social Welfare Bureau, offers a comprehensive network of family and child welfare services that are accessible to all Hong Kong residents. These include preventive and remedial services for orphans, abused and/or neglected children, children of incarcerated adults, and children with disabilities (Social Welfare Department, 2016a, 2017a, 2017b, 2017d).

For orphaned children or those whose parents cannot look after them at home, the government provides residential child care services in crèches (for children under 3 years) and in child care centers (children aged 3–6). There are no small-group homes for children under 6 years. In addition to residential care, Hong Kong has a foster care system for young children whose parents cannot take care of them adequately for various reasons. Foster parents are provided with numerous forms of support, including incentive payments and regular training workshops and talks on topics related to the care of foster children (Social Welfare Department, 2016a). Though less common, adoption is another option for children who are orphaned or whose parents are unable to care for them (Social Welfare Department, 2017a).

There were a total of 874 reported cases of child abuse in calendar year 2015, including both physical abuse (48.5%) and sexual abuse (31.2%) (Social Welfare Department, 2016b). The SWD has specific protocols in place to protect children from abuse. After a suspected case has been reported, social workers from the Family and Child Services Units of the SWD contact the child's family and assess the home environment and the child's condition, and conduct a risk assessment. If required, the social worker will send the child to a hospital for medical examination and treatment, or arrange a temporary living situation. Intensive treatment for victims is provided in 11 centers in Hong Kong. A multidisciplinary case conference with doctors, social workers, teachers, and psychologists is held after the intervention (Social Welfare Department, 2015).

For moderately to severely disabled children under age 6, training and care is provided in day or residential special care centers. These centers are overseen by the SWD but operated by NGOs. Parents pay a nominal fee of about $45 (HK$354) per month for day care services and slightly more for residential care. Government grants are provided for parents who cannot pay this fee.

Children with identified special needs are enrolled in integrated kindergartens-cum-child care centers or in special child care centers, where they receive specialized services such as occupational therapy and speech therapy. Space in these centers is limited; in 2015, for instance, there were 2,900 children aged 0–6 on the waitlist. In response to this overwhelming demand, the government introduced the Pilot Scheme on On-site Preschool Rehabilitation Services, which allows children with special needs to receive specialized services (e.g., speech therapy) in kindergartens and child care centers that cater for normally developing children (Social Welfare Department, 2017c).

To address economic inequalities, the Hong Kong government and NGOs also provide financial assistance for young children from low-income families. The Comprehensive Social Security Assistance Scheme provides cash assistance to bring incomes of needy households up to prescribed levels to meet basic livelihood needs (Social Welfare Department, 2016c). Additional funds are given to low-income, single-parent families and those with a child with a disability.

Parenting Education

The Grandparent Scheme, a two-year pilot project launched by the SWD in 2016, is a novel parenting education initiative (Social Welfare Department, 2016d). Catering to 540 trainees, it provides child care courses to help grandparents become well-trained caregivers in the home setting. The Grandparent Scheme represents an important and culturally attuned approach to parent education, as Hong Kong grandparents often play a significant caregiving role. It is also a notable response to the need for cost-effective, high-quality child care that is in line with traditional Chinese cultural beliefs about the importance of the family.

Center-Based Child Care and Education

To ensure equality of access to ECEC, the Hong Kong government encourages a wide range of service options. Center-based care and education services for children from birth to 6 are provided in private child care centers, kindergartens, kindergartens-cum-child care centers, kindergartens-cum-mixed child care centers, and special child care centers, as detailed in Table 5.1. Child care centers offer day care to children from birth to 3, with a focus on providing stimulating environments to enhance their growth and development. This is particularly important for children from lower socioeconomic backgrounds, in order to give them the chance to develop their full potential. Kindergartens-cum-child care centers provide care and education for children aged 2 to 6, whereas kindergartens provide services for children from 3 to 6 years. Twenty-nine kindergartens-cum-mixed child care centers also provide services for children from birth to 6 years.

All kindergartens are privately run, and they are classified either as nonprofit (84%) or private independent (16%), depending on their sponsoring bodies. Only nonprofit kindergartens receive government financial subsidies (e.g., through PEVS or FQKEP); private independent kindergartens do not receive any fiscal support from the government and are free to charge parents high fees. Kindergartens are further classified as local schools (86%), which follow the *Guide to the Pre-Primary Curriculum* (Curriculum Development Council, 2006), or as non-local schools (14%), which do not. All nonprofit kindergartens must be local schools, but private independent kindergartens may choose whether to follow the guide. The government plays a significant role in supporting and monitoring the quality of all kindergartens in Hong Kong, regardless of their sponsoring body or local/non-local designation.

Kindergartens have no mixed-age groups, and they are divided internally into three levels: nursery class for 3-year-olds, lower kindergarten class for 4-year-olds, and upper kindergarten class for 5-year-olds. The majority of kindergartens provide half-day sessions of three hours each. This allows two different groups of children to be served on the same premises, one group in the morning and another in the afternoon, which may take place with the same principals and teachers. A smaller number of kindergartens provide whole-day (7 to 7½ hours per day) or long whole-day kindergarten services (10 hours per day). This stands in contrast to child care centers, the majority of which offer whole-day programs. There is an unmet need for subsidized full-day services from kindergartens (D. Lee, personal communication, October 9, 2017).

Occasional Child Care

Occasional child care services look after children when their parents have an unexpected need for short-term care. Provision of such services prevents

Table 5.1. Center-Based ECEC in Hong Kong

Setting	Special Child Care Center (CCC)	Residential CCC	CCC	KG-cum-Mixed CCC	KG-cum-CCC		KG
					2-3	3-6	
Ages of children	0-6	0-6	0-3	0-6	2-3	3-6	3-6
No. of centers	39	5	26	29	8		1,014
No. of children served/places	1,841	341	2,154	Not available	Not available		184,032
Overseen by	Social Welfare Department			Joint Office for KGs and Child care Centers			Education Bureau
Legal basis	Child care Services Ordinance and Regulations			Child care Services Ordinance Regulations & Education Ordinance and Regulations	Education Ordinance and Regulations		Education Ordinance and Regulations
Curriculum	Operation Manual from Social Welfare Department			KG Education Curriculum Guide (since September 2017)			
Quality monitoring	Service Performance Monitoring System (since 1999)			Quality Assurance Framework (since 2000)			
Teacher training	Certificate/Diploma/Degree in Child care or Equivalent			Qualified KG Teacher or Certificate/Diploma/Degree in Early Childhood Education or Equivalent			

young children from being left unattended at home. Occasional child care is available on full-day, half-day, or hourly bases at some child care centers and kindergartens-cum-child care centers.

SUPPORTING SERVICES: SYSTEMIC COMPONENTS

Instructional Components

Philosophical and Practical Approaches to Pedagogy

Hong Kong's historical roots have had a profound, and sometimes conflicting, influence on its approach to pedagogy. Its Chinese heritage has instilled the Confucian value of education as the vehicle for self-improvement, moral development, and upward social mobility. This, in turn, drives a pedagogical philosophy that emphasizes order, hierarchy, self-discipline, obedience, memorization, and academic achievement. In contrast, the legacy of British rule is reflected in an emphasis on inquiry, individuality, and critical thinking. Preschool pedagogy in Hong Kong can therefore be characterized as a dynamic fusion between traditional Chinese beliefs and Western notions of appropriate practice for young learners (Rao et al., 2009).

On the classroom level, finding a balance between these two approaches can be challenging. While the government curriculum promotes child-centered pedagogy, Hong Kong parents often insist on formal literacy and numeracy instruction in kindergartens and expect children to be given homework (Fung & Lam, 2008). Indeed, these traditional Chinese views about early education mitigate the effectiveness of government efforts to discourage didactic teaching (Rao, Ng, & Sun, 2016; Rao, Sun, & Zhang, 2014). Several observational studies have documented the use of direct instruction (Li & Rao, 2005; Ng & Rao, 2013), the deployment of a textbook-based approach, and an emphasis on copying words and sentences and completing worksheets (Ng & Rao, 2013) in kindergartens. More recent studies, however, report an increase in child-centered pedagogical approaches in kindergartens (Lau & Rao, 2018), suggesting that the balance may continue to shift.

Curriculum Matters

Historically, separate curricular guidelines existed for kindergartens and child care centers, but these were amalgamated in 1996 to form the *Guide to the Pre-Primary Curriculum*, which was further revised in 2006 and 2017 (Curriculum Development Council, 1996, 2006, 2017). This is regarded as the local curriculum and must be adhered to by kindergartens that receive governmental funding under the FQKEP (or previously under PEVS).

Developed with the goal of providing pedagogical coherence across diverse delivery systems, the *Guide* includes curriculum goals and frameworks, guidelines for whole-school curriculum planning, catering for diversity, an interface between kindergarten and primary school, and teacher professional development. The 1996, 2006, and 2017 reforms to the *Guide* reflect changing global views of the role of ECEC and demonstrate responsiveness to global trends.

The 2017 iteration, titled *Kindergarten Education Curriculum Guide: Joyful Learning through Play, Balanced Development All the Way*, reflects the government's belief that the curriculum for 2- to 6-year-olds should be holistic. Six learning areas are specified in the guide: *Physical Fitness and Health, Language, Early Childhood Mathematics, Nature and Living, Self and Society,* and *Arts and Creative Expression.* The aim is to nurture children toward balanced development, as well as to foster interest in learning and exploration, inquisitive minds, positive attitudes and values, self-confidence, and adaptability—overall, the development of good learning habits. Echoing and incorporating the deeply embedded Confucian belief that the ultimate goal of education is socialization, there is a strong emphasis on moral development as an educational objective. The *Guide* focuses on how children learn about themselves, how they develop the concept of right and wrong, how they express their emotions and feelings, and how they get along with others (Curriculum Development Council, 2017).

All PPE institutions that receive government funding must follow the *Guide.* That stated, they have some leeway in implementation, and curriculum and pedagogy are often swayed somewhat by parents' desire for an academic curriculum that prepares children for primary school admissions (Ng, Sun, Lau, & Rao, 2017). Not surprisingly, some of the kindergarten pedagogy implemented at the classroom level has been found to reflect instructional practices deployed in primary schools (Rao et al., 2014, 2016).

Program Monitoring

All ECEC programs are in the private sector, but the government has sole responsibility for regulation. Programs must meet health, safety, and pedagogical quality benchmarks to be granted an operating license, with regular inspection visits determining whether these licenses will be renewed. Government inspections are thus high-stakes events. The government has used its monopoly of the regulation system to enhance the quality of PPE programs by increasing the stringency of operating requirements.

Stand-Alone Child Care Centers

All education and care services for children from birth to 3 are registered and monitored by the SWD and must comply with its Service Quality Standards.

The SWD also monitors special child care centers (birth to 6 years). The Service Performance Monitoring System aims to improve the quality of services so that they are efficient and customer-focused, and to ensure accountability for public funds (Social Welfare Department, 2017e). The system is based on 16 Service Quality Standards, divided into three broader categories: Essential Service Requirements, Service Quality Standards, and Output Standards (Social Welfare Department, 2012, 2017e). Programs serving children aged 0–3 are required to submit annual reports on the three components to the SWD. In addition to annual self-assessments, the SWD conducts review visits/surprise visits and on-site assessment of centers at least once every three years (Education Bureau, 2012). These SWD reviews are not made publicly available.

Kindergartens and Kindergartens-Cum-Child Care Centers

All kindergartens and kindergartens-cum-child care centers are monitored by the Joint Office for Kindergartens and Child Care Centers, which is housed in the Education Bureau. Although there is a Joint Office for Kindergartens and Child Care Centers, the standards developed by the Social Welfare Department are used to evaluate the quality of services for children under 3 years old and the Quality Assurance Framework of the Education Bureau is used for the evaluation of the quality of services for children 3 and over who attend kindergartens. Since the introduction of the Quality Assurance Framework in 2000, kindergartens have been required to undergo annual school self-evaluations and external reviews. School self-evaluations require schools to prepare and submit a school report that outlines an evaluation of the effectiveness of current work plans and strategies for the next school year. Stakeholder surveys are also conducted to collect views of parents, teachers, and non-teaching staff on school performance (Education Bureau, 2017d).

In 2007, all kindergartens joining the PEVS were required to undergo a more stringent quality review requiring more documentation, which has continued under the FQKEP. Kindergartens are evaluated using 16 indicators under four domains: *Management and Organization, Learning and Teaching, Support to Children and School Culture,* and *Children's Development* (Education Bureau, 2017b). Kindergartens are then classified as excellent, good, acceptable, or unsatisfactory; in order to meet prescribed quality review standards for the PEVS/FQKEP, kindergartens must be deemed "acceptable" (at a minimum) in all four domains. Compliance with prescribed standards of quality is necessary for operating licenses and government funding to be granted. The Education Bureau may withhold or terminate funding to service operators should they fail to make improvements to reach prescribed standards of performance. Government monitoring thus ensures continuous quality improvement of kindergartens and demonstrates the importance given to quality assurance.

Unlike SWD reports on child care centers, which are not publicly available, inspectors' reports of kindergartens are uploaded onto the Education Bureau website. To facilitate parental choice and transparency, kindergartens are also encouraged to upload their school reports and development plans onto their school websites. Open access to inspection reports is an important portal for parents to gain information on program operations.

Workforce

The Hong Kong government's financial support for both preservice and inservice training of early childhood teachers over the past two decades illustrates its commitment to responsive policymaking. Driven by the belief that teacher quality influences early childhood program quality, the government has enacted incremental increases to professional requirements for all ECEC professionals. It has also made significant progress in harmonizing the historically separate trainings for kindergarten staff and child care center staff.

Professional Certification

Kindergarten Qualifications. The enhancement of professional certification qualifications for kindergarten teachers has been a gradual process. Minimum academic entry qualification was first introduced in 2001, with prospective teachers mandated to complete Secondary Five (equivalent to Grade 11), with five passes in the Hong Kong Certificate of Education Examination (now the Hong Kong Diploma of Secondary Education Examination). In 2003, this was extended to require that all newly appointed kindergarten teachers obtain Qualified Kindergarten Teacher certification. By 2004–2005, the percentage of teachers with Qualified Kindergarten Teacher status had risen to 93%, up from 23.6% a decade prior (Rao & Li, 2009). Finally, with the implementation of PEVS in 2007, all teachers in kindergartens who joined the scheme were required to attain a certificate in ECEC or its equivalent (Education Bureau, 2017c). In 2015–2016, 91.2% of kindergarten teachers held a Certificate of Education in Early Childhood Education, up from 69.5% in 2010–2011 (Education Bureau, 2017a). As a result of this steady rise in professional requirements, many inservice kindergarten teachers study for certificates, diplomas, or degrees on a part-time basis.

Child Care Qualifications. Historically, the academic qualifications for child care workers were lower than those of kindergarten teachers, with child care workers only required to complete a Director of Social Welfare–recognized training course, including courses for nursery workers, crèche workers, and playgroup leaders. Today, an increasing number of recognized programs are offered, including those that can prepare students to become kindergarten teachers.

Harmonization. For many years, kindergartens and child care centers were guided by different staffing requirements. This changed beginning in 2005, when the Hong Kong government initiated harmonization efforts. Kindergarten qualifications and child care qualifications are now recognized by both the Education Bureau and the SWD (Education and Manpower Bureau, 2003). Teachers with ECEC qualifications are therefore eligible for employment in either setting, the only exception being that training courses for child care workers offered by the SWD that focus on birth to 3 years are not recognized for employment in kindergartens that focus on children over 3 years.

This harmonization has been accompanied by increased government investment in teacher training, which over recent years has expanded the number of preservice programs and the number of tertiary institutes that offer such programs. Approved preservice training courses in early childhood education, which qualify for both kindergarten teachers and child care workers, are now offered in ten institutions, including community colleges, schools of continuing education, and universities (Education Bureau, 2016a).

Professional Support

The newfound emphasis on quality is also reflected in the school-based professional support services to teachers in kindergartens and kindergartens-cum-child care centers that are organized by the Education Bureau (such services are not provided to child care centers, which focus more on care rather than education). Teachers are provided advice by government inspectors on implementing the curriculum guide, catering to learner diversity, and supporting children's transition to primary education (Education Bureau, 2017e). Notably, an increasing number of professional support programs on teaching Chinese to non-Chinese-speaking children in kindergartens have been implemented in recent years, in response to the government's prioritization of better-quality language teaching for ethnic minority children. These children accounted for about 4% of preschool students (excluding White students) in the 2016–2017 school year (Hong Kong Legislative Council, 2017b).

The Education Bureau also provides inservice training events, primarily to kindergartens or kindergartens-cum-child care centers, in the form of seminars and school-based programs in special educational settings. They aim to enhance teachers' professional knowledge of strategies for managing student diversity, and to discuss the latest developments in education and curriculum for children with special educational needs (Education Bureau,

2016c). These schemes illustrate the government's commitment to an educational system that allows all students to develop to their full potential and reflects the government's concern with promoting equality and equity.

Transitions

In Hong Kong, there is a great deal of pressure from parents for kindergartens to "train" children in primary school content that will increase their chances of gaining entry to the better primary schools. In response to this situation, the government has recommended guidelines on the smooth transition from kindergarten to primary school (Curriculum Development Council, 2006, 2017). Examples of activities to support children's transition to primary school include seminars, simulations of primary school settings in kindergartens, visits to primary schools, and meetings among primary school teachers, students, and parents.

STRUCTURAL COMPONENTS

Governance

Hong Kong has a split-system approach to service organization, with responsibility shared between the Department of Health, the Hospital Authority, the SWD, and the Education Bureau. There is also a split-age approach, with the Education Bureau overseeing educational services for children above 3 years and the SWD for those under 3 years. Nonetheless, the territory's small size, high population density, and efficient transport system help facilitate interministerial coordination. There are regularly scheduled meetings among the various departments that provide services for children. Overall, services are well coordinated despite the split system, as evidenced by the numerous schemes that the government has initiated.

An example of efforts to promote cross-departmental coordination and integrative efforts is the Comprehensive Child Development Service (CCDS) scheme, which was initiated in 2005. It offers early identification and timely intervention to reduce health inequalities and to help parents raise healthy and well-adjusted children. The distinctive feature of the CCDS is that it involves interdisciplinary and cross-sectorial collaboration among the Education Bureau, the SWD, the Department of Health, and the Hospital Authority. Under the CCDS, a referral and reply system enhances close collaboration among kindergartens, child care centers, MCHCs, and Integrated Family Service Centers/Integrated Service Centers (overseen by the SWD) in the identification and provision of services for children with special learning needs (Department of Health, Education Bureau, & Social Welfare Department, 2008).

Another example of cross-departmental coordination is the Joint Office for Kindergartens and Child Care Centers, which registers and monitors all services for 3- to 6-year-olds. Consolidating registration and monitoring in one authority is accomplished by an office that is staffed by officers from both the SWD and Education Bureau, although the Education Bureau has a much larger role. Helping to harmonize services, the establishment of the CCDS and the Joint Office for Kindergartens and Child Care Centers suggests a trend in governance toward more interdepartmental coordination to provide effective and efficient services.

Finance

Government funding for kindergarten education is provided through the FQKEP, which replaced the PEVS in September 2017. Both schemes provide subsidies for half-day services (15 hours a week), but in different ways. Under the PEVS, which took a demand-side approach, all families with children aged 3–6 were provided with vouchers, which could be used at participating (i.e., nonprofit) kindergartens. These kindergartens offered the local curriculum, met quality benchmarks set by the government, and charged a tuition fee not exceeding specified fee thresholds.

In contrast, the FQKEP takes a supply-side approach, providing funding directly to participating kindergartens, instead of parents, on a per-capita basis. The amount of these subsidies is expected to increase over the years, and additional funding will also be available for kindergartens offering whole-day programs and long-whole-day programs. Like the PEVS, the FQKEP limits fees, requiring that kindergartens wishing to charge fees seek special approval. For the 2017–2018 academic year, 30 of 500 kindergartens under the FQKEP scheme received permission from the government to charge fees of up to $512 (HK$4,000) (Chiu, 2017). It is likely that these permissions have been granted because government subsidies are not enough to defray the schools' operating expenses or to finance improvement of the schools' educational facilities.

Though FQKEP primarily subsidizes half-day services, working parents often require full-day services for their children. Thus, additional demand-side funding for ECEC is provided to families who qualify for social assistance through the Kindergarten and Child Care Center Fee Remission Scheme, and to families of children below the age of 3 who attend child care centers through fee remission.

Overall, there has been a substantial increase in government funding for pre-primary education in the past 12 years. In 2005–2006, just before the launch of the PEVS, government expenditure on pre-primary education was merely $154 million (HK$1.2 billion); by 2015–2016 it had risen to $500 million (HK$3.9 billion). In 2017–2018, the government's investment in pre-primary education was $864 million (HK$6.7 billion) (Legislative

Council Panel on Education, 2017). This massive injection of funds indicates that the government's laissez-faire policy toward PPE is rapidly dissipating and reflects the government's newfound view that equitable early childhood education is the key first step in fostering human capital.

Engagement Components

Family, Community, and School Linkages

The FQKEP stresses the importance of parent engagement and encourages kindergartens to set up parent-teacher associations. Kindergartens are also encouraged to provide opportunities for parent participation in school activities and foster home-school communication (Education Bureau, 2016b). Further, the government encourages parents and kindergarten staff to make good use of community resources to enrich children's learning and life experiences. For example, the Neighborhood Support Child Care Project, which covers all 18 districts in Hong Kong, is a formalized child care service for children under 9 (Social Welfare Department, 2016a). Intended to provide needy parents with more flexible child care services, the project provides care in home settings through "neighborhood nannies," who are volunteers but may receive an honorarium.

Other Influences

Hong Kong does not have a central unit for child-related research. However, the Census and Statistics Department of the Hong Kong government provides relevant, reliable, and timely benchmark information on demographic and socioeconomic characteristics of the population for public policy formulation and academic research purposes. Data on service usage are collected on an annual basis by different governmental bureaus, such as the Education Bureau, the SWD, the Department of Health, and the Central Policy Unit. These bodies also conduct research related to their own policy domains. Importantly, however, no standardized child assessments are conducted. More evidence is needed to inform decisions that will improve the effectiveness of government-funded ECEC services.

Universities and NGOs bear the major responsibility for conducting basic and policy-relevant ECEC research, often with financial support from the government. Findings from both local (albeit limited) and overseas studies are often referred to as a basis for responsive policy planning. For instance, in making its recommendations to the government about the implementation of free kindergarten education, the Committee on Free Kindergarten Education (2015) set up the Sub-committee for Objectives, Teacher Professionalism, and Research to review policy-relevant, local ECEC research from 2013 to 2015.

There is a growing acceptance of the importance of rigorous and relevant evidence for problem analysis, policy formulation, policy implementation, and program evaluation. A preliminary search through Google Scholar reveals a gradual increase in the number of peer-reviewed journal articles published, with growth in output correlating with key policy changes in Hong Kong. The increase in research on early childhood education in 2016–2017 may particularly reflect anticipation of the FQKEP and responsive policymaking, as the government is showing greater willingness to fund relevant local research. Importantly, program evaluation is always an integral part of new ECEC initiatives, such as the PEVS and FQKEP.

CONSIDERING THE HONG KONG ECEC SYSTEM

According to the Theory of Change that guided this analysis, contextual, sociocultural, and temporal factors shape the inputs, outputs, and outcomes of an ECEC system. The Theory of Change posits that a solid infrastructure must be in place in order to achieve the desired systemic outputs of quality, equity, sustainability, and efficiency. This section presents the status of these systemic outputs in Hong Kong, followed by an analysis of the status of the systemic inputs that combine to yield these results.

Systemic Outputs

Analysis of four systemic outputs—quality, equity, sustainability, and efficiency—provides key context to understanding the current status of the ECEC system in Hong Kong. The following subsections discuss the government's recognition of the importance of each of these outputs and outline efforts that have led to progress as well as challenges.

Valuing Quality

The Hong Kong government has promoted quality ECEC since the 1990s. Diverse approaches to quality enhancement are under way, with policies focusing on increasing workforce quality by raising benchmarks for employment in kindergartens and kindergartens-cum-child care centers. The Hong Kong government also advances a strong culture of quality assurance and inspection. For example, the SWD and Joint Office for Kindergartens and Child Care Centers offer robust inspection services, evaluating programs based on well-defined systems of standards with inspection data then being used to drive quality. Moreover, data that are regularly collected, compiled, and analyzed by the Education Bureau are used to plan professional support to kindergarten teachers and enhance the quality of services. This emphasis on dissemination and use expands the reach of good practices. As such, the

Hong Kong government recognizes the importance of quality services and demonstrates a continued commitment to strategic investments in quality enhancements.

Valuing Equity

While efforts to promote ECEC quality continue, innovative funding initiatives to promote equitable access to health, welfare, and education services have also gained momentum. Equity in access for education, for example, is realized in universal primary and secondary education and, in ECEC, in the almost 100% enrollment rate in PPE. No child is deprived of schooling because of financial insufficiency, with support for families provided through the Fee Remission Scheme in addition to the former PEVS and the current FQKEP.

Moreover, equity in access is reflected in the government's support for children and families with diverse needs. Various targeted CED services and supports are provided for children from needy families, children from ethnic minority backgrounds, children with special educational needs, and children at risk of developmental delay. Such efforts promote their inclusion in mainstream education and facilitate their well-being, learning, and development.

Despite these achievements, however, two realities characterize the Hong Kong context. First, while children generally do have access to services, there is a good deal of variation in the nature and quality of those services. Despite the Education Bureau's stringent monitoring and quality assurance mechanisms for kindergartens, which are intended to ensure that all kindergartens reach an "acceptable" level of quality, variations in the quality of kindergartens persist (Chan & Rao, 2013; Ng & Rao, 2013). Children from higher-income family backgrounds still tend to attend better-resourced, independent (i.e., non-FQKEP-participating) kindergartens that have more qualified and experienced teachers and better facilities. Second, there are concerns about access to specialist services for children with special needs, particularly their access to special child care centers, kindergartens that offer integrated services, and residential child care centers. Despite ongoing efforts, access to identification, assessment, support, and placements remain limited.

Valuing Efficiency

Attention has also been accorded to promoting systemic efficiencies through infrastructure development so that various components (e.g., finance, governance, quality assurance) align and support one another. By this definition, the PPE system for Hong Kong's 3- to 6-year-olds is efficient. The harmonization of pre-primary services has resolved the problem of overlapping governance of education and care services catering to children of the same age group. Moreover, it has improved the efficiency of service monitoring for children over 3 years. Cross-departmental collaborations, such as the interministerial and interdisciplinary Comprehensive Child Development Service, further contribute to the efficiency of the ECEC system. Notably, however, the system for children under age 3 remains underdeveloped.

Valuing Sustainability

ECEC programs in Hong Kong are well sustained primarily because of high demand, marketization, and recurrent government funding. The government's fiscal commitment and continuous improvement of the infrastructure subsystems contribute to the sustainability of the system. Moreover, the government is also committed to scaling up and sustaining new services, often developed by NGOs, if they have been deemed effective, thus fostering their durability.

ECEC sustainability, however, is constrained by two conditions. First, real estate prices in Hong Kong are very high and continue to increase, impacting the financial sustainability of kindergartens. Given this, market-driven services face a real challenge remaining financially viable and operative. So severe is this condition that much of the public funding for PPE under the FQKEP will be used to pay rising rent costs to private property owners. For the FQKEP to be sustainable, the government will need to address this pressing rental issue. Second, to further sustain the ECEC system in Hong Kong, more support for data and research is needed to enable evidence-based policymaking and the improvement of services provided to children and families. A databank on child development is needed to centralize data for optimal use. Further, more local and systematic research should be conducted so that the unique needs and situations pertinent to Hong Kong are reflected in empirical data.

Analyzing Systemic Inputs

Three major elements of the infrastructure are crucial to understanding the output achievements, each of which has helped shape the current status of the ECEC system in Hong Kong. These are discussed in the following subsections.

Citizen Engagement and Responsive Policymaking

The British colonial government's laissez-faire attitude toward ECEC, as well as the beliefs that underpinned the pre-handover policy (e.g., child care as a parental responsibility and free-market economy), continue to be evident today. For instance, the Hong Kong government still does not provide universal subsidies for center-based care for children under 3. Nonetheless, the post-handover period was accompanied by important reforms to the ECEC system, shifting the policy zeitgeist from a hands-off approach to one that is far more interventionist (Wong & Rao, 2015). In this process of change, the government has been remarkably responsive to the needs of the population, and to the use of data to inform strategies and policies. Indeed, contemporary Hong Kong is an exemplar of responsive policymaking.

In designing its comprehensive strategy of responsive policymaking, the Hong Kong government has paid special care to diverse constituents and data sources, taking account of: (a) characteristics of the local population, including demographic trends; (b) civil society demands (e.g., parents' requests for extended hours of service); and (c) global trends in ECEC policy and practice (e.g., enhancing pre-primary teachers' professional qualifications and providing early intervention services to children with special educational needs). Motivated by concerns with inequities and the quality of the workforce, and by effective lobbying by stakeholders, responsive policymaking was legitimated.

Such engagement took place as policies were being formed and implemented at the turn of the century but continues today, as the government now exerts considerable effort to ensure that stakeholders have numerous channels to provide feedback on proposed and implemented initiatives. For example, a review of the PEVS was held three years earlier than initially planned because of public dissatisfaction with policy, providing tangible evidence of the responsive policymaking.

Coherent Ideology as a Platform for Integrated Action

Although Hong Kong has achieved considerable advancements through its responsive policymaking, progress has not always been as rapid as citizens or professionals in the field desire. In part, this has been attributed to: (a) the lack of a clear government position on ECEC development; (b) the absence of a forward-thinking plan for educating teachers; and (c) the lack of strong government intervention to educate parents on the early years.

With regard to a clear position on ECEC development, there is concern that the split governance system encourages different departments to simply focus on their sphere of services, without seeing children or families in their totality. For example, more collaboration between the Department of Health and the Education Bureau is needed regarding the provision of care for young children who are sick and unable to attend school while their parents work. To stave off these and other problems, such efforts could encompass more comprehensive planning across the fields of education, care, welfare, and health, as well as town planning, labor and manpower, and technology. Currently, the split-governance design may inhibit departments from seeing the overall needs of families—"the big picture"—but also precludes long-term solutions to endemic, systemic problems. Moreover, such division results in an underemphasis on the birth-to-3-year-old population. In other words, without a cohesive vision and more elaborated mechanisms for cross-ministry planning, the development of a comprehensive ECEC system with sufficient and integrated services may be inhibited.

Funding and Strategic Investments

Two fundamental and complementary ideologies guide Hong Kong's investments in young children and frame its contemporary commitment to proportionate universalism. First, Hong Kong has historically aimed to maximize the potential of its labor force and, in so doing, the future welfare of the society. Armed with new research, the government recognizes that investing in young children meets both of these human capital goals. Hong Kong's economic predisposition is therefore shifting toward investment in the early years as a strategic vehicle for maximizing social returns.

Second, Hong Kong is a vibrant market economy that thrives on entrepreneurialism and supports the functioning of the private sector. This ideological predisposition frames the ways in which Hong Kong sees fit to support ECEC services. Stated simply, marketization of ECEC prevails, with all services for young children being outsourced to the private sector. With essential direct service provision in the private sector, the government then uses its leverage, via regulation and fiscal incentives, to drive quality and equity. Regulatory drivers include the provision of regulations and the implementation of a monitoring system. Fiscal incentives have led to increases in provision, especially for older children.

This marketization has produced many positive effects. Governmental incentivization has led to broader coverage of the 3- to 6-year-old population. Achievement gaps between children from middle-class and less privileged backgrounds are less marked at age 5 than at age 3—a stunning outcome that suggests that preschool education is effective in mitigating achievement gaps prior to school entry (Rao et al., 2013). As a strategy, then, government fiscal and regulatory investments and incentives have yielded improvements in quality and equity. In this sense, the Hong Kong government is using its policy strategy—one typical of market-driven economies—to direct change with a (not so) light touch.

Nonetheless, there are disadvantages. A market-driven strategy ultimately privileges the market, which, in the case of ECEC, privileges parents by allowing them to make critical choices regarding the nature, amount, and type of services for their children. It does not, however, privilege all parents equally; those with greater resources have greater options. Moreover, parental choice means that there is no guarantee that services will be equitable in quality, as rich parents can avail themselves of more expensive and often better-funded services. Such choice ultimately means that the Hong Kong kindergarten market by itself has not been able to produce the equity needed for the healthy and holistic development of all young children.

Beyond these concerns at the macro level, there are important quality concerns that impact ECEC provision at the micro level, notably in the programs and curricula. As has been noted previously, kindergarten operators are forced to bend to market forces, including parental demands for more structured pedagogy and curriculum. Recognizing this challenge, academics and some service providers suggest that government control over the pre-school sector is insufficient and that Hong Kong cannot depend on market forces alone to provide high-quality, universally available services for young children.

Within this context, Hong Kong seems to be veering toward a doctrine of proportionate universalism (Marmot & Bell, 2012) in terms of ECEC funding. For example, in principle, the new FQKEP funds services for all children and families, hence the attribution of "universalism." But with the addition of the means-tested Kindergarten and Child Care Center Fee Remission Scheme and other financial assistance for families in need, funding is actually provided proportionate to the level of disadvantage. Hence a funding strategy of proportionate universalism is emerging, one that is manifest with regard to children from low-income families and those with special learning needs and from ethnic minority backgrounds. These youngsters will be given more support than in the past, tilting the strategic ECEC funding approach from *equality* to *equity* as it funds and supports PPE.

MOVING FORWARD: POTENTIAL NEXT STEPS

Taking Hong Kong's unique culture, size, population density, and emerging as well as embedded ideological predispositions into consideration, developing and improving the ECEC system has been, and will continue to be, challenging but feasible. As noted herein, even without a commitment to integrated governance structures, Hong Kong has made considerable strides toward enhancing the quality, equity, efficiency, and sustainability of its ECEC services. Building on the efforts undertaken to date, six recommendations are offered for consideration.

Shared Spaces

Hong Kong has a high population density and a small geographic footprint. Further compounded by high rent costs, many ECEC facilities have neither sufficient indoor space for children to have essential learning experiences nor outdoor play areas. One way to deal with this is would be to have common spaces shared by many kindergartens. For example, each district in Hong Kong could have a large ECEC facility with expansive outdoor areas that could be frequented on different days of the week by children from different kindergartens in that district.

Hybrid Model of Subsidization

The hybrid models of subsidization of PPE acknowledge both market forces and social engineering. The government's funding model gives parents wider choices of kindergartens while its monitoring system controls the quality of private sector kindergartens. By maintaining the link between funding and kindergarten quality, the government can continue to be a positive force in the system by progressively enhancing standards for quality, equity, efficiency, and sustainability.

Promoting and Scaling Up Innovation

Through the PEVS and now the FQKEP, the government funds kindergarten education and limits the fees that can be charged to parents. There are concerns, however, that these financial restrictions may dampen kindergarten's curriculum innovations—the cornerstone of producing effective systemic outcomes. The government must therefore take on the burden of fostering and scaling up innovation. The government should provide incentives to kindergartens to develop noteworthy practices and take responsibility for scaling up effective innovations.

Dealing with Inequity

There is considerable income inequity in Hong Kong. Elite kindergartens and kindergartens-cum-child care centers, which comprise about 16% of the market and are attended by about 20% of 3- to 6-year-olds, are not subject to the FQKEP. They charge higher fees, are better resourced, and employ teachers with higher professional qualifications. The government should progressively increase the benchmarks for setting and monitoring teacher quality so that all kindergartens and child care centers are resourced at similar levels.

Enhancing Services for Children Under 3

There is a great need for subsidized ECEC for the birth-to-3-year-old age cohort. Such services will enable mothers to engage in paid employment, aligning with both Hong Kong's historic values that emphasize work and its population policy. The government has recently commissioned a consultancy to advise on the long-term development of child care services. Depending on the findings, the government may provide universal free child care for children ages 2 to 3, which would represent an advancement in Hong Kong's ECEC system.

Research

As noted earlier, there is a lack of policy-relevant ECEC research currently being conducted in Hong Kong. Reliable general population demographic data are collected regularly and systematically, but data on conditions of children and usage of ECEC services are insufficient. Although there has been growth in ECEC research over the last decade, a central databank on child development and an overall increase in funding for research should be priorities in the future in order to inform policy planning and evaluate program effectiveness.

CONCLUSIONS

Set amidst a small geographical footprint, rich cultural heritage, robust quality assurance processes, and hybrid models of subsidization, Hong Kong's ECEC policy is thriving. It is characterized by continuity in its sustained emphasis on quality, and change in its newfound focus on equity. Accompanying this ethos, Hong Kong's dynamic ECEC system has supported a responsive policy strategy that takes account of the needs of children, parents, society, and the economy. With these efforts has come an increased, and still maturing, focus on the ECEC infrastructure. The government is aware that for Hong Kong to remain "Asia's World Class City," strategic planning must include its youngest citizens. This explains the emphasis on PPE and the move to FQKEP, which requires that private kindergarten operators follow government guidelines more closely (e.g., implement more play-based learning).

Hong Kong does not have an integrated ECEC system, and there are no plans for it to move in that direction. Despite this, there is quality provision and universal access to kindergarten. To remain a highly responsive system, government benchmarks for quality should grow increasingly stringent. Moreover, continuing responsive policymaking and policy implementation, coupled with increased investment, will ensure that all children in Hong Kong benefit from high-quality early education and care.

REFERENCES

Census and Statistics Department. (2013). Thematic household survey report no. 51. Retrieved from statistics.gov.hk/pub/B11302512013XXXXB0100.pdf

Census and Statistics Department. (2017). Hong Kong 2016 population by-census: Gathering population data for future blueprints. Retrieved from bycensus2016. gov.hk/en/index.html

Chan, W. L., & Rao, N. (2013). Variation in the qualities of instruction methods adopted by different kindergartens in Hong Kong. *The International Journal of Early Childhood Learning, 19*(2), 21–41.

Chiu, P. (2017, September 12). Hong Kong parents still paying kindergarten fees for schools under free scheme. Hong Kong: *South China Morning Post.* Retrieved from scmp.com/print/news/hong-kong/education-community/article/2110715/ hong-kong-parents-still-paying-kindergarten-fees

Committee on Free Kindergarten Education. (2015). Children first, right start for all: Report of the committee on free kindergarten education. Retrieved from edb. gov.hk/attachment/en/edu-system/preprimary-kindergarten/kg-report/Free-kg-report-201505-Eng.pdf

Curriculum Development Council. (1996). *Guide to the pre-primary curriculum.* Hong Kong: Author.

Curriculum Development Council. (2006). *Guide to the pre-primary curriculum.* Hong Kong: Author.

Curriculum Development Council. (2017). *Kindergarten education curriculum guide: Joyful learning through play, balanced development all the way.* Hong Kong: Author.

Department of Health. (2011). Developmental surveillance scheme. Retrieved from fhs.gov.hk/english/health_info/child/13033.pdf

Department of Health. (2016). Health facts of Hong Kong 2016 edition. Retrieved from dh.gov.hk/english/statistics/statistics_hs/files/Health_Statistics_pamphlet_ E.pdf

Department of Health. (2017). Child health. Retrieved from fhs.gov.hk/english/main _ser/child_health/child_health.html

Department of Health, Education Bureau, & Social Welfare Department. (2008). *Pre-primary children development and behaviour management—Teacher resource kit.* Hong Kong: Authors.

Education and Manpower Bureau. (2003). Education and manpower bureau circular no. 20/2003: Harmonisation of pre-primary services. Retrieved from edb. gov.hk/attachment/en/edu-system/preprimary-kindergarten/harmonisation-of-preprimary-services/background/embc03020e.pdf

Education Bureau. (2012). Handbook on quality review for kindergartens. Retrieved from edb.gov.hk/attachment/en/edu-system/preprimary-kindergarten/quality-assurance-framework/qr/handbook_on_qr_eng.pdf

Education Bureau. (2016a). Approved course list (2016/17 academic year). Retrieved from edb.gov.hk/attachment/en/edu-system/preprimary-kindergarten/ preprimary-voucher/approved%20course%20list_e.pdf

Education Bureau. (2016b). Education bureau circular no. 7/2016: Free quality kindergarten education. Retrieved from applications.edb.gov.hk/circular/upload/ EDBC/EDBC16007E.pdf

Education Bureau. (2016c). Special education services. Retrieved from edb.gov.hk/ en/edu-system/special/policy-and-initiatives/special-edu-serv/

Education Bureau. (2017a). Kindergarten education. Hong Kong: Government Printer. Retrieved from edb.gov.hk/en/about-edb/publications-stat/figures/kg.html

Education Bureau. (2017b). Performance indicators (Pre-primary institutions). Retrieved from edb.gov.hk/en/edu-system/preprimary-kindergarten/quality-assurance-framework/performance-indicators-pre-primary-institutions/index.html

Education Bureau. (2017c). Pre-primary Education Voucher Scheme. Retrieved from edb.gov.hk/en/edu-system/preprimary-kindergarten/preprimary-voucher/index.html

Education Bureau. (2017d). Quality assurance framework. Retrieved from edb.gov.hk/en/edu-system/preprimary-kindergarten/quality-assurance-framework/index.html

Education Bureau. (2017e). School-based support services for kindergartens. Retrieved from edb.gov.hk/en/edu-system/preprimary-kindergarten/sch-based-support-for-kindergartens/index.html

Education Commission. (2000). Review of Education System Reform Proposals. Retrieved from info.gov.hk/archive/consult/2000/Full-Eng.pdf

Education Department. (1959). *Annual report by director of education, 1958–59.* Hong Kong: Government Printer.

Education Department. (1972). *Annual report by director of education, 1971–72.* Hong Kong: Government Printer.

Fung, C. K. H., & Lam, C. C, (2008). The pre-primary education voucher scheme of Hong Kong: A promise of quality education provision? *Education Journal, 36*(1–2), 153–170.

Government of the HKSAR. (2015). Hong Kong 2015 yearbook. Retrieved from yearbook.gov.hk/2015/en/index.html

Hong Kong Legislative Council. (2017a). Replies to initial written questions raised by Finance Committee members in examining the estimates of expenditure 2017–18 (Reply Serial No.: FHB(H)446). Retrieved from legco.gov.hk/yr16-17/english/fc/fc/w_q/fhb-h-e.pdf

Hong Kong Legislative Council. (2017b). Replies to initial written questions raised by finance committee members in examining the estimates of expenditure 2017–18 (Reply Serial No.: EDB553). Retrieved from edb.gov.hk/attachment/en/about-edb/press/legco/others/17-18-EDB-2-e1.pdf

Lau, C., & Rao, N. (2018). Early childhood education in Hong Kong. In J. Roopnarine, J. E. Johnson, S. Quinn, & M. Patte (Eds.), *Handbook of international perspectives on early childhood education.* New York, NY: Routledge.

Legislative Council Panel on Education. (2017, January 24). 2017 policy address education bureau's policy initiatives (LC Paper No. CB(4)456/16-17(01)). Retrieved from legco.gov.hk/yr16-17/english/panels/ed/papers/ed20170124cb4-456-1-e.pdf

Li, H., & Rao, N. (2005). Curricular and instructional influences on early literacy attainment: Evidence from Beijing, Hong Kong and Singapore. *International Journal of Early Years Education, 13*(3), 235–253.

Localiiz. (2017, January 16). Public or private? A guide to healthcare in Hong Kong. Retrieved from hk.localiiz.com/public-or-private-a-comprehensive-guide-to-healthcare-in-hong-kong/#.WMjQ0NKGNpg

Marmot, M., & Bell, R. (2012). Fair society, healthy lives. *Public Health, 126,* S4–S10.

Ng, M. L., & Rao, N. (2013). Teaching English in Hong Kong kindergartens. *The International Journal of Literacies, 19*(3), 25–47.

Ng, S. S. N., Sun, J., Lau, C., & Rao, N. (2017). Early childhood education in Hong Kong: Progress, challenges and opportunities. In N. Rao, J. Zhou, & Sun, J. (Eds.), *Early childhood education in Chinese societies* (pp. 147–169). Dordrecht, The Netherlands: Springer.

Opper, S. (1992). *Hong Kong's young children: Their preschool and families*. Hong Kong: Hong Kong University Press.

Rao, N., & Koong, M. (2000). Enhancing preschool education in Hong Kong. *International Journal of Early Childhood, 32*(2), 1-11.

Rao, N., & Li, H. (2009). Quality matters: Early childhood education policy in Hong Kong. *Early Child Development and Care, 179*(3), 233–245.

Rao, N., Ng, S. S. N., & Pearson, E. C. (2009). Preschool pedagogy: A fusion of traditional Chinese beliefs and contemporary notions of appropriate practice. In C. K. K. Chan & N. Rao (Eds.), *Revisiting the Chinese learner: Changing contexts, changing education* (pp. 255–279). Hong Kong: Comparative Education Research Centre, The University of Hong Kong.

Rao, N., Ng, S. S. N., & Sun, J. (2016). Early learning experiences of young Chinese learners in Hong Kong: The role of traditional values and changing educational policy. In R. B. King & A. B. I. Bernardo (Eds.), *The Psychology of Asian learners* (pp. 635–649). Dordrecht, The Netherlands: Springer.

Rao, N., Sun, J., Ng, S. S. N., Ma, K., Becher, Y., Lee, D., Lau, C., Zhang, L., Chow, C. B., & Ip, P. (2013). The Hong Kong Early Child Development Scale: A validation study. *Child Indicators Research, 6*, 115–135. Retrieved from link. springer.com/article/10.1007%2Fs12187-012-9161-7

Rao, N., Sun, J., & Zhang, L. (2014). Learning to learn in early childhood: Home and preschool influences in Chinese learners. In C. Stringer & R. Deakin (Eds.), *Learning to learn for all: Theory, practice and international research*. Abingdon, UK: Routledge.

Social Welfare Department. (2012). Service performance monitoring system performance assessment manual. Retrieved from swd.gov.hk/doc/ngo/Manual/Performance%20Assessment%20Manual-September%202012-Eng.pdf

Social Welfare Department. (2015). Procedural guide for handling child abuse cases: Revised 2015. Retrieved from swd.gov.hk/doc/fcw/proc_guidelines/childabuse/Procedural%20Guide%20for%20Handling%20Child%20Abuse%20Cases_Revised%202015_eng_21122016.pdf

Social Welfare Department. (2016a). Foster care service. Retrieved from swd.gov.hk/en/index/site_pubsvc/page_family/sub_listofserv/id_fostercare/

Social Welfare Department. (2016b). Newly reported child abuse cases from January to December 2015. Retrieved from swd.gov.hk/vs/stat/stat_en/201501-12/stat-en.pdf

Social Welfare Department. (2016c). Social security. Retrieved from swd.gov.hk/en/index/site_pubsvc/page_socsecu/

Social Welfare Department. (2016d). Pilot project on child care training for grandparents. Retrieved from swd.gov.hk/en/index/site_pubsvc/page_family/sub_listofserv/id_projectcct/

Social Welfare Department. (2017a). Adoption service. Retrieved from swd.gov.hk/en/index/site_pubsvc/page_family/sub_listofserv/id_adoptionse/

Social Welfare Department. (2017b). Child care services. Retrieved from swd.gov.hk/en/index/site_pubsvc/page_family/sub_listofserv/id_child cares/

Social Welfare Department. (2017c). Pilot scheme on on-site pre-school rehabilitation services. Retrieved from swd.gov.hk/oprs/index_en.htm#toc

Social Welfare Department. (2017d). Residential child care services. Retrieved from swd.gov.hk/en/index/site_pubsvc/page_family/sub_listofserv/id_residchild care/

Social Welfare Department. (2017e). Service performance monitoring. Retrieved from swd.gov.hk/en/index/site_ngo/page_serviceper/

Wong, J. M. S., & Rao, N. (2015). The evolution of early childhood education policy in Hong Kong. *International Journal of Child Care and Education Policy*, 9(1), 1–16. Retrieved from ijccep.com/content/9/1/3

World Health Organization. (2016). Proportion of births attended by a skilled attendant—2007 updates. Retrieved from apps.who.int/iris/bitstream/10665/69949/1/WHO_RHR_07.16_eng.pdf

CHAPTER 6

Progress via Innovation and Investment

Setting the Stage for Greater Harmonization in the Republic of Korea

Mugyeong Moon and Eva Landsberg

The Republic of Korea, traditionally referred to as the "country of morning calm," has in recent years been rebranded as "dynamic Korea" and "creative and innovative Korea" (Presidential Council on National Branding, 2014). These monikers reflect the fast-paced, future-oriented transformation of the nation, which over the past 60 years has achieved nearly unrivaled economic development. Much of this success has been attributed to Korea's unique education system, which has long included early childhood education and care (ECEC). Driven by persistent low birth rates, concerns over equity of opportunity, and a prescient eye toward the development of future generations, ECEC has been elevated to prominence in Korean society and politics.

HISTORY, VALUES, AND VISION

The Republic of Korea's political history has uniquely contoured the emergence of its ECEC system. Following a 36-year period of Japanese colonial governance, Korea achieved independence from Japan in 1945, when it was divided along the 38th parallel and occupied by the Soviet Union in the North and the United States in the South (the Republic of Korea). The North Korean Communist Army's invasion of the south in 1950 signaled the outbreak of war and led to the rise to power of an authoritarian military government in the Republic of Korea. Civil society struggles in the postwar period ultimately led to the election of the civilian government of Kim Young-sam in 1992 (The Academy of Korean Studies, 2017).

For factual details on early childhood in the Republic of Korea, see Appendix E

128

The political upheaval of the mid-20th century left ECEC largely neglected, with priority accorded to the development of elementary and secondary education systems. Despite this, over three key periods, and emanating from a variety of rationales, ECEC has now emerged as the foundation of Korea's education system and a key pillar of its public services. In the first of these periods, from the 1960s through the 1980s, the war-torn nation concentrated on economic growth through its Five-Year Economic Development Plan, designed to stabilize and enrich Korean society. With few natural resources to develop, however, the government focused on cultivating its human capital, beginning with its youngest citizens (Korea Educational Development Institute & Ministry of Education, 2015). ECEC policy was thus developed through the Five-Year Plans. Standards for the educational environment for young children were enacted in 1962, and in 1976, the nation established its first four kindergartens attached to public primary schools (Na & Moon, 2003). Throughout the 1980s, with the implementation of the Early Childhood Education Promotion Act in 1982, the number of kindergartens and teacher training institutes, along with children's ECEC participation rates, increased dramatically. Notably, due to scarce resources and a political agenda that privileged rapid expansion, Korea took a "quantity over quality" approach throughout this period (Korea Educational Development Institute & Ministry of Education, 2015).

As the nation's economy matured through the 1990s, the number of working mothers grew, leading to calls for significant increases in ECEC services. In this second period of ECEC development, the government initiated a three-year expansion of child care services, with the aim of supporting maternal employment. This effort also involved some investment in service and staff quality. Because growth occurred primarily in the private sector, however, it raised pressing issues of universality, equity, and transparency.

In the 21st century, the Republic of Korea now faces a dual impetus for investment in ECEC. First, though the nation achieved the remarkable distinction of being the first country in OECD history to rise from "recipient nation" status to join the Development Assistance Committee, inequality and social polarization have been deepening. Characterized by the newly coined term "*Sujeo* (spoon-and-chopsticks) *class theory*," there are concerns that children are being provided vastly different opportunities from the beginning of their lives based on the social, cultural, and economic backgrounds of their families, rather than their own abilities and efforts (Ministry of Education, 2017b). As a result, a new equity focus has risen to prominence, with the government committed to providing high-quality, universal early childhood services so that children from vulnerable and underprivileged families are offered equal learning opportunities.

Second, and perhaps the strongest influence on Korean ECEC currently, a looming "population cliff" derived from persistent low fertility rates has compelled the government to explore a range of child-rearing support policies. Increases in dual-income families, single-parent families, divorced families, families in which grandparents raise their grandchildren, married couples with no children, and multicultural families have all heightened the demand for social supports for children's services (Choi et al., 2015; Moon, Cho, & Kim, 2016). This is complicated by concurrent concerns over lessening family roles in child-rearing, as the number of children in full-day ECEC programs rises. The nation's 21st-century outlook on ECEC, therefore, necessitates strong government investment through an array of diverse, flexible child-rearing supports.

RANGE OF SERVICES

Health and Nutrition Services

A wide range of health and nutrition services are available for young children and their families, encompassing health checkups and screenings, vaccinations, parenting education and counseling, and pre- and perinatal care. For nearly all Korean children, these health services are provided through the National Health Insurance (NHI) Service, which covers almost 100% of the population; families may also elect to enroll in additional private insurance. A very small percentage of the total population are not included in the NHI because they are beneficiaries of the Medical Aid insurance program, which covers populations such as very-low-income or North Korean refugee families, or families of wounded or deceased veterans and public safety personnel. Medical services are provided primarily at private doctors' offices and hospitals, which are licensed and regulated by the Ministry of Health and Welfare (National Health Insurance Service, 2017b).

During a woman's pregnancy, the government provides Citizen-Happiness Vouchers (500,000 KRW, or approximately $500, for the pregnancy of a single child; approximately 900,000 KRW, or $900, for multiple birth pregnancies) intended to cover related health care costs (in addition to those covered by the NHI) at designated medical centers. Further financial supports are available to young (age 18 or under) and low-income mothers (Ministry of Health and Welfare & Social Security Information Services, 2017).

After a child's birth, insurance covers neonatal screenings for the six most common diseases, and, thereafter, child health checkups are provided up to seven times, from 4 to 71 months old (typically, the first checkup is conducted within 4 to 6 months, the second within 9 to 12 months, and once annually after 18 to 24 months). Health checkups involve services such as: (a) measuring height, weight, and head circumference; (b) developmental screenings; (c) counseling; and (d) general health and hygiene education

(National Health Insurance Service, 2017a). A series of 16 vaccinations are available freely to all children up to the age of 12.

Specialized services are also available. The Nutrition Plus project, which targets pregnant mothers and children under the age of 6 who have nutritional risk factors (e.g., anemia, low birth weight, poor growth or nutrition), provides specialized care. Children with disabilities and their families are supported through care services, disability examination subsidies, and disabled child-rearing allowances for developmental rehabilitation services, parent counseling, and extended child care services.

Female workers are granted a total of 90 days of paid maternity leave, which can be taken before and after childbirth. Three days of paid paternity leave, in addition to two unpaid days, are provided to fathers (National Law Information Center, 2017). Further parental leave is granted for one year to each parent for children age 8 and under (parents may overlap their years). The paid salary during most of this leave is 40% of the normal monthly wage, with an upper limit of approximately $900 (1 million KRW).

Due to low numbers of fathers taking parental leave, however, the government has increased the parental leave benefit of the second user to cover 100% of the normal wage in the first three months (Ministry of Employment and Labor, 2017a). Since 2010, the number of fathers taking leave has been increasing, a positive reflection of the ongoing national effort to counteract low birthrates by promoting male participation in child-rearing (Ministry of Employment and Labor, 2017b).

Child Protection Services

Child protection services, designed to ensure the healthy upbringing of children under age 18 who do not have guardians deemed capable of raising them, focus on orphans and runaway, abused, and neglected children (Social Welfare Act, Article 3, 2017). These services include: (a) support for a target child's capacity to live independently; (b) financial support for foster care; (c) center-based social services; and (d) the Child Development Account (CDA), a matching fund between the local government and a sponsor in order to support a child's entry into society and the workforce, called a Seed Account (Ministry of Health and Welfare, 2017a).

The Ministry of Health and Welfare operates specialized institutions for child protection (50 total) that prevent and protect against child abuse. These institutions receive child abuse reports, conduct field surveys, and provide professional linked services to abused children (Kim, Park, Lee, & Lee, 2016). Shelters for child victims and temporary protection shelters offer integrated, residential services to children in need of immediate protection.

The Ministry of Health and Welfare also runs the Dream Start project, designed to provide customized and integrated services to vulnerable children, such as those from low-income families, single-parent families, or backgrounds of abuse, to support their growth as healthy and happy members of society. As of 2015, there were 229 Dream Start Centers with a total of 125,562 recipients enrolled (124,200 children and 1,362 pregnant women). The centers offer integrated case management through home visits and continuous monitoring, as well as partnerships with community sponsors.

Smile Centers, operated by the Ministry of Justice, are specialized institutions that provide mental and psychological treatment services to crime victims and their families who have been mentally traumatized by crime. As of 2016, a total of 10 Smile Centers operate nationally (Kim et al., 2016).

ECEC Services

Korean ECEC is provided in child care centers and kindergartens, or through home visiting services. Though these may be public or private, ECEC is generally market-driven, with over 75% of children being served in private, for-profit settings. Overall enrollment rates in ECEC services are high and increase as children grow older, from 15.9% of children under 1 year, to 70.1% of 1-year-olds, 85.8% of 2-year-olds, 89.5% of 3-year-olds, 90.8% of 4-year-olds, and 91.1% of 5-year-olds (Korea Institute of Child Care and Education, 2016).

Child Care Centers. Child care centers, which serve children aged 0–5, are overseen by the Ministry of Health and Welfare. They provide full-day care for 12 hours a day, typically from 7:30 a.m. to 7:30 p.m. Child care centers may be either public or private, although most are private, with public centers catering to just 12.1% of children. Private centers may be founded by legal corporate bodies, home-based providers, employers, or parents. Incentivized by the government, a growing proportion of child care centers are based in the workplace.

As of 2017, over half (51.9%) of child care centers are family day cares, where children are mostly served in the home of a certified child care provider. Though numerous, these family day cares serve fewer than a quarter of children enrolled in child care (23.7%) because their enrollments are capped at 20 children (Ministry of Health and Welfare, 2017b). Like child care centers, family day cares fall under the purview of the Ministry of Health and Welfare. Family day care has been criticized for low service quality and low levels of teacher education (Yoo, Lee, & Lee, 2016).

Kindergartens. Overseen by the Ministry of Education, kindergartens serve children between the ages of 3 and 5. They operate for 4–5 hours daily and often provide 3–4 hours of afterschool programs. Like child care centers, kindergartens may be public or private, although over three-quarters of children are served in private settings. Private kindergartens may be established and run by corporate bodies or private entities, including individual service providers, and may be nonprofit or for-profit. Public kindergartens, on the other hand, may be attached to elementary schools or be independent entities composed of four or more classrooms.

Home Visiting Child Care Services. A third type of ECEC provision, home visiting child care, is intended for families who may require individualized or additional services (e.g., employed single parent or a disabled parent, low-income households, multi-child households). Overseen by the Ministry of Gender Equality and Family, home visiting child care services are designed to reduce the child care burden for parents and may complement other forms of center-based care. Home visiting child care may be offered on an hourly basis for children under the age of 12, or on a full-time basis for children under 3 years, with service fees subsidized by the government between 25% and 75%, depending on income (Ministry of Gender Equality and Family, 2017).

SYSTEMIC/STRUCTURAL COMPONENTS

Structural Components

Split Governance. The Republic of Korea's ECEC system has a split system of governance, with responsibility shared between two national-level ministries. The Ministry of Education (formerly called the Ministry of Education, Science, and Technology, or MEST) oversees all kindergartens (serving children aged 3–5), while the Ministry of Health and Welfare oversees all child care centers and family day cares (serving children aged 0–5). Historically, the Ministry of Gender Equality and Family has also played a significant role in ECEC, particularly for children aged 0–2. In 2004, it was made responsible for administering child care services due to concerns that the needs of working mothers were not being met; however, this responsibility was shifted back to the Ministry of Health and Welfare in 2008. The shifting balance of power among national-level ministries is representative of the numerous societal rationales for ECEC that exist in Korea; it also signals the need for greater coordination.

ECEC policy planning is largely centralized, with the two national-level ministries (Education, and Health and Welfare) setting most standards and regulations for their respective areas of oversight. Since 2011, they have worked together to develop, and in parallel to implement, the Nuri Initiative, a broad-spanning project that represents the core of early childhood education policies for children aged 3–5. It includes a common curriculum, a common government-provided subsidy, and a common teacher training program, which apply across all ECEC programs for 3- to 5-year-olds (i.e., both kindergartens overseen by the Ministry of Education and child care centers overseen by the Ministry of Health and Welfare).

To ensure effective implementation of national directives, such as components of the Nuri Initiative, each ministry distributes supervisory responsibility to lower levels of governance. The Ministry of Education is supported by 17 Local Education Offices and 178 District Offices of Education, which oversee kindergartens across nine metropolitan cities and eight provinces. Fifteen of the Local Education Offices operate Early Childhood Education and Development Institutes, which provide information on ECEC to parents and communities, develop new programs, conduct training of kindergarten teachers, and implement kindergarten program evaluations. Meanwhile, the Ministry of Health and Welfare operates 230 child care–related divisions (e.g., Division of Youth or Division of Women and Family), which supervise child care centers across municipalities, counties, and districts. Comprehensive child care support centers serve similar functions to Early Childhood Education and Development Institutes, for the child care sector.

The dual and parallel ECEC governance structure evokes some concerns over efficiency and equity; these are particularly prominent with regard to funding and quality disparities between kindergartens and child care centers. For the past two decades, the Korean government and diverse stakeholder groups have attempted to consolidate this split system but have been hindered due to a lack of consensus on specific ways to do so as well as insufficient funding to carry this out (Chang et al., 2013; Moon, Park, & Kim, 2017; Rhee, Kim, Shin, & Moon, 2008). In 2013, recognizing the complications that arise from a dual governance approach, the president designated a higher governance body, the Office for Government Policy Coordination (part of the Prime Minister's Secretariat) to bridge the gaps and address persistent issues occasioned by split governance (Office for Government Policy Coordination, 2013). Notable functional integration has emerged from the efforts of this boundary-spanning entity. Through the Nuri Initiative, the curriculum for children aged 3–5 has been consolidated, a single subsidy has been established to heavily support ECEC services in both child care centers and kindergartens, and a harmonized quality assurance (monitoring) system is planned. The Republic of Korea's ECEC system thus demonstrates the effectiveness and efficiency of designating a boundary-spanning mechanism—in this case, a higher governance body, the Office for Government Policy Coordination—when power and funding dichotomies exist at the ministerial level.

Finance. The Korean government offers substantial subsidies to cover child care and education for all children aged 0–5, irrespective of household income or background (Ministry of Education, Science and Technology & Ministry of Health and Welfare, 2011). Some money is given directly to providers, but Korea has largely adopted a demand-side approach, with voucher cards called "i-Happiness Cards" provided directly to families who apply for them. Introduced in 2015, the cards—which harmonized the formerly separate voucher systems for kindergarten and child care centers—can be used to pay for ECEC services for children aged 0–5.

Every child aged 0–2 is entitled to a subsidy (provided to families via i-Happiness cards) intended to cover free full-day care in public or private child care centers. Financial backing for this subsidy is shared by the central government (approximately 65%) and local governments (approximately 35%). Local funding is provided equally by general accounts of upper-level local governments (i.e., metropolitan cities and provinces) and lower-level local governments (i.e., small cities, counties, and districts) (Suh & Lee, 2014). In order to regulate costs, the Ministry of Health and Welfare has established a universal (national) ceiling on maximum fees that child care centers, whether public or private, can charge for tuition.

ECEC financing for children aged 3–5 was transformed in 2012–2013 by the Nuri Initiative—an expansive policy agenda designed to improve functional harmonization of ECEC. While providing some supply-side funding through supplementary "Nuri allowances" to ECEC teachers, the Initiative has made the most significant reforms to demand-side financing. Every child aged 3–5 is entitled to a $200 (220,000 KRW) per-month subsidy through their i-Happiness Card, which is intended to cover half-day (4–5 hours a day, i.e., 20–25 hours a week) of Nuri-Curriculum education in child care centers or kindergartens. It is anticipated that the Nuri subsidy, regardless of whether it is used in a kindergarten or child care center, will be fully funded by Local Offices of Education. The Nuri Initiative thus marks a notable harmonization between the financing of the two settings.

Although the subsidies on the i-Happiness Card (child care subsidies for children aged 0–2 and Nuri subsidies for children aged 3–5) are intended to make ECEC free to all families, in reality, parents typically bear some of the cost, particularly in costly private kindergartens. Unlike in child care centers, fees in private kindergartens have traditionally been left unregulated, although the government issued a recommendation that fees be "frozen" following the initiation of the Nuri subsidies. Kindergartens also charge additional fees for afterschool programming, which are only partially subsidized by local governments. Thus, parents may pay additional fees up to almost double amount of the Nuri subsidy per month (Lee, Kim, & Lee, 2016).

This lack of kindergarten fee regulation stems from the fact that kindergarten has historically not been part of public school systems, and until recently was left largely in the hands of private providers. Over the past decade, growing social awareness of the importance of early childhood has led the Korean government to seek to increase the public nature of pre-primary education. With substantial public funds now being channeled (via Nuri subsidies) to for-profit private kindergartens with unregulated fees, there are increasing demands for such kindergartens to be more financially transparent and to be bound by the same financial regulations as other ECEC settings. However, a reform attempt by the Ministry of Education designed to increase harmonization in accounting rules (Kim et al., 2015; Ministry of Education, 2012, 2017a; Woo, Park, Jun, & Jung, 2012) stalled in the face of fierce resistance from private kindergartens. It serves as a prescient reminder of the challenges countries face when attempting to revise fiscal schemes, particularly within a split system.

Instructional Components

Pedagogical Approaches and Curriculum. Two consecutive national curricula encompass Korean ECEC. The first, the National Standard Child Care Curriculum (3rd Edition), applies to children aged 0–2, who are served in child care centers. It was first implemented in 2007 for children aged 0–5 through an effort by the Ministry of Gender Equality (since 2008, the Ministry of Health and Welfare) to create a child care agenda and guidelines for child care teachers. Following the 2012–2013 adoption of the Nuri Curriculum for all children aged 3–5, the National Standard Child Care Curriculum was revised and implemented exclusively for younger children (ages 0–2), with modifications designed to strengthen its continuity and consistency with Nuri.

The aforementioned Nuri Curriculum now applies to all children aged 3–5, whether they are enrolled in child care centers or kindergartens. It was developed in 2011 through the consolidation of the erstwhile National Kindergarten Curriculum (1969–2011) and the National Standard Child Care Curriculum (2007–2011) as it applied to children aged 3–5. As part of the broader Nuri Initiative, this curriculum represents a significant functional harmonization in the ECEC sector, fostering consistent, high-quality pedagogy and practice in both kindergartens (overseen by the Ministry of Education) and child care centers (overseen by the Ministry of Health and Welfare).

The Nuri Curriculum aims to help children develop good character and basic knowledge and skills, thus establishing a strong foundation for them to grow into responsible citizens of a democratic society. Specifically, it is based on five desired outcomes: (a) to cultivate basic habits, order, consideration for others, and cooperation; (b) to help young children have respect for people and nature, and obtain a good understanding of their culture; (c) to foster creative minds through holistic development; (d) to strengthen linkages with the elementary school curriculum; and (e) to place an emphasis on self-directed learning experiences in the five learning areas and establish an integrated, play-centered program designed to run for 4–5 hours daily. These learning areas are: (a) Physical Activities, Health, and Safety; (b) Communication; (c) Social Relationships; (d) Arts Experience; and (e) Inquiries into Nature. Within these areas are 20 categories, 63 subcategories, and 136 details. Above all, the Nuri Curriculum emphasizes play-based and interest-based approaches, with the idea that children should learn through their daily life experiences. Active interactions between children, between children and teachers, and between children and their environment are supported through a mixture of large- and small-group and individual activities, indoor and outdoor activities, active and quiet activities, and integrated activities based around themes.

For children aged 3–5, formative child evaluations are conducted by teachers based on Nuri content and objectives, and they focus on the individual characteristics of each child and her level of development and developmental change. Teachers utilize a variety of tools, including observation, analysis of education outcomes, and interviews, to create well-rounded, comprehensive evaluations. These are then compiled as reference materials for each classroom's teaching staff to use to: (a) better understand individual children; (b) make decisions to support their learning; (c) improve teacher-child interactions; (d) reorganize the Nuri Curriculum on the classroom level; (e) inform discussions with parents; and (f) prepare children's overall academic record.

The Nuri Curriculum is intended to align well with both the National Standard Child Care Curriculum that precedes it and the primary and secondary school curricula that follow it. Alignment is progressing, with the Ministry of Education conducting a revision of the competency-based primary and secondary school curricula to align them more closely with the Nuri Curriculum. As such, the revised curricula will emphasize the importance of knowledge production and utilization, rather than rote knowledge acquisition.

The Korean national government and local governments have led several initiatives to promote the quality of Nuri Curriculum implementation. For instance, to identify and highlight good practice, the Ministry of Education selects "50 Outstanding Kindergartens" based on their curriculum planning and implementation of character and creativity education (Ministry of Education, 2015). The 17 Local Offices of Education also hold contests of good educational programming in kindergartens under their supervision in order to promote educational quality. Many local governments also provide individual ECEC services with customized in-depth consultations of pedagogy and curriculum implementation by dispatching senior practitioners and experts. Such consultation is found to be highly helpful, especially for child care teachers, who tend to have less time for professional development due to their long working hours (Choi et al., 2012; Moon, Lee, & Kim, 2016).

The Ministry of Education (formerly MEST) supports a unique supplementary program in kindergartens designed to foster science and technology learning. Called the robot learning (R-learning) program, it deploys teacher-assisting robots in kindergarten classrooms. This initiative emerged as part of the future-oriented Plan for the Advancement of Early Childhood Education in 2009, which sought to emphasize science and technology as key components of 21st-century learning (Ministry of Education, Science, and Technology, 2009). As part of the R-learning program, MEST hosted explanatory and educational programs for teachers and developed new educational content that included the robots. Initial assessment of the impacts on children, teachers, and institutions suggested that innovative robot-assisted education offered positive impacts and was an area of potential future growth (Lee, Lim, & Byeon, 2015).

Monitoring Quality of Services. Reflecting the split system of ECEC governance, two systems of ECEC monitoring currently exist in the Republic of Korea: the Child Care Accreditation System (CAS), introduced in 2005, and the Kindergarten Evaluation System (KES), introduced in 2008. Participation in both the CAS and KES, in their entirety, is voluntary on the part of providers, but participation in the systems is tied to government subsidies (e.g., Nuri subsidies), resulting in high rates of participation and compliance. In 2015, a total of 96.3% of kindergartens participated in the evaluation, and 78.8% of child care centers achieved accreditation (Korea Institute of Child Care and Education, 2016).

With regard to content, the CAS was created by benchmarking the Australian accreditation system (see Chapter 2) and is heavily focused on structural quality. To become accredited, child care centers must meet rigorous and detailed service operation requirements on measures such as safety and teacher-to-child ratios. In total, the CAS is composed of 6 areas (environment, health, safety, curriculum, child care activities and teacher-child interaction, and management), 50 indicators, and 308 elements (Ministry of Health and Welfare, 2017b). Under the fourth round of evaluation in 2017, CAS was revised to include more process quality indicators such as child-teacher interactions and communication and engagement with parents and the public. Accreditation is overseen by the Korea Child Care Promotion Institute at the central level, in collaboration with Comprehensive Child Care Support Centers at the local level. It is conducted through a combination of self-evaluation, written evaluation, and on-site evaluation, with an "expert committee" review following the on-site evaluation. Results are then made available to the public.

In comparison to the CAS, the KES generally includes a stronger emphasis on process quality and is far less detailed with regard to service operation requirements. It consists of just 4 areas (curriculum, learning environment, health and safety, and operational management), 11 indicators, and 30 elements. The Ministry of Education supports the KES structurally by providing common indicators and manuals and running a database for the evaluations. Evaluation is led, however, by the Local Offices of Education, which establish and implement specific evaluation plans, compile evaluation results, train evaluators, and verify all information. The process of evaluation is similar to that of the CAS, involving a self-evaluation, written evaluation, and on-site evaluation, with results ultimately being made available to the public to inform parental choice and incentivize improvement.

Recognizing the inefficiencies and quality disparities that arise from split systems of monitoring, the Korean government, as a part of its broader ECEC integration project, recently began the process of creating a consolidated quality assurance system. This new system is intended to harmonize the CAS and KES, consolidating quality indicators and creating commonality in service quality between kindergartens and child care centers (Kwon, Lee, Bae, & Yoon, 2016). Projected to be in effect by the end of 2017, the effort was stymied by resistance from Local Offices of Education and other kindergarten stakeholders, who expressed concerns that the new system would achieve harmonization by lowering quality and introducing too many detailed indicators. As a result, integration has yet to be fully achieved.

Workforce Training. In light of the Nuri Initiative's success in harmonizing the curriculum for 3- to 5-year-olds across all settings, workforce training (pre- and inservice) for child care and kindergarten teachers is needed. Currently, significant disparities exist between the two systems, with kindergarten teachers generally trained more intensively under a more streamlined system than child care teachers. Entry requirements, inservice training, budgets for teacher training, and salary subsidies all differ as well. Though much discussed, harmonization has yet to be achieved. This section describes the current split systems of workforce training.

Despite an explosion in the number of child care services in the 1990s, the Office of Management of Child Care Teacher Certificate was set up by the Ministry of Health and Welfare in 2007, with the goal of more efficiently preparing the child care workforce. An important first step was replacing the term "child care giver" with "child care teacher," emphasizing that child care center staff provide more than protection and care. Nonetheless, child care teachers' low entry qualifications and irregular training backgrounds have yielded an overall lack of parental trust in the quality of child care services (Moon & Kim, 2013). In contrast, kindergarten teachers' comparatively rigorous academic and training backgrounds (51% held bachelor's degrees in 2015) have helped solidify the status of kindergartens in Korea as educational institutions, or "schools," for pre-primary children.

Entry qualifications for kindergarten and child care teachers differ. Prospective kindergarten teachers graduate from an early childhood education department at a 2-, 3-, or 4-year college or university with a Second-Level teacher license, and then acquire their First-Level teacher license after three years of field experience and inservice training. In contrast, prospective child care teachers may graduate from a 2-, 3-, or 4-year college or university with their Second-Level license but are also permitted to instead complete a one-year training after high school graduation and receive a Third-Level teacher license. Unlike the department-centered training of kindergarten teachers, child care teachers acquire their license on a credit basis; in other words, they can attain their minimum 51 credits in a wide range of 13 departments (e.g., Child Development, Child Care, Child Welfare, Nursing), rather than a single specific one.

Inservice training for kindergarten teachers is distinguished into two types: (a) training to develop teaching skills and understanding of the most recent theories; and (b) training to obtain higher qualifications and career promotion (i.e., Level-1 teacher, assistant director, and director license). This second category of training involves courses on general liberal arts, the teaching profession, and specialized areas (e.g., play, arts, or science), spread over at least 90 hours in 15 days, to become a Level-1 teacher, master teacher, or assistant director. Those wishing to become directors must spend at least 180 hours in training, spread over at least 25 days. Teachers must then earn at least 60 out of 100 possible points on the inservice training evaluation in order to qualify for a higher level.

Inservice training for the child care workforce is also stipulated. Under the Child Care Act (Article 23, Enforcement Ordinance 11, 2014), child care teachers and directors must receive training at least once within three consecutive years. Otherwise, their licenses will be suspended. This general training consists of 15 courses spread over 40 hours, including courses on character and liberal arts, health and safety, and specialized knowledge and skills. Training for higher qualifications consists of 21 courses in 80 hours: character and liberal arts, health and safety, and specialized knowledge and skills, plus a 2-hour evaluation exam (Ministry of Health and Welfare, 2016).

Workforce Compensation. Compensation of ECEC teachers varies significantly between child care and kindergarten, and between the public and private sectors. In comparison to kindergarten teachers, child care teachers have lower salaries and receive far fewer allowances or benefits. They may receive holiday allowance, vacation allowance, and an allowance for implementing the Nuri Curriculum. According to the National Survey on Child Care, the average monthly sundry allowance of a beginning child care teacher is approximately $236 (260,000 KRW) (Ministry of Health and Welfare, 2015). Private child care centers offer, on average, the lowest sundry allowance of $191 (210,000 KRW), and workplace child care centers offer the highest, at $391 (430,000 KRW).

Kindergarten teachers are generally better paid than child care teachers, but disparities exist between public kindergartens—where salaries are set by the government—and private kindergartens, where salaries are set by individual providers. Public kindergarten teachers receive equal pay to elementary and secondary teachers, with salaries ranging among 40 scales depending on academic background and major. Since 2011, public kindergarten teachers' salaries have been steadily increasing; for instance, they rose 3.7% between 2016 and 2017. These are supplemented by additional allowances, which may include allowances for: (a) teaching the Nuri Curriculum; (b) good attendance; (c) administrative work; (d) working in rural areas; (e) working overtime; (f) being a good public servant; and (g) long service. They are granted benefits such as parental leave allowance, tuition fee subsidies for their children, and family allowance. Many additional allowances are available, including health activity allowances, household support supplements, and position allowances (Kim, Moon, & Lee, 2015). Private kindergarten teachers also may receive many of these allowances as supplements to their provider-set salaries.

Transitions. The introduction of the Nuri Initiative has rekindled efforts to smooth the transition from ECEC to primary school. In part because the Ministry of Education oversees both kindergartens and primary schools, there are regularized and innovative transition efforts taking place between those settings, as compared to child care centers. For instance, under the Early Childhood Education Act, kindergarten directors are expected to prepare and manage "kindergarten life records" for each child in accordance with standards defined by the Ministry of Education. These records are then shared with elementary school teachers. Further, in 2017 the Ministry of Education developed a manual for kindergarten teachers to help children's transitions to school, with an accompanying workshop covering how to use it successfully.

Public kindergartens attached to elementary schools have an advantage in promoting continuity in children's learning experiences. In these kindergartens, 1st-grade (Primary 1) teachers typically give an orientation to elementary school life to kindergarten parents near the end of the school year. However, private kindergartens and child care centers are less likely to have such well-formed connections with elementary schools due to different physical locations and/or different overseeing ministries.

Engagement Components

Family Involvement. The Korean government has several methods of engaging parents in ECEC, accelerated by a societal recognition of the value of family and the desire to engage parents in the upbringing of their children. These efforts fall broadly into three categories. The first, parent engagement through monitoring and oversight, promotes active parental engagement in the quality and operation of their children's ECEC services. Many of these initiatives stem from the national level. For instance, the Korean government mandates that every kindergarten and child care center establish an operation committee composed of parents, teachers, the director, and a relevant community member, so as to enhance operational transparency and strengthen linkages with families and the community. These committees hold meetings to review and revise: (a) program-level operating regulations; (b) institutional budgets and accounts; (c) methods of operation of education and care; (d) parental fees; (e) cooperation efforts with the local community; and (f) the health, safety, and nutrition of children. Another example of this form of engagement is parental satisfaction surveys, which are incorporated into the National Survey on Child Care for all types of child care centers and kindergartens, public or private. The surveys are then published online through the Ministry of Health and Welfare (Ministry of Health and Welfare, 2016). Furthermore, city mayors and provincial governors organize parent monitoring teams to help inspect and monitor the quality of child care centers in their jurisdiction.

The second category of parental engagement efforts supports direct parent involvement in ECEC classrooms. For example, in 2015, as part of an effort to prevent child abuse and encourage greater parental participation in ECEC, the Ministry of Health and Welfare introduced the concept of "open child care centers." This initiative promotes openness of center spaces, encouraging spontaneity of parents participating in daily classroom routines and flexibility of child care center operations so as to accommodate families and communities (Kwon et al., 2016).

The third area of parental engagement is parent education—initiatives to increase parents' knowledge of child development in the early years and increase their confidence in their abilities as role models and parents. For instance, the Division of Parent Support, established by the Ministry of Education, Science, and Technology in 2009, aims to strengthen the competence of parents as part of lifelong (adult) learning by providing parent education and counseling through designated Parent Support Centers nationwide. These centers, which initially served parents of older children, have gradually expanded to serve kindergarten parents as well. The Ministry of Gender Equality and Families runs both Healthy Family Support Centers and Multicultural Family Support Centers, which provide similar, but more targeted, education. The Ministry also launched a national Korean Parent

Education Project in 2017, which delivers standard parent education programs based on parenting life cycles. Further, there are self-organized parent groups, such as the Good Parents Association and Fathers' Association, which are designed to promote effective parenting and advocate for the rights of parents.

Research, Demonstration, and Evaluation. Aside from teacher-implemented child evaluations, which are kept at the classroom level, very little child outcome data are collected within the Korean ECEC system. In contrast, program data are collected and published through the CAS and KES monitoring systems. These data are supplemented by national surveys on child care and kindergarten, conducted every 3 and 5 years, respectively. Each of these surveys collects service, workforce, and household data from a sample of settings. Results are ultimately published online, where they are publicly available, and data are used to develop the Five-Year National Plans for early childhood education and for child care. A census of basic child care and kindergarten statistics is also conducted each year.

Research-based policymaking is one of the strengths of Korea's ECEC system. The nation's active research community—featuring 13 academic associations and rich research manpower—produces work on a wide variety of topics related to ECEC. Historically, the majority of academic research has focused on programs and pedagogies at the micro level. In recent years, however, there has been a rise in university professors' involvement in policy research, thanks to growing recognition of the societal importance of ECEC as well as a growing stream of dedicated funding from the government.

The Korean government's investment in ECEC research and development is evidenced by the establishment of a dedicated research body, the Korea Institute of Child Care and Education (KICCE), one of 26 research institutes operating under Korea's National Research Council for Economics, Humanities, and Social Sciences. KICCE annually produces over 80 government-funded policy research projects on a range of ECEC-related issues, providing empirical data, suggesting effective policy measures, and collaborating with other research bodies. KICCE's work includes: (a) longitudinal studies (e.g., the 2006–2027 Panel Study on Korean Children); (b) demonstration studies (e.g., a pilot research project for kindergarten-child care center cooperation); (c) pricing indices (e.g., the KICCE child-rearing price index); and (d) program development for disadvantaged children and their families. The research community has thus made considerable contributions to address issues of equity, quality, sustainability, and efficiency in Korean ECEC services. Particular areas of focus in recent years have been impact evaluation studies of policies on child outcomes, and the development of valid measurement tools to foster equity and quality, along with government accountability.

SYSTEMIC INSIGHTS: INNOVATION AND INVESTMENT

The unique story of ECEC in the Republic of Korea has yielded particular ECEC strengths, discussed below.

Shared Recognition of the Importance of ECEC

Korean society's collective recognition of the significance of ECEC serves as a powerful driving force behind the government's policy implementation. The Korean government does not need to "make the case" to the citizenry that the early years are a critical period of development; it is widely accepted—and now, even expected—that the government will provide "free" (heavily subsidized) education and care for young children, just as it provides free compulsory education to elementary and middle school. This has resulted in Korea being one of the few nations worldwide to fund full-day care for its very youngest citizens, those aged 0–2.

Numerous rationales have driven Koreans' collective embrace of ECEC investment. Having emerged from its politically unstable past as a uniquely future-oriented society that values innovation and growth, Korea now faces the worrying reality of an aging population and a persistently low birthrate. These demographic issues have elevated early years policy to a level of national significance. Thus, there is widespread support for policies geared at supporting working mothers and making the act of raising young children easier and more affordable. Furthermore, deeply held and intertwined societal values of education and equity have been effectively harnessed as a powerful rationale for investment. By representing free, high-quality ECEC as a necessary foundational component of an education system and, more broadly, of a true meritocracy, the government has created a durable, evocative justification for its commitment to free education and care.

Centralized Governance and Strong Implementation Power

In the earliest stages of Korea's ECEC system development, the national government single-handedly planned and executed a majority of policies, as the sociopolitical climate put the highest priority on national economic development. Over time, though implementation power has been increasingly distributed to local levels of government, the central government continues to set the ECEC agenda and enact national-level policies of profound significance (e.g., the components of the Nuri Initiative). In large part, this is due to the high level of significance accorded to the early years. Acute issues of female workforce participation/economic growth, low birthrates, and equitable educational opportunities demand broad and durable responses, ones that are best formulated at a high level of governance. As such, the central Korean government has accorded much focus to the ECEC system infrastructure, enacting policies related to quality, equity, efficiency, and sustainability. Over time, however, it has ceded a great deal of *implementation* responsibility to the local governments, which now hold primary responsibility for funding and quality assurance. The national government now primarily oversees curriculum content and initial and qualification-promotional teacher training. Broadly, therefore, Korea has highly centralized (split) ECEC governance with regard to policy planning and making, but it has distributed implementation responsibilities to the local level, a trend that is expected to continue and expand in the future.

The Nuri Initiative: Successful Implementation of Functional Integration

Perhaps the Republic of Korea's most remarkable achievement within its ECEC system, the Nuri Initiative represents the planned, purposeful, and successful implementation of a variety of functional integrations. Against the backdrop of a fundamentally split ECEC system, with responsibility divided between two ministries, the Nuri Initiative has steadily sought consolidation. A holistic, child-centered national curriculum has been developed and implemented for all children aged 3–5, regardless of setting. A government guarantee of "free" (heavily subsidized) education and care for all children 3–5 has resulted in a single voucher system that applies across settings. A harmonized quality assurance system is planned that will standardize monitoring. Demands for consolidated teacher training, predicated on the fact that all ECEC staff now use the same curriculum for their 3- to 5-year-old children, are growing. Notably, under the Nuri Initiative, all of these functional harmonizations, though significant in scope, have been achieved *without* deeper, structural consolidation. As such, Korea presents a powerful exemplar demonstrating the possibilities for integration that exist even in the face of seemingly intractable governmental divides.

Systemic Policy Planning

The Republic of Korea's process of policy planning, through its national Five-Year Plans, creates a unique opportunity for systematic ECEC planning within a broader social policy framework. Every 5 years, as part of its national plan, Korea develops and implements both a midterm early childhood education plan and a child care plan. These contain distinct policy goals and a clear vision, focus areas, implementation strategies, timelines, estimated budgets, and expected outcomes and effects; they are based, in part, on data generated from the two national surveys of child care and kindergarten, respectively. Working in parallel, the Ministry of Education and the Ministry of Health and Welfare rigorously monitor their respective progress on implementing their plans, and they publish annual reports on their status. These interim results are then used to guide the next iterations of the plans. This unique systematic cycle of goal-setting, reflection, and re-evaluation promotes a high level of reflectiveness and clarity in ECEC policymaking.

Participatory Approaches to Policymaking

Historically, driven by pressing economic development needs, Korea followed a strictly top-down system of policymaking and implementation with regard to ECEC. In recent years, however, the nation has seen significant advancement in the openness and responsiveness of these processes, largely by seeking out stakeholder participation and operating forums for two-way communication between government bodies and the public. For instance, the early childhood committees of central and local governments now feature more diverse perspectives from stakeholders of different backgrounds, including parents. The 5-year midterm plans for ECEC are reviewed in open seminars, hosted by the central government, that include local government officials, academic professionals, teachers, parents, and NGOs. This inclusion of public feedback, which is not only welcomed but actively fostered, has magnified the effectiveness of policy revisions. At various intervals, the government also solicits feedback through numerous other channels, such as surveys.

Continuous Innovation for Various Stakeholders

As an innovation-driven society, Korea has demonstrated a strong commitment to improving and elevating its ECEC system for parents, teachers, and traditionally underserved groups. One example of innovation for parents is the online ECEC Information Disclosing System, which was first developed in 2012. This website shares information on all public and private ECEC institutions in an easy-to-understand manner, so as to help parents make informed choices for their children. Further, starting in 2009, the unique Intergenerational Wisdom-Sharing Teacher role employs experienced, retired school teachers with expertise in particular subject matters to provide educational activities in afterschool programming both in public and private kindergartens.

Innovation is also seen in Korea's approach to providing ECEC for disadvantaged children, who have been traditionally underserved. To eliminate social barriers, reduce inequity, and cultivate their human capital, the Korean government invested in the Support Programs for the Development of Young Children's Basic Learning Abilities project. This provided training to 20,000 kindergarten staff, as well as direct support to 1,529 developmentally delayed children and 582 multicultural children. Recently, the Korea Arts and Culture Promotion Agency conducted a program to bring artists into child care centers and kindergartens in disadvantaged areas so as to reduce gaps in artistic and cultural experiences. Together, these innovative initiatives represent the Korean government's commitment to continual improvement and its embrace of forward-thinking initiatives.

CHALLENGES, IMPLICATIONS, AND RECOMMENDATIONS

Among the generic elements of effective ECEC systems discussed previously, several have special bearing on the Korean context. First, due to a current split system of ECEC, fostering more coordination and integration is of paramount importance to enhancing effectiveness and efficiency. Second, improved financing and quality monitoring is critical, as Korean ECEC is market-driven and the majority of children are served in for-profit, private settings that still burden parents financially in spite of the Nuri subsidies. Third, parents' strong aspirations for their children's education may have ambivalent effects on national efforts to drive quality; parental expectations and government policies must be reconciled.

A Split ECEC System

Above all, the greatest challenge of the Korean ECEC system is its fundamentally split nature, which is manifest in virtually every system element, from administrative auspices to legal bases, regulations and standards, financing, quality assurance, curriculum, teacher training, and service delivery systems. This dilemma is well recognized. Functional integration efforts have been ongoing for almost two decades, most notably through the Nuri Initiative, and have achieved success in the harmonization of the curriculum for 3- to 5-year-olds, the voucher card system, and, soon, the service monitoring system. However, many functions—such as teacher qualifications and initial training—remain split. Korea thus faces a profound strategic question moving forward: Will the nation continue to approach integration on a piecemeal basis, undergoing legal and implementation battles for each element of the system? Or will it take on the perhaps more politically difficult task of addressing the underlying problem—split governance— to achieve more durable, structural integration? More than distinctions in nomenclature, this represents a fundamental shift from a focus on limited functional integration efforts to more comprehensive structural integration.

Financing: The Need for Realistic Subsidies

A key tenet of the Nuri Initiative is the provision of free ECEC to all children aged 3–5, across all settings, regardless of family background or income. However, Nuri subsidies do not in reality cover the full costs of education and care. Parents who send their children to private kindergartens, for instance, may pay up to $400 per month to do so, because kindergarten providers are free to set their own fee rates and Nuri subsidies have not been increased since their launch. Additional fees in child care centers also represent a burden to parents, although less so than in kindergartens because child care fees for both public or private centers are capped by the government. Thus, although Korean ECEC is "free" on paper, the current funding situation does not meet demand, thus raising issues of equity. There are multiple approaches the government could take to address this. It could set a ceiling on private kindergarten fees, thus limiting the additional costs borne by families, but this would hinder the traditionally market-driven approach to ECEC. The government could also raise the amount of subsidy provided by the Nuri voucher to a more realistic level that reflects the real market price for ECEC services. Although logical, this approach may be less viable due to budgetary concerns.

Gaps in Access and Quality

On a national level, the overall quantity of ECEC services in the Republic of Korea is sufficient to offer total coverage, with 18% of services having vacant places for children (Yang, Lee, Chung, & Kim, 2016). On the local level, however, uneven distribution of services results in an abundance of slots in some areas and persistent gaps in services in other areas. Moreover, well-known disparities exist in the quality of services available. Though the child care subsidy generously supports 12 hours a day of care at low cost to parents, parents do not always have high confidence in the quality of child care centers. Such quality issues are particularly pertinent in rural and poor urban areas, which have difficulty recruiting and retaining high-quality teachers. To simultaneously address issues of both access and quality, in 2016 the newly elected Korean government announced a goal to increase the capacity of public kindergartens and child care centers to ultimately cover up to 40% of all children aged 0–5, up from 23.6% and 12.1%, respectively. These public settings are particularly needed in urban areas with high populations of young children (Choi, 2017).

Imbalance Between Public and Private Services

Korea's market-driven approach to ECEC, which results in a system driven primarily by for-profit, private providers, raises a number of concerns with regard to quality, equity, and transparency. As government funds continue to flow into for-profit kindergarten and child care centers through Nuri subsidies, the need to regulate and control these private settings to a greater degree has become evident. In particular, there are calls for the regulations of for-profit providers to be the same as those for nonprofit providers, to ensure public transparency. This has, unsurprisingly, faced resistance from the for-profit sector. One potential strategy to reduce the imbalance between private and public quality without as much backlash may be for the government to provide the salaries of all ECEC teachers, regardless of setting and founding body. Such an approach would incentivize private providers to accept greater quality control, financial transparency, and accountability.

Diversifying Support for Child-Rearing
Beyond Subsidies for Child Care Services

The government's universal subsidy system allots the i-Happiness voucher card to any child aged 0–5. Families must apply for the card, but it is provided without regard to family income, parents' working status, or background. As a result, there are concerns that some children who are enrolled in child care centers do not "need" the child care services because they have nonworking parents at home—an unintended consequence of the government's policy. In 2015, a reform was initiated to differentiate support between children with working and nonworking mothers, but it was met with heavy resistance and is now under alteration. Instead of limiting children's equal access to vouchers, a more effective approach may be to offer a greater variety of child-rearing supports, beyond subsidies for child care and education services. This might include parental leave or cash support for raising children at home, to move the ECEC system away from a strict center orientation.

Extracurricular (Enrichment) Programs and Lack of Play

Traditionally, Korean society has privileged functional education and tangible outcomes—a value system that is seemingly at odds with the national government's holistic, play-based Nuri ECEC curriculum. As a result, many parents enroll their children not only in the heavily subsidized Nuri Curriculum hours, but also in afterschool or extracurricular programs, which focus on reading, writing, arithmetic, English, and sometimes sports, art, and music. These hours are offered in the same settings as Nuri ECEC, and in private academies called *Hagwons*. They heavily emphasize cognitive, "academic" learning, and rarely allow significant time for play (Lee & Lee, 2010). Although at odds with the government's view of child development, many parents consider these enrichment activities to be important tools to help their children become academically competitive in their later school years. The implications of this are twofold. First, it means that many children spend the vast majority of their waking hours away from the home, thus raising parents' concerns about their ability to foster strong parent-child relationships. Second, it suggests that much work is to be done in reconciling parents' academic expectations with the government's view of early learning, as there is an evident discrepancy.

Durable Investment in Scaling Up Innovation

Remarkable innovation—one of the hallmarks of the Korean ECEC system—carries with it the persistent and interrelated challenges of durability and scalability. The early years landscape is rife with examples of new initiatives, most operating on a small scale (e.g., the master teachers system or the study leave system). Too often, however, the creativity and excitement around these projects is not matched by dedicated, sustainable funding, and thus they may fail to be scaled up or continued. For example, the Exemplary Kindergartens and Child Care Centers on Character Education project was conducted with 264 institutions based on rigorous selection criteria from 2012 to 2015, but it was ultimately discontinued due to limited budgets. Another example is the Recommendation System of Extracurricular Activities in Kindergartens, which was initiated in 2010 in order to identify and recommend quality enrichment programs by a central-level review committee. Though the recommendation system worked well early on, it is currently inactive because of financial constraints and lack of acceptance from private kindergartens.

Even the Nuri Initiative, one of the Korean system's most notable innovations, has been delayed and modified due to funding issues (e.g., Local Offices of Education and provincial governments have been unable to generate sufficient funds for kindergarten and child care vouchers). Thus, while innovation should continue to be encouraged, it should be matched with a future-oriented eye toward scalability and durability of funding.

CONCLUDING REMARKS

Above all, the Republic of Korea's framing value, *"Hong-ik-In-gan"* (홍익 인간), or "live and work for the benefit of all mankind," serves as the basis for its strong early education system. Driven by powerful rationales for economic development, equity, and demographic change, ECEC has emerged as a foundational pillar in this future-oriented society. Alongside the government's commitment to free child care for all children aged 0–2, the remarkable Nuri Initiative has advanced the pledge to provide free ECEC for all children aged 3–5. Further, the Initiative has affected significant functional consolidation, through a unique Nuri Curriculum for all children aged 3–5, a single subsidy voucher, and a harmonized quality assurance system. Nearly a decade after Nuri's introduction, Korea now finds itself at a new crossroad with regard to funding and governance. Yet, armed with a tenacious commitment to its children, Korea's continued commitment to investment and innovation in its ECEC system will remain unaltered, building on the past to prepare the future.

REFERENCES

The Academy of Korean Studies. (2017). Encyclopedia of Korean Culture. Retrieved from intl.aks.ac.kr/english/viewforum.php?f=88

Chang, M. L., Lee, M. H., Moon, M., Kim, E. S., Choi, Y. K., Kim, E. Y., Yoo, H. M., & Choi, E. Y. (2013). A mid-term roadmap toward the integration of early childhood education and care. Seoul, Republic of Korea: Korea Institute of Child Care and Education.

Child Care Act. (2014). In-service training of child care teacher, Article 23, Enforcement Ordinance 11.

Choi, E. Y. (2017). Strengthening the public nature of early childhood education: Possibilities and limitations. The 4th KICCE Policy Symposium. Retrieved from kicce.re.kr/kor/publication/04_03.jsp?mode=view&idx=23049&startPage=0&listNo=136&code=etc03&search_item=&search_order=&order_list=10&list_scale=10&view_level=0

Choi, E. Y., Choi, Y. K., Kim, J. G., Kim, M. J., & Kim, K. M. (2012). Developing models of the consulting system for the implementation of the Nuri Curriculum. Seoul, Republic of Korea: Korea Institute of Child Care and Education.

Choi, Y. S., Ko, S. J., Kwon, H. K., Nam, Y. J., Bae, H. B., Sung, M. A., Song, M. S., & Yang, H. A. (2015). Talk about families in Korea: Current status and issues. Seoul, Republic of Korea: Hawoo Publisher.

Kim, E. S., Park, J. A., Choi, H. M., Kim, A. R., Jung, B. S., & Lee, D. H. (2015). Consolidating financing and accounting rules in kindergartens and child care centers. Seoul, Republic of Korea: Office of National Policy Coordination & Korea Institute of Child Care and Education.

Kim, E. Y., Park, W. S., Lee, J. H., & Lee, H. M. (2016). Creating a safe ECEC environment: Perceptions on child abuse and improvement measures. Seoul, Republic of Korea: Korea Institute of Child Care and Education.

Kim, G. S., Moon, M., & Lee, M. K. (2015). Current status of and measures to promote rights of early childhood teachers. Seoul, Republic of Korea: Korea Institute of Child Care and Education. Retrieved from kicce.re.kr/kor/publication/02.jsp?mode=view&idx=18979&startPage=20&listNo=88&code=report01&search_item=&search_order=&order_list=10&list_scale=10&view_level=0

Korea Educational Development Institute & Ministry of Education. (2015). Education for the future: Korean education policy development. Seoul, Republic of Korea: Korea Educational Development Institute.

Korea Institute of Child Care and Education. (2016). Key statistics of early childhood education and care in Korea. Retrieved from kicce.re.kr/kor/publication/04_04. jsp?mode=view&idx=23299&startPage=0&listNo=93&code=etc04&search_item=&search_order=&order_list=10&list_scale=10&view_level=0

Kwon, M. K., Lee, M. W., Bae, Y. J., & Yoon, J. Y. (2016). *Enhancing the applicability of consolidated indicators of child accreditation and kindergarten evaluation*. Seoul, Republic of Korea: Korea Institute of Child Care and Education.

Lee, B. M., & Lee, S. J. (2010). Early education: Anxious parents and busy children. *Humane Citizen, 18*, 85–107.

Lee, Y. J., Kim, J. H., & Lee, M. K. (2016). *Analysis on outcomes of the Nuri Initiative*. Seoul, Republic of Korea: Korea Institute of Child Care and Education.

Lee, Y. S., Lim, S. J., & Byeon, S. J. (2015). Analysis on R-learning environment. *The Journal of Korea Robotics Society, 10*(2), 79–89.

Ministry of Education. (2012, June). The rule of finance and account for private kindergartens (Press release). Retrieved from moe.go.kr/boardCnts/view.do?boardID=294&boardSeq=30690&lev=0&searchType=S&statusYN=W&page=1&s=moe&m=0503&opType=N

Ministry of Education. (2015, December). Selecting 50 outstanding kindergartens of the curriculum implementation. Retrieved from moe.go.kr/boardCnts/view.do?boardID=294&boardSeq=61631&lev=0&searchType=S&statusYN=W&page=1&s=moe&m=0503&opType=N

Ministry of Education. (2017a, February). The accounting manual and system for private kindergartens to enhance their public transparency (Press release). Retrieved from moe.go.kr/boardCnts/view.do?boardID=294&boardSeq=70581&lev=0&searchType=C&statusYN=C&page=1&s=moe&m=0503&opType=N

Ministry of Education. (2017b, March). Directions and tasks of educational welfare policy to cope with the economic and social polarization (Press release). Retrieved from moe.go.kr/boardCnts/view.do?boardID=294&boardSeq=70667&lev=0&searchType=C&statusYN=C&page=1&s=moe&m=0503&opType=N

Ministry of Education, Science, and Technology. (2009, December). Plan for the advancement of early childhood education. Retrieved from cafe.daum.net/preschoolseongbuk/5QSX/1260?q=%C0%AF%BE%C6%B1%B3%C0%B0%20%BC%B1%C1%F8%C8%AD%20%B9%E6%BE%C8

Ministry of Education, Science, and Technology & Ministry of Health and Welfare. (2011, December). *The Nuri Initiative expanded to 3- and 4-year-olds*. Retrieved from moe.go.kr/boardCnts/view.do?boardID=294&boardSeq=35194&lev=0&searchType=null&statusYN=W&page=450&s=moe&m=0503&opType=N

Ministry of Employment and Labor. (2017a). Parental leave. Retrieved from moel.go.kr/policy/policyinfo/woman/list5.do

Ministry of Employment and Labor. (2017b). e-Nara Index: Current status of maternity and parental leave (2009–2016). Retrieved from index.go.kr/potal/main/EachDtlPageDetail.do?idx_cd=1504#link

Ministry of Gender Equality and Family. (2017). *Child care service*. Retrieved from mogef.go.kr/eng/pc/eng_pc_f007.do

Ministry of Health and Welfare. (2015, December). Initiating customized part-time child care starting from July, 2017 (Press release). Retrieved from mohw.go.kr/react/al/sal0301vw.jsp?PAR_MENU_ID=04&MENU_ID=0403&page=

1&CONT_SEQ=329296&SEARCHKEY=TITLE&SEARCHVALUE=%B8%
C2%C3%E3%C7%FC%20%BA%B8%C0%B0%C1%A6%B5%B5

Ministry of Health and Welfare. (2016, May). Child care fees per child have been reduced to 41% compared to those in 2012 (Press release). Retrieved from mohw.go.kr/react/al/sal0301vw.jsp?PAR_MENU_ID=04&MENU_ID= 0403&page=2&CONT_SEQ=332248&SEARCHKEY=DEPT_NM&- SEARCHVALUE=%BA%B8%C0%B0%C1%A4%C3%A5%B0%FA

Ministry of Health and Welfare. (2017a). 2017 guide to social welfare. Retrieved from mohw.go.kr/react/jb/sjb030301vw.jsp?PAR_MENU_ID=03&MENU_ID= 032901&CONT_SEQ=338690&page=1

Ministry of Health and Welfare. (2017b). 2017 guide to child care. Retrieved from central.childcare.go.kr/ccef/community/data/DataSl.jsp?BBSGB=385&flag =Sl&BID=60640

Ministry of Health and Welfare & Social Security Information Services. (2017). Comprehensive Citizen-Happiness Voucher. Retrieved from voucher.go.kr/common/ main.do

Moon, M., Cho, S. I., & Kim, J. M. (2016). *Korean perspectives on becoming a parent and values on parenting.* Seoul, Republic of Korea: Korea Institute of Child Care and Education. Retrieved from kicce.re.kr/kor/publication/02.jsp?- mode=view&idx=21738&startPage=0&listNo=109&code=report01&search_ item=&search_order=&order_list=10&list_scale=10&view_level=0

Moon, M., & Kim, M. J. (2013). *National framework on qualifications of early childhood workforces.* Seoul, Republic of Korea: National Research Council of Economics, Social Science and Humanities.

Moon, M., Lee, G. R., & Kim, H. S. (2016). *Monitoring quality of teacher implementation of the Nuri Curriculum.* Seoul, Republic of Korea: Korea Institute of Child Care and Education.

Moon, M., Park, C. H., & Kim, M. J. (2017). *2018–2022 mid-term plan for early childhood education.* Seoul, Republic of Korea: Korea Institute of Child Care and Education.

Na, J., & Moon, M. (2003). Early childhood education and care policies in the Republic of Korea. OECD *Thematic Review of ECEC Policy: Country background report.* Retrieved from oecd.org/korea/27856763.pdf

National Health Insurance Service. (2017a). Health-in: Health check-up of young children. Retrieved from hi.nhic.or.kr/aa/ggpaa001/ggpaa004_m01.do#

National Health Insurance Service. (2017b). NHI Program. Retrieved from nhic.or. kr/static/html/wbd/g/a/wbdga0401.html

National Law Information Center. (2017). *Paternity leave.* Retrieved from easylaw. go.kr/CSM/CsmOvPopup.laf?csmSeq=739&ccfNo=3&cciNo=2&cnpClsNo=4

Office for Government Policy Coordination. (2013, December). Completing the integration of ECEC within the presidential term by reflecting parental needs (Press release). Retrieved from opm.go.kr/pmo/news/news01.jsp?mode=view& article_no=48918

Presidential Council on National Branding. (2014). *Dynamic Korea.* Retrieved from 100.daum.net/encyclopedia/view/31XXXXXX3549

Rhee, O., Kim, E. S., Shin, N. R., & Moon, M. (2008). Developing models to integrate early childhood education and care in Korea. *International Journal of Child Care and Education Policy, 2*(1), 53–66.

Social Welfare Act. (2017, May). Article 3, Children under 18 years old in need of social protection. Retrieved from law.go.kr/eng/engLsSc.do?menuId=1&query=Child+Welfare+Act&x=25&y=26#liBgcolor2

Suh, M. H., & Lee, H. M. (2014). *Trends of increases in early childhood financing and its impacts.* Seoul, Republic of Korea: Korea Institute of Child Care and Education.

Woo, M. S., Park, K. H., Jun, H. J., & Jung, B. S. (2012). *Legislating the finance and accounting rules for private kindergartens: Proceedings for public hearing.* Seoul, Republic of Korea: Ministry of Education, Science, and Technology.

Yang, M. S., Lee, G. R., Chung, J. W., & Kim, J. M. (2016). *Evaluation on the supply policy of public early childhood education and care.* Seoul, Republic of Korea: Korea Institute of Child Care and Education.

Yoo, H. M., Lee, G. R., & Lee, M. K. (2016). *Enhancing quality of child care services for children under three: Focusing on family daycare centers.* Seoul, Republic of Korea: Korea Institute of Child Care and Education.

CHAPTER 7

A Careful Balancing Act

Evolving and Harmonizing a
Hybrid System of ECEC in Singapore

Rebecca Bull and Alfredo Bautista

The *Lion City* (or *Singapura*) presents a fascinating story of rapid transformation and success. This holds true whether speaking about the economy, the well-being of the citizenry, the nature of the overall services provided, or the evolution of early childhood care and education (ECEC). This chapter unveils how such progress came to be achieved in ECEC, delineating the challenges that such success evokes. Ultimately, it is a story of carefully hewn harmonization and balance.

VISION AND VALUES

Singapore was founded in 1819 as part of the British Empire, and its trading ports attracted migrants from China, India, and other parts of Asia. However, Singapore's prosperity suffered a blow during World War II, when it was occupied by the Japanese Empire. Despite reverting to British control when the war ended, growing nationalism led to self-governance in 1959. In the country's first general election, the People's Action Party won a majority of seats in Parliament and Lee Kuan Yew became the first prime minister. Following a brief union with Malaysia in 1963, Singapore was finally established as an independent and sovereign nation in 1965.

After years of turbulence and political instability, and despite lacking natural resources, the nation developed rapidly through the 1970s. The government focused on two goals: ensuring a thriving economy and establishing a politically stable and socially cohesive nation. To this end, Singapore embarked on a modernization program to establish a manufacturing industry, foster external trade, and contribute to the development of its workforce

---

For factual details on early childhood in Singapore, see Appendix F

through investments in public education. By the 1990s, it had become one of the most prosperous countries in the world. A pragmatic rather than ideological approach to policy implementation (Quah, 2016) has efficiently and successfully attended to the needs of the nation over the past decades. Today, the country's population, with the world's highest confidence in the national government (Legatum Institute, 2016), is enjoying a degree of government effectiveness, regulatory quality, policymaking transparency, and rule of law unseen in other countries. The government's stability and clear sense of direction have been central to the rapid development of the country in all sectors.

Singapore has historically depended on the strength and influence of family structures (Lee, 2012). Families are the primary source of emotional, social, and financial support, contributing to social stability and national cohesiveness, as they help raise socially responsible individuals and deepen the bond Singaporeans have with their country. The family plays a key role in keeping society orderly and maintaining a culture of hard work, thrift, filial piety and respect for elders, scholarship, and learning. Clearly inspired by Confucius's ideas of civil order, Lee considered these values to be ones that make for a productive society and advance economic growth. Indeed, Confucian societies believe that governments cannot and should not take over the important role of the family, which should be capable of fulfilling the needs of those individuals who belong to it. Such beliefs are reflected in Singapore's adoption of a neoconservative approach to social welfare, with an emphasis on dignity and self-reliance (e.g., employment, individual savings, home ownership) through asset-building policies. Beyond self-reliance, the family and community are seen as the first line of support for the poor, and only after passing through these options should individuals turn to the state for assistance.

In the late 1980s, however, there was a sense that the foundational values of the population were slowly shifting from communitarianism to individualism, as a result of Singaporeans' long exposure to Western influences. Policy leaders were concerned that this trend would negatively affect Singapore's social and racial cohesion, its economic growth, and its competitiveness. To prevent these consequences, the government introduced five shared national values (Parliament of Singapore, 1991): (a) nation before community and society above self; (b) family as the basic unit of society; (c) community support and respect for the individual; (d) consensus, not conflict; and (e) racial and religious harmony. Meritocracy, pragmatism, and honesty are also cited as key elements for Singapore's success (Lee, 2012). Meritocracy constitutes a form of "national ideology," the overall societal conception being that opportunities should be equalized, with individuals rewarded on the basis of their merit or abilities and not on arbitrary factors such as race and gender.

Over time, Singapore's small land size and lack of natural resources have motivated policymakers to invest in human capital, and hence in mainstream education, which has been critical to ensuring the survival and prosperity of the nation. The government's decision to move all schooling (from the primary level onward) into the public sector in the initial years of modernization was understandable in the context of traditional Asian societies, which place high value on education. Early childhood education and care (ECEC) was not a high priority at that time. Over time, given Singapore's limited workforce and declining birthrate, every individual has become increasingly important to ensuring the sustainability of the nation. Today, ECEC is seen as the first opportunity to nurture Singapore's most precious asset: its young children, the human resource that will be key to economic and social development in the near future. In line with the country's family-centered values, over the last decade the government has implemented pro-family policies that address national needs and priorities.

Such policies have had significant implications on the availability, affordability, and quality of ECEC services. The issue of affordability has been particularly important for addressing other national priorities, such as the reduction of inequality and social disadvantage. The cost of raising quality, without passing on that cost to parents, has resulted in the government investing substantial resources into ECEC. National ECEC spending is more than double that of five years ago. Resources have been utilized to: (a) regulate, govern, and harmonize the sector; (b) better educate and professionalize the ECEC workforce; (c) provide more financial support to parents and service providers; and (d) develop curricula and pedagogical frameworks to guide the (primarily private) sector. Building on this momentum, the Prime Minister announced in 2017 that annual government spending in the ECEC sector will double again, from $605 million[1] to $1.2 billion, by 2023 (Prime Minister's Office Singapore [PMO], 2017). This increased expenditure will support continued expansion and quality enhancement of affordable ECEC center-based care. It will also support the transformation of the ECEC profession through: (a) the establishment of a new National Institute of Early Childhood Development (NIEC); (b) new efforts to attract and develop the pipeline of ECEC professionals; and (c) the creation of more structured career pathways for ECEC educators and leaders.

RANGE OF SERVICES

Health Services

At the time of Singapore's independence, the Ministry of Health (MOH) focused on meeting the basic health needs of the populace—ensuring proper sanitation procedures, controlling infectious diseases, and guaranteeing access to medications and clean food. Over time, economic growth helped raise health standards and build a sustainable care system. Primary care services were provided through maternal and child health clinics, which served as one-stop centers for immunization, health promotion, health screening, well-women programs, and counseling. Health care is now provided by government and private hospitals, and by community-situated polyclinics. Routine antenatal care is provided from 12 weeks gestation, with follow-up checks every two to four weeks depending on the stage of the pregnancy. All births are attended by skilled physicians. Following birth, the National Childhood Immunization Program legislates that all children receive immunizations for diphtheria and measles, and it provides optional immunizations against other diseases such as tuberculosis, poliomyelitis, measles, mumps, and rubella. The National Immunization Registry monitors and ensures that children receive immunizations at the appropriate time. Approximately 96% of children are vaccinated against key childhood diseases (World Health Organization [WHO], 2014), with major childhood diseases virtually eliminated. The overall high quality of health provision, education, and maternal and infant care has resulted in Singapore now having some of the lowest rates of maternal, neonatal, and infant mortality in the world.

Parents are given a health booklet when their child is born, which provides information on the schedule for immunizations, developmental assessments, and developmental milestones. Developmental assessments by a health professional (e.g., growth monitoring, feeding history, hearing tests, and physical examinations) are conducted monthly for the first six months, with the regularity decreasing afterward. Parents are encouraged to complete a prescreening questionnaire prior to their child's assessments. The questionnaire asks about developmentally appropriate behaviors and skills, and it indicates the age at which 90% of children would be expected to achieve them. The screening checklists include risk indicators for developmental conditions; if a developmental delay is suspected, children are referred to the MOH-funded Child Development Program (CDP), which identifies and treats developmental and behavioral problems. Approximately 90–95% of children referred to CDP have their first referral between ages 2 to 3.

To support working parents in managing their work and family responsibilities, particularly in the perinatal period, pro-family measures have resulted in changes to leave policies, which have extended leave allowances for both mothers (up to 16 weeks) and fathers (up to 2 weeks) and allowed for a split leave between the two parents (up to 4 weeks). A government-paid maternity benefit is provided for mothers not eligible for maternity leave. Policy amendments are also acknowledging changing family dynamics. For instance, all mothers (married or unmarried) receive the same maternity leave entitlement, and the leave for adoptive parents has been increased.

With good health standards in place, the government has turned its focus to health education, with the Health Promotion Board (HPB) established to undertake national health promotion and disease prevention efforts. The Ministers of State for Health and Education are jointly leading an interagency task force to guide the development of NurtureSG, a plan to enhance health outcomes among the young (MOH, 2016). The HPB also established a Health Promoting Pre-School framework, giving accreditation to preschools that have comprehensive health promotion practices. As a result, recent changes to center-based care and education include doubling the time scheduled for physical activity from 30 minutes to one hour daily (half of which should be spent outdoors). Furthermore, over 70% of preschools now provide healthier food and drinks.

Protective Services

The Children and Young Persons Act provides for the welfare, care, and protection of children under 16. The Ministry of Social and Family Development (MSF) is the lead agency for protective services and chairs the Inter-Ministry Workgroup on Child Protection (IWCP), which sets the strategic policy direction for service planning and development in child protection and defines the responsibilities of the various partners. Legislation and policies related to family and child welfare target the preservation and strengthening of the family unit through proactive and preventive programs that aim to keep the child in family-based care rather than out-of-home residential care.

In recent years, initiatives aimed at strengthening services and interagency collaborations have contributed to a more progressive, responsive, and robust Child Protection System (CPS) (MSF, 2016), with better integration between agencies and ministries (e.g., police, health care institutions, schools, voluntary welfare organizations, and child care centers) and better training to increase the competency of stakeholders. The CPS works with various stakeholders to deliver a child-centered, family-focused, and community-based intervention. For example, Family Service Centers (FSCs) and Child Protection Specialist Centers (CPSCs) serve as community-based focal points and social service providers for families. FSCs work with low-risk cases such as families who need caregiving support, financial assistance, or counseling to cope with stressors, whereas CPSCs deal with cases deemed to be of moderate risk (e.g., excessive discipline, drug-addicted parents).

Care and Education Services

There are no regulated or monitored forms of in-home care and education in Singapore. Informal arrangements for in-home care, which serves

approximately 80% of children under the age of 2, are usually with extended family or foreign domestic workers, focusing on physical care with no
planned learning program for the child. With regard to center-based care,
kindergartens provide half-day educational programs, Monday to Friday,
for children aged 3–6 years, whereas child care centers provide both care
and education programs for children between 18 months and 6 years of age.
Some centers also provide infant care programs for infants between 2 and
18 months. Infant and child care centers offer longer and more flexible service provision compared to kindergartens, providing up to 12 hours daily,
from Monday to Saturday. With the exception of 15 public kindergartens
overseen by the Ministry of Education (MOE), preschool[2] provision is sup-
plied by for-profit and not-for-profit private operators.

Between 2007 and 2017, the number of places in child care centers
more than doubled from 62,911 to 143,468, and enrollment increased from
50,290 to 108,351; conversely, enrollment in kindergarten decreased from
approximately 82,000 to 59,620 (Department of Statistics, 2016; PMO,
2017). This is explained by more parents choosing to enroll their children
in child care because they require full-day care for their children when they
return to work, and the provision of basic financial subsidies for children
registered in a licensed child care center, which is not available for children
enrolled in kindergarten. Further, between 2012 and 2016, the number of
infant care places increased from 4,722 to 7,032, with enrollment increasing
from 2,604 to 4,306. Overall enrollment in center-based care is approximately 21% for children under the age of 2 years, 79% for children aged
2–4 years, and 90% in the one or two years prior to primary school. ECEC
is not compulsory, although the government strives to ensure that all children attend center-based care for at least one year prior to entering primary
school. For children not attending preschool, MOE works with community
leaders to persuade families to enroll their children for at least six months
prior to school.

In his 2017 National Day Rally speech, the prime minister announced
important changes intended to lay a stronger foundation for young children and provide better support for families. First, MOE will increase the
number of MOE kindergartens from 15 in 2017 to 50 by 2023, serving
approximately 20% of children aged 5–6 years. Second, the two largest
government-supported operators in Singapore will set up new Early Years
Centers (EYCs) catering to children aged 2 months to 4 years. Children
enrolled in EYCs will be guaranteed a place in a nearby MOE kindergarten
to smooth the service continuum for parents and children. These measures
constitute a significant expansion in the capacity of Singapore's ECEC system, with over 40,000 new full-day preschool places being added (a 30%
capacity increase).

Although there is no statutory support for the inclusion of children with disabilities in preschool, different service options are available. Children in the two years prior to primary school entry with mild developmental needs (e.g., speech and language delays, behavioral problems) receive intervention through the Development Support Program, a 6- to 15-week program conducted by learning support educators and/or a psychologist/therapist within the preschool. For children aged 2–6 years with mild to moderate disabilities, 14 child care centers offer the Integrated Child Care Program. These centers receive additional funding to deploy at least one professional trained in special needs to provide extra guidance (e.g., curriculum modification curriculum, development of an Individual Education Plan); no specific physical, learning, or emotional therapy is provided.

For children with moderate to severe needs, the Early Intervention Program for Infants and Children (EIPIC) provides therapy and educational services. EIPIC centers are run by voluntary welfare organizations, providing 5–12.5 hours of therapy per week. The therapy received depends on the needs of the child but may include physical and occupational therapy, speech and language therapy, and/or psychological support, as well as caregiver training and support. EIPIC is not a substitute for preschool education, but 70% of children attending EIPIC do not attend preschool due to the severity of their needs or the lack of suitable preschools. Fees for all services are means-tested, as are fees for mainstream preschool.

Integrating Service Provision

Recent pilot efforts (e.g., KIDS 0-3, KidSTART, Circle of Care) are pursuing an integrated approach to provision across comprehensive early development (CED) services, including health, protective, care, and educational services. For example, KidSTART involves hospitals, social services, family services, and preschools working to proactively identify and support families through home visits, parent education, supported playgroups, and enhanced support to preschools. Home visits provide expectant and new mothers with practical knowledge on child growth, health, and nutrition. Weekly community-based playgroup sessions help build parental skills and develop peer support networks. Finally, enhanced support to preschools ensures that additional resources are provided to improve engagement with and support for parents, and to improve children's school readiness. This may include addressing barriers to preschool attendance and referrals to programs to support children's developmental needs. Ultimately, the aim of these pilot schemes is to establish and validate a sustainable model of integrated support for vulnerable families and children that is scalable to a national level.

SYSTEMIC/STRUCTURAL COMPONENTS

Structural Components

Governance. Responsibility for CED policy lies at the national level, where it is divided among ministries. Although responsibility for all health-related matters falls under the purview of MOH, responsibility for protective care and education services is overseen by MSF (previously the Ministry for Community, Youth, and Sport, or MCYS) and MOE. Key responsibilities of MSF include: (a) protection and social welfare for children and families; (b) promotion of strong families through relationship support; (c) administration of financial supports and statutory entitlements for children and families; and (d) service provision to individuals with disabilities. A statutory board under MSF, the National Council of Social Services, acts as a coordinating body for voluntary welfare organizations, many of which provide services supporting child care, children with disabilities, community services, and welfare and family protection.

MOE focuses on directing the formulation and implementation of educational policies, including those related to curriculum, pedagogy, and assessment. The MOE Preschool Education Branch (PEB) provides curriculum guidance to the ECEC sector and oversees the operations of MOE kindergartens. SkillsFuture Singapore, a statutory board under MOE, aims to develop a high-quality system of education and training that meets the evolving needs of the nation. As such, MOE, via postsecondary institutions and institutes of higher learning, plays a key role in ensuring the quality of preservice and inservice education provided to ECEC professionals.

ECEC has been governed as a combination of both split and parallel systems. Historically, child care centers and kindergartens came under separate purviews (MSF/MCYS and MOE, respectively); had different policy objectives (custodial care versus education); and were regulated under different legislation. The parallel system reflected the fact that both ministries provided preschool education to children aged 4 to 6 years, and both were guided by the same curriculum framework. The split system applied because MSF also had responsibility for children aged 2 months to 3 years. Although the late 1990s and early 2000s saw MCYS and MOE forming high-level interministerial committees tasked with aligning and improving the quality of preschool education (Khoo, 2010), it was only in 2012 that the prime minister announced the establishment of a new autonomous statutory board to oversee ECEC (PMO, 2012).

Established in 2013, the Early Childhood Development Agency (ECDA) integrated the capabilities of MOE, PEB, and the MSF Child Care Division, removing the overlap of responsibilities pertaining to ECEC matters. Serving as a single point of contact for new and existing ECEC professionals, parents and families, and child care center and kindergarten operators, ECDA's key responsibilities include: (a) overseeing measures to enforce and incentivize quality of ECEC programs, including regulation, quality assurance, and the provision of resources such as curriculum frameworks; (b) facilitating the training and professional development of ECEC professionals; (c) creating a master plan for infrastructure and manpower resources to support the ECEC sector; (d) providing subsidies and grants to keep quality preschool programs affordable; (e) conducting public education and outreach; and (f) uplifting the image and professionalism of the sector through strategic partnerships and programs.

Finance. In the highly privatized ECEC sector, a hybrid model of funding has emerged, in which families make private contributions to the costs of ECEC services while the government provides both supply- and demand-side subsidies. All families are expected to make a minimal contribution, even if only a few dollars, in order to foster a feeling of internal agency and responsibility regarding their child's health, development, and learning, and to prevent a sense of entitlement. Families are encouraged to save for their children's care and education through co-savings schemes, wherein savings deposited by parents are matched dollar-for-dollar by the government. Equitable access to center-based care and education has been made possible by ensuring affordability via basic entitlements for children enrolled in full-day, center-based care, and via additional tiered subsidies targeted to middle- and lower-income households (regardless of type of provision). Through regulation and a quality rating system, the government offers more financial incentives for providers who meet quality *and* affordability criteria. Typical support includes subsidized operating costs, subsidies for staff salaries and training, and infrastructure development. Such targeted support helps providers offer high-quality ECEC to low-income families.

With regard to government expenditure, the Family Development Program (encompassing the Family Development Group and ECDA) takes the largest share of MSF's budget. In 2016, the Family Development Group received a budget increase of 18.7%, mainly due to enhancements to statutory entitlements such as government-paid leave schemes, whereas ECDA received a budget increase of 23% due to initiatives to raise the accessibility, affordability, and quality of ECEC services. These included support provided to more families and operators through infant care, child care, and kindergarten subsidies, and the enhanced Anchor Operator (AOP) and Partner Operator (POP) Schemes (Singapore Budget, 2016), which provide funding support to select preschool operators to increase access to high-quality and affordable ECEC. ECDA provides funding directly to centers to enable them to keep fees low, assuring a monthly maximum fee payable by parents of approximately $1,078 for full-day infant care, $616 for full-day child care, and $123 for kindergarten. AOP and POP preschools are selected on the basis of financial stability, governance processes, high-quality programming, affordability, ability to increase capacity, and commitment to investing in quality improvement and continuing professional development. Through the expansion of AOP, POP, and MOE kindergartens, two in three preschoolers will have a placement in a government or government-supported quality preschool by 2023 (Early Childhood Development Agency [ECDA], 2017).

As in ECEC, Singapore has adopted a hybrid fiscal model of health care that combines government subsidies with patient co-payments. Medisave is a mandatory savings account in which individuals put aside 8–10.5% of their monthly income to meet family health care expenses. All parents of newborns receive a government grant of $2,880, which can be used to defray the costs of their child's health care or pay for the national health insurance plan, MediShield Life (National Population and Talent Division, 2017). All Singapore citizen newborns are automatically covered by this national health insurance plan from birth. The government offers significant support to keep premiums affordable, including providing subsidies to those with lower incomes. The position of the government is that nobody will lose national health insurance coverage due to inability to afford premiums, and no individuals will be denied care if they are unable to pay. An endowment fund has been established by the government to support individuals in such circumstances.

Instructional Components

Philosophical and Practical Approaches to Pedagogy. Before 2003, preschool education (particularly the two years prior to compulsory education) was perceived as preparation for primary school, with a focus on academic skills through didactic teaching approaches. In recent years, however, competition driven by globalization has resulted in demands for changes to pedagogical practices. The government now argues that the definition of school readiness is not mastery of the Primary 1 syllabus, but rather that children are ready for school when they are eager to learn and have confidence; perseverance; and the ability to communicate, make friends, and understand socially appropriate behaviors (Tan, 2017).

A major step for quality enhancement was the development and refinement of two curriculum frameworks: the Early Years Development Framework (EYDF) for children aged 2 months to 3 years (ECDA, 2013a) and the Nurturing Early Learners (NEL) Kindergarten Curriculum Framework (MOE, 2013) for children aged 4 to 6 years. These frameworks were designed to ensure curricular continuity, and advocate for the adoption of child-centered pedagogical approaches. Both EYDF and NEL make explicit the learning and developmental expectations of children at different ages, and encourage a holistic and play-based approach to children's development and learning.

The NEL Framework highlights six core principles that guide teaching and learning: (a) an integrated approach to learning; (b) teachers as facilitators of learning; (c) engagement of children in learning through purposeful play; (d) authentic learning through quality interactions; (e) children as constructors of knowledge; and (f) holistic development. The framework emphasizes an integrated approach (around a theme, story, or project) to support learning in six areas: aesthetics and creative expression, discovery of the world, language and literacy, motor skill development, numeracy, and social and emotional development.

The desired outcomes of preschool education, articulated by MOE and aligned with the longer-term desired outcomes of education, deemphasize academic learning achievements. Instead, they focus on developing young children with positive outlooks who have the skills, knowledge, and dispositions to prepare them for lifelong learning. Ultimately, preschool education is seen as the foundation from which children grow to become hardworking citizens who value order and are law-abiding, respectful, and considerate toward others (Lim & Lim, 2017). As such, perseverance, reflectiveness, appreciation, inventiveness, sense of wonder, curiosity, and engagement are encouraged.

The existing curriculum and pedagogical frameworks are hybrid in nature, combining elements of Chinese and Western ideology. The way in which NEL describes the teacher's roles and responsibilities reflects traditional Confucian values of respect for elders and authority, scholarship, and learning, with the teacher portrayed as a facilitator, mediator, and guider of children's learning who establishes learning goals and activities. A paradigmatic example of how Western ideas have been adapted (rather than adopted) in Asian educational systems is the NEL Framework's notion of purposeful play (in contrast to unstructured free play), where the teacher designs the environment and provides resources with specific learning objectives in mind.

Program Monitoring. Child care centers and kindergartens have historically been regulated under the differing regulatory requirements of the Child Care Centers Act and the Education Act, respectively. Until recently, the focus of mandatory external inspection was almost entirely on structural variables such as physical space, safety requirements, staffing, hours of operation, type of services offered, and administrative procedures. Licenses for child care centers were issued for a period of 6 to 24 months, and needed to be renewed at the end of each period. As such, licensing was considered as ongoing monitoring. In contrast, kindergartens were registered one time only, with no requirement for regular license renewal. However, in February 2017 Parliament passed a new Early Childhood Development Centers (ECDC) Act to harmonize the requirements for all center-based provision. Under a common licensing framework, all center-based care (with the exception of kindergartens operated by MOE) is subject to the same regulatory and monitoring requirements, with licenses granted for up to 36 months. The Act also gives ECDA more investigative power to ensure that preschools uphold standards, and grants ECDA more flexibility in handling less serious offenses through a wider range of regulatory sanctions (e.g., fines, shortening of license tenures).

Beyond the mandatory level of licensing of preschool centers, the Singapore Preschool Accreditation Framework (SPARK) is a quality rating scale used for self-assessment and external certification of quality for preschool programs delivered to 4- to 6-year-olds. Participation in SPARK is not mandatory, but the government incentivizes quality improvement efforts by offering more financial subsidies to centers that attain SPARK certification. Quality improvement focuses on both process and structural variables, including leadership, planning and administration, staff management, resources, curriculum, and pedagogy. Approximately 40% of preschools in Singapore are SPARK-certified.

Workforce. One key challenge in the rapidly growing ECEC sector has been to ensure sufficient numbers of well-qualified professionals to meet expanding demand. Preservice training was ad hoc and brief when first introduced in the early 1970s. In the late 1990s, the Steering Committee on Preschool Education made the alignment and improvement of the quality of training of child care and kindergarten teachers one of its key missions. The Early Years Qualification Accreditation Committee (EYQAC) and the Preschool Qualification Accreditation Committee (PQAC), an interministerial collaboration between MCYS and MOE, were established to provide guidance on the content and training of ECEC professionals for the 0–3 and 4- to 6-year age groups, respectively. EYQAC and PQAC set accreditation standards for preservice training covering entry requirements, course administration, course content (aligned with the curriculum frameworks), modes of assessment and supervised teaching practice, and quality of faculty. EYQAC and PQAC now function under ECDA.

A variety of employment opportunities, outlined in three distinct career paths, are available to fit diverse educational and skill profiles. Professionals in the Educarer track work with children aged 2 months to 4 years, whereas those in the Teaching track work with children aged 18 months to 4 or 6 years, depending on their qualifications and experience. Professionals in the Leadership track oversee center operation for all age groups. These career tracks transcend service provision (e.g., teachers can work in both child care centers and kindergartens). The minimum qualifications for Educarers, Teachers, and Leaders are an accredited certificate (1 year of post-secondary education), a diploma (2 years of postsecondary education), and an advanced diploma, respectively, from an ECDA-approved training program. This is lower than the qualification level for primary school teachers, most of whom hold bachelor's degrees.

Both MOE and ECDA provide financial awards to help candidates cover the cost of their programs; in return, recipients may be required to work in the sector for a specified time period. Though the number of professionals has grown substantially to a pool of 16,000, the Early Childhood Manpower Plan unveiled in 2016 indicated a need to attract another 4,000 professionals by 2020. Strategies to encourage more individuals into the profession included the articulation of a skills framework providing clarity on the three career pathways and possibilities for career progression, and the offering of nontraditional routes into training, including professional conversion courses, place-and-train modes, and apprenticeships.

Fostering the professional growth of staff is key to ECDA's efforts to raise the quality of the Singapore ECEC sector. The Continuing Professional Development (CPD) framework (ECDA, 2013b) provides ECEC personnel with structured pathways to develop and update their knowledge, skills, and dispositions, while customizing professional development (PD) to the specific needs and progressive levels of competencies of each professional. ECDA encourages (but does not mandate) all ECEC professionals to participate in a minimum of 20 hours of PD per year. Although PD courses are heavily subsidized by the government (usually covering 80% or more of the cost), opportunities to participate in PD are not equitable across the sector (Ang, 2012).

Finally, the government has announced a range of strategies to promote and retain workforce personnel and foster leadership, mentorship, and collaboration. The ECDA Fellows program expands opportunities for ECEC leaders to develop their own careers and mentor other ECEC professionals to enhance the quality and image of the sector. The ECDA Fellows also develop sector-wide resources for PD, curriculum leadership, and sector partnerships. The Fellows are appointed based on their professional expertise in teaching and learning, ability to foster creativity and innovation, and strong leadership in building a culture of professionalism and collaboration among ECEC personnel. Other programs, such as the Professional Development Program (a new initiative introduced by ECDA) and Principal Matters (started in 2016 by the Lien Foundation) also aim to support the growth of ECEC professionals who have the potential to take on leadership roles in their organizations.

In August 2017, the government announced that MOE will establish the National Institute of Early Childhood Development (NIEC) to centralize strategic matters related to the training and professional development of ECEC professionals (e.g., curriculum design and development, academic governance), and to enhance the rigor and quality of training programs. Under the ambit of Singapore's National Institute of Education (NIE), NIEC will consolidate the training provided by postsecondary and higher learning institutes. NIEC will offer certificate-level and diploma-level pre-employment training (PET) courses for postsecondary students (with all students supported by a training award providing full sponsorship and an allowance), continuous education and training (CET) courses for mid-careerists, and inservice upgrading and CPD courses to further develop the competencies of in-service teachers and leaders. It is hoped that organizing all students under one institution will help develop a stronger sense of fraternity and belonging in the profession. Upon graduation, students will be awarded NIEC qualifications, which will be a recognized endorsement of the quality and rigor of the program. NIEC will benefit from NIE's expertise in curriculum, pedagogy, teacher training, and research to help strengthen the nexus between research, training, and practice.

Transitions. Historically, ECEC has functioned separately from the school system, with different ministries overseeing ECEC and primary education, and with ECEC being provided by private operators while primary schooling is nationalized. As a result, preschools and primary schools did not have formalized links. However, there are multiple efforts to facilitate children's transitions within ECEC and from ECEC to primary education. To ensure curricular and pedagogical continuity, the two curriculum frameworks for the early years (EYDF and NEL) are aligned with each other, and also with the longer-term desired outcomes of mainstream education. There is now a greater emphasis on nonacademic skills and active learning in the first two years of primary school, aligning with children's experiences in preschool (MOE, 2009). Strategies for supporting transitions are assessed in the SPARK quality rating system, with the minimal expectation that centers will familiarize children with the primary school setting.

Circle of Care, a recent pilot initiative, aims to ease transitions by formalizing the working relationship between preschools and primary schools, focusing on vulnerable families who may require greater support in the transition process. The initiative arranges preschool "clusters" grouped around an anchor primary school in order to enable regular meetings between preschool educators, primary school teachers, social workers, counselors, and pastoral care teams.

Engagement Components

Families and Communities. With family and community support recognized as national core values, policies and frameworks encourage parents, families, and communities to actively participate in ECEC. To foster family engagement, standards on parental collaboration are included in the SPARK certification process. The curriculum frameworks also spell out various parental engagement strategies that allow parents and ECEC professionals to develop a shared sense of responsibility for children, thus supporting continuity and consistency of care between the home and preschool. However, there are no mandatory requirements nor monitoring of the implementation of these practices; consequently, practices vary substantially across the sector.

The various ministries, agencies, and nongovernment organizations (e.g., self-help groups, voluntary welfare organizations) involved in ECEC have initiatives in place to promote family empowerment, education, and advocacy. At a basic level, some initiatives focus on the mere provision of information about relevant ECEC issues, typically through guides and online resources. Initiatives of higher intensity involve the provision of seminars and programs. For example, the Association for Early Childhood Educators–Singapore (AECES), a professional body committed to collaborating with the community, organizes conferences and workshops in which ECEC professionals offer parental empowerment and education initiatives. Programs such as the MSF-coordinated FamilyMatters! also aim to empower parents with the necessary knowledge and skills to build strong and happy families.

Beyond parents and families, initiatives also foster the engagement of community partners in ECEC. Through the Innovation Guidance Project launched by ECDA in 2014, centers are encouraged to collaborate with community partners (e.g., National Heritage Board, National Parks Board) to enhance children's learning experiences. Other initiatives are led by government bodies, which have implemented programs focused on health-related issues (e.g., the Healthy Meals in Child Care Centers program, run by HPB), as well as programs aimed at providing comprehensive and integrated support to vulnerable children and families (e.g., KidSTART). Finally, philanthropic organizations and private associations also play an important role in the promotion of community engagement and home–center partnerships.

Other Influences (Research, Advocacy, Foundations, Media). Over the past few decades, Singaporean policies and regulations, curricula, accreditation frameworks, and teacher preparation models have been influenced by Western theories and practices. However, there is increasing awareness of the need to produce knowledge that is locally relevant and situated. Today, government attention to ECEC has resulted in significantly expanded domestic research efforts, including: (a) longitudinal studies on health, parenting, and education on child outcomes; (b) survey studies on social and family issues; (c) studies of pedagogy and practice; (d) policy formulation and review research; and (e) basic science and neuroscience research. MSF, MOE, and ECDA have specific divisions responsible for reviewing and synthesizing literature and undertaking research projects. Singapore's small geographical size allows a close working relationship between government ministries and research institutes, with civil servants and researchers regularly meeting to discuss alignment of research interests with the research needs of the government. The majority of ECEC research in Singapore is government-funded, with most being commissioned or competitively awarded to researchers at autonomous universities.

Philanthropic and nongovernment organizations also play a vital role in their involvement and financing of research, and in advocacy for the ECEC sector. For example, the Lien Foundation commissioned the Starting Well report (Economist Intelligence Unit, 2012) and the Vital Voices for Vital Years report (Ang, 2012), which voiced stakeholders' concerns about the ECEC sector in Singapore. Although the government had already started to focus attention on ECEC far in advance of such reports, they did serve as catalysts for the rapid initiation of new policies. Professional associations also play a central role in supporting the ECEC infrastructure. For example, AECES has supported the government in the delivery of language assistance and mental wellness programs to preschools, through the recruitment, training, and deployment of para-educational professionals. The Association of Early Childhood and Training Services (ASSETS) has collaborated with the Ministry of Manpower (MOM) and ECDA on projects designed to boost productivity and improve retention in the ECEC sector, and to develop technology to aid preschools in their day-to-day processes and administrative duties.

SYSTEMIC INSIGHTS

According to the Theory of Change, program- and boundary-spanning entities (e.g., education, social protection, health) and infrastructure subsystems (e.g., governance, finance, standards, human capacity, assessment, data and accountability, family and community engagement, and transitions) are the requisite conditions for an effective ECEC system. Based on the information presented here, some of the requisite conditions for an effective ECEC system are clearly in place in Singapore, whereas others are still under development. Some limitations in the infrastructure make it difficult to conclude that the system outputs of quality, equitable access, efficiency, and sustainability have been realized to their full potential. Furthermore, the lack of available data makes it difficult to corroborate the linkages from system inputs to child and family outcomes. Notwithstanding the difficulties of drawing definitive conclusions about effectiveness, it is clear that Singapore has made tremendous efforts to address the quality, equity, efficiency, and sustainability of ECEC services, achieving significant improvements in a short period of time.

Policy changes within the ECEC sector have been made possible by a strong and stable political base and responsive policy implementation to address the wider social and economic needs of the country. Addressing these national priorities has resulted in a flurry of enthusiasm and effort, supported by a manifold increase of financial investment from the government. The current ECEC system in Singapore can be best conceptualized as a hybrid model, with the public sector playing a key role in governing, regulating, and financing, and the private sector playing a key role in the ECEC service delivery. However, the planned expansion of government-run and government-supported preschools clearly represents a shift toward public-sector provision.

Accompanying this movement to greater public-sector control has been an increase in the centralization of governance. Previously, ECEC was one part of a large portfolio of services under two different ministries, each of which was responsible for monitoring different aspects of service provision regulated under different legislative acts. Consolidating matters related to ECEC under one autonomous agency, ECDA, emphasizes Singapore's heightened focus on ECEC, and ensures that there is no preferential focus on welfare or care versus education. In a hybrid ECEC sector, one of ECDA's chief responsibilities is to align the values and goals of the multiple groups and organizations playing key roles in ECEC via regulation (e.g., licensing, accreditation), sponsorship (e.g., subsidies), and advocacy (e.g., multi- and intra-agency collaborations).

More specifically, and as the sole regulatory authority for center-based care and education, ECDA has harmonized the licensing and regulation of all center-based provision, ensuring that: (a) all center-based provision meets minimum quality standards; (b) all provision is subject to the same accountability criteria; and (c) programs are monitored regularly by trained personnel. Similarly, the goal of introducing a quality improvement framework with a focus on both structural and process factors has been to allow providers to reflect on, and receive external assessment and certification of, their quality.

The same attention to harmonizing quality can also be seen in the government's approach to developing and maintaining a well-trained, compensated, and respected workforce. There is now closer regulation of the content of preservice training and of the quality of training providers. Innovative programs have been initiated for both the professional development of sector leaders and the deployment of sector leaders as advocates and mentors. Skills maps and career progression pathways have been articulated as part of the broader national effort to provide a common reference for the skills and competencies required in the ECEC sector. The recent decision to centralize the preservice training of ECEC professionals under the NIEC represents an important next step toward quality enhancement and harmonization.

Meritocracy and equality of opportunity are core tenets of Singaporean society. As such, it is believed that every child, regardless of background, should be given equal opportunities to succeed. However, the government has also articulated that meritocracy alone will not ensure social mobility. With increasing social and economic inequality, and a system of private preschools and health care providers with high variation in cost, Singapore has made it a priority to be vigilant about providing all citizens with access to a comprehensive range of CED services. The combined efforts of the government and nongovernment organizations have been important to ensuring a move toward equitable access to ECEC. Increased government regulation of the sector (e.g., through teacher training and qualifications, licensing, and increased financing of providers who can meet quality enhancements and affordability targets), and the provision of sufficient funding for baseline services and additional funding for targeted populations, means that all children can access ECEC services that meet a baseline quality standard. Current financial subsidies incentivize parents to place children in full-day child care (because basic non-means-tested subsidies are not available for children attending kindergarten). With the transition to more programs offering the equivalent of full-day care, as seen in MOE kindergartens with afterschool care, the government will need to reconsider whether basic subsidies should be available to all families, regardless of their choice of service provision.

Providing equal access to services does not necessarily align with equitable access to services. Some children and families will need additional or compensatory support to ensure that the opportunities available to them are equitable with the opportunities available to the wider community. To ensure equitable access, new policy initiatives (e.g., KidSTART, Circle of Care) proactively target low-income and vulnerable children. Further efforts are needed, however, to support access to services for other groups of children. For instance, accessing center-based care is more difficult for infants and toddlers, with lower enrollment attributed to personal choice on the part of parents, lack of places, and lack of affordability. In February 2017, the government announced that there would be an expansion of infant care provision from 4,000 to 8,000 places by 2020. As such, there may be increased access to services, but this may not be available to all parents due to the high costs involved. This expansion also requires training more ECEC professionals to work with younger children but in so doing highlights the paradox of deploying the least qualified professionals to teach children in the most formative years. The lack of focus on this age group is also underscored by the fact that there are currently no incentives for infant care to make quality improvements; however, ECDA is developing an analogue of the SPARK quality framework for use in settings catering to children aged 2 months to 3 years.

Another group lacking equal opportunities for preschool access is children with disabilities. Children with disabilities have fewer options for center-based care, and some attend center-based care for just a few hours per week. The government recently announced that it will study the feasibility of an inclusive preschool model (MSF, 2017) to improve the social integration of children with special needs. Nongovernment organizations have already piloted such a model, and the over-subscription of child care places for both typically developing children and children with special needs provides evidence that the public will subscribe to this inclusive model of ECEC provision.

There is both an economic and a value rationale that results in the expectation that ECEC programs and services should be sustainable. The recent increased investment in the ECEC sector is motivated by the need not only to respond to the threats of widening social income gaps, but also to prepare citizens with the knowledge, skills, and values that will be relevant to future society and economy. ECEC is seen as the first opportunity to develop the 21st-century competencies essential for an innovative society and economy. It is also one of the earliest opportunities to instill the national values, particularly racial and religious harmony, that will be critical for future world challenges. On a more pragmatic level, the government's decision to adopt a hybrid model, leaving ECEC service provision primarily in private hands but with strong monitoring structures, reflects a clear concern with the sustainability of the sector. Nationalizing the ECEC sector like mainstream education would have had huge financial implications on the national budget and may not have been sustainable. The decision to instead adopt a mixed model ensured the sustainability of private sector delivery with public quality safeguards.

Challenges and Implications

Developing the ECEC Workforce to Address Quality, Efficiency, and Sustainability Challenges. Building a high-quality ECEC workforce is one of the biggest endeavors that must be undertaken in the development of an effective ECEC system. Despite the highlighted efforts, and consistent with the views of study respondents, a range of challenges must still be addressed. The first is reducing staff turnover and dropout. Data from MOM indicate that only 56.5% of fresh ECEC graduates remain in the teaching force one year after graduation. Reasons cited for leaving the sector included: (a) low salary (initial salaries are reasonable but remain fairly stagnant); (b) perceived low prestige of the profession; (c) lack of professional autonomy, esteem, or respect by the public; and (d) perceived lack of career advancement (Craig, 2013).

Furthermore, with the increase in the number of preschool centers, current demand for ECEC professionals is high, and staff are able to take advantage of the expanding private sector by moving from one center to another for marginally more pay. This has created a volatile employment market (Ang, 2012), with study respondents noting that good teachers may be poached by providers who can offer a higher salary. High turnover of ECEC professionals results in a lack of stability in the care and education of children, and difficulty establishing professional communities within centers. Standardizing pay and benefits across the sector may help to mitigate the high turnover rate, and may also weaken the effect of ECEC professionals choosing centers based on pay packages, instead encouraging them to choose centers that resonate with their ECEC philosophy. Recently announced measures designed to enhance the status, compensation, and training of ECEC professionals may also help mitigate this challenge (PMO, 2017).

A second challenge is how best to facilitate the engagement of ECEC professionals in continuing professional development (CPD). Many respondents acknowledged that the current working conditions of ECEC professionals do not allow them adequate time to engage in CPD and that CPD opportunities are not available equitably. Strategies must be developed to afford all ECEC professionals sufficient time and opportunity to engage in CPD. Similar to the mainstream education system in Singapore, this may include mandating minimal no-teaching periods (known as "white time") and providing assistant teachers and/or community and parental involvement so that ECEC professionals can be released to engage in CPD.

A third challenge is the development of high-quality and efficient ECEC leadership. Investments should be made in developing not only transformational leadership and curriculum/instructional leadership, but also system leadership—that is, developing skills and attitudes in extending and deepening networks and collaboration with individuals, groups, and organizations, which could in turn increase leaders' own organizational capacity. Such delivery models are seen in the school system, where cluster superintendents develop, guide, and supervise the school leadership teams in a designated cluster of schools to ensure that schools are effectively run. Cluster superintendents play an important role in personnel and financial management and ensure that there is networking, sharing, and collaboration among the clustered schools. This model could be adopted in the ECEC sector, and it may be one way to sustain the momentum of innovative leadership programs such as ECDA Fellows, Principals Matter, and the Professional Development Program. Some of the larger preschool providers are already implementing such a model, promoting staff to become executive principals.

Supporting High-Quality and Efficient Transitions Across Settings. Although Singapore is aware of the importance of linking ECEC to the compulsory school system and is currently exploring various strategies to aid transitions (e.g., pedagogical continuity, informal induction experiences, targeted transition support for at-risk children), decentralization of transition responsibilities to private ECEC providers has resulted in varying levels of transition quality. Despite the curriculum frameworks' inclusion of national guidelines on transitions, structural impediments render coordination across sectors challenging. These include teachers' lack of time due to shortage of staff in centers, limited knowledge and external support, and inaccessibility to primary schools due to physical distance or lack of institutional connections. To overcome some of the structural impediments to transitions, plans for the building of new primary schools should include space for preschools. The locating of all MOE kindergartens within primary schools, partnered with a number of surrounding Early Years Centers, will be a strong first step toward addressing transition challenges within the ECEC sector.

Another way to support transitions is through professional continuity, which requires that ECEC center leaders, primary school principals, ECEC staff, and primary school teachers are prepared for collaboration and transitions through initial training and ongoing professional development, and that they receive relevant and sufficient support to facilitate transitions. Current discrepancies in the status and educational background of ECEC and primary school staff might create tensions, affecting relationships and, in turn, the quality of cooperation. However, alignment of working conditions, content, and level of qualifications would require change at a systemic level; ECEC could be reconceptualized as spanning the age range of 0–8 years, wherein professionals across the age range build on common knowledge and professional practice to support a holistic, continuous learning environment. This would mean strengthening the role of ECEC professionals as an indispensable feature of mainstream schooling, as well as providing opportunities for primary school teachers to be trained and engaged in preschool practices and pedagogies (Ang, 2012).

If such systemic change is not viable, initiatives to support collaboration and shared understanding might include joint training of ECEC and primary school staff, or the creation of collaborative professional learning groups. The government could also look at opportunities to reskill inservice primary school teachers, or provide training to preservice primary school teachers that would enable them to work with younger children. This may support children's transition from the preschool to the primary school through teacher looping. The centralization of training for ECEC professionals in the NIEC provides the ideal opportunity to begin consideration of training overlaps and alignment of professional standing between ECEC staff and primary school teachers.

Balancing Beliefs, Expectations, and Practices of Different Stakeholders. The government has taken a strong stand in its vision that ECEC should support children's holistic development through play-based pedagogy and that prematurely formalizing preschool, via a strong academic focus, may be dangerously counterproductive. However, these Western notions of how children learn and should be taught, which are clearly articulated in

Singapore's curriculum frameworks, run counter to cultural beliefs and academic priorities held by many parents and teachers in a largely Chinese society with Confucian values (Lim-Ratnam, 2013). Some ECEC professionals have expressed doubt that play can be substituted for academic rigor and, on account of parents' demands, hesitate to remodel their existing practices (Nyland & Ng, 2016). Furthermore, as private businesses, preschools are dependent on maintaining enrollment figures to ensure sustainability. ECEC professionals may therefore face pressure from providers to concede to parents' requests to include more academic work in the curriculum.

These tensions have a number of important implications. If parents perceive a preschool's curriculum to be less academically rigorous, they may take preventive action such as enrolling their children in additional private tuition classes. This action would exacerbate inequity in opportunities, as lower-income families cannot afford such additional support, resulting in the growth of social disparity when children enter primary school. Second, it will be impossible to quantify the impact of the holistic and child-centered pedagogical approach unless evidence of a clear link exists between a provider's planned curriculum and what is actually enacted in the classroom.

More needs to be done to ensure that parents and ECEC professionals have a common understanding of national policy goals. Numerous initiatives seek to foster parenting education and empowerment, and MOE and ECDA have made concerted efforts to educate parents about the importance of developing children holistically to be lifelong learners. However, there is no research to monitor parent or center engagement with these initiatives, it is not clear if parents are truly embracing these ideas, and there are no data that can testify to the effectiveness of these initiatives. Furthermore, research suggests that teachers may not be adequately prepared to teach using play-based pedagogies, or they may be struggling to adjust or reevaluate their beliefs about how children learn (Ng, 2011; Bull et al., 2016).

Repositioning deeply rooted and strongly held cultural beliefs and practices will be difficult. Additional efforts should be undertaken that ensure parents' active involvement in program activities and center decisionmaking, and ECEC professionals should be provided additional support not only to put into practice play-based pedagogies, but also to be able to identify and document children's learning and development in such activities. Enhancement of family and center partnerships may help to reduce tensions between parents' expectations and the expectations of ECEC professionals, in order to align their pedagogical practices with national curriculum frameworks. However, such change may be embraced only when local evidence is provided to both parents and teachers that such curricular and pedagogical adjustments do not leave children at a disadvantage when they enter school, and in fact may provide a more positive experience for children.

Efficient and Sustainable Use of Data to Drive Improvement Efforts. One of the biggest challenges to determining whether initiatives to improve quality have achieved their goal is the lack of data or research evidence directly linking policy initiatives to measured outcomes or actual practices. It is not clear what prospective plans are in place at the point of policy implementation to measure the impact of ECEC efforts. The ability to evaluate effectiveness is also limited by the lack of system-level data on child and family outcomes. The dearth of child outcome data might be partially due to resistance to national-level evaluations, particularly at a time when the government is trying to deemphasize the importance of high-stakes summative assessments and ability comparisons. Conducting national evaluations is also challenging both methodologically and administratively, as there is no statutory requirement for children to attend preschool and the provision of services is largely in the hands of the private sector. Despite these constraints, having child outcome data at a national level would be of immense value to inform, evaluate, and improve the efficiency of system performance. However, the collection of such data should not put an additional burden on ECEC staff. One model would be to standardize the measurement and documentation of children's learning and development, replacing the current methods of documentation that are decided at the center level. The collation of this information should be supported by information systems that can deliver meaningful and actionable information in realistic time frames. These assessments could then be used at the national level for summative evaluation (e.g., of policy changes and pilot programs), and for formative purposes at the center level to support individual children's learning and development.

There is currently no designated body to coordinate, oversee, or provide strategic direction for research in the early years. Although many organizations are engaged in ECEC research, establishing a national body dedicated to advancing research on ECEC—which could draw together expertise from multiple domains including health, social policy, education, psychology, and neuroscience—would allow evaluation and monitoring of initiatives using multiple sources of evidence. The promotion of programmatic research studies would support collaboration between the various organizations that have interest in the ECEC sector and would encourage the efficient use of funding for ECEC research. It would also optimize and support sustainable collaborations between the relatively small number of academics and professionals currently conducting research on ECEC in Singapore and would help to ensure that data collection efforts are not unnecessarily duplicated across agencies. Finally, engaging researchers at the point of policy planning would allow for prospective (rather than retrospective) research efforts to evaluate policy changes. The need to build a body of evidence-based research over the short and long term that will measure and evidence the impact of preschool services, policy, and practice was articulated by many study respondents and echoes the sentiments expressed by Ang (2012) that the pertinent questions "What works?," "Why does it work?," and "What impact will it have on children and families?" should be firmly embedded in policy and practice.

As well as harmonizing research efforts, the ECEC system needs to better use and share data across its different parts. Multiple sources of data are currently collected, including monitoring data collected from centers as part of the licensing regulations, data from ECEC researchers, data collected by health professionals, and national data held by ministries (e.g., subsidy support to families). The government recognizes the need to better collect, use, and share data to inform policies, and efforts are currently in place to improve data exchange and use within public services. The focus of such work should be to consider how to develop data exchange systems to make data-sharing possible to nongovernmental organizations and to develop professional capacity for integrating, managing, and analyzing large and secondary sources of data.

CONCLUDING THOUGHTS

The Singapore government is focused on two goals: ensuring a thriving economy and maintaining a politically stable and socially cohesive nation. Singapore is proud to have progressed from Third to First World status in a very short period of time. Human resources are the nation's most precious asset, and the education and nurturing of every child is seen as critical to economic development. Singapore is world-renowned for its successful educational system, and this success has been attributed to its strong investment in educational infrastructure, curriculum design, research, and teacher education and professional development at the primary, secondary, and tertiary levels. Now the government focus has turned to the early years, as there is greater realization that high-quality health, care, and education for young children positively impact the later years. Investment in young children is critical not only for addressing the current national priorities, but also for ensuring the continued prosperity of the nation. Slowed economic growth may produce social challenges, including intergenerational transmission of wealth inequalities and lower social mobility. Enhancing support for children with a weaker start by making preschools more affordable, more accessible, and higher quality is a crucial element of ensuring that "birth is not destiny" and that all children receive the support they need to maximize their development and learning potential.

The government's approach to intervening in ECEC has been to set broad parameters to start the process of evolving a harmonized ECEC sector that meets affordability and quality criteria while preserving the diversity that comes from having private market provision. A key theme of the Singaporean story is the careful balancing act that has been required to set this evolution in motion: (a) balancing increasing public regulation with the freedom expected from a private market; (b) balancing competition versus collaboration in a lucrative free market; (c) balancing policy-borrowing from Western cultures with policy adaptation to the local context; (d) balancing public and private financing of services; (e) balancing family expectations and professional beliefs; and (f) balancing the rapid pace of implementation with the time needed for thorough evaluation. Striking the right balance will require continued vigilance and innovative policies on the part of the government.

NOTES

1. All financial information is provided in US$ at an exchange rate of SG$1 = US$0.72.

2. We use the generic term *preschool* to refer to all forms of center-based care, regardless of the age of the child.

REFERENCES

Ang, L. (2012). Vital voices for vital years: A study of leaders' perspectives on improving the early childhood sector in Singapore. Retrieved from lienfoundation. org/sites/default/files/vitalvoices_1.pdf

Bull, R., O'Brien, B. A., Khng, K. H., Ng, E. L., Bautista, A., Lee, K., Poon, K., & Karuppiah, N. (2016, October). Singapore Kindergarten Impact Project (SKIP), unpublished interim report to MOE and ECDA, Singapore.

Craig, T. (2013, November 8). Pre-school teachers: Leaving before they've even started. Retrieved from m.todayonline.com/singapore/pre-school-teachers-leaving-theyve-even-started

Department of Statistics. (2016). Population trends: 2016. Retrieved from singstat. gov.sg/docs/default-source/default-document-library/publications/publications_ and_papers/population_and_population_structure/population2016.pdf

Early Childhood Development Agency. (2013a). Early years development framework for child care centers. Retrieved from ecda.gov.sg/growatbeanstalk/Documents/ EYDF%20eng_secured.pdf

Early Childhood Development Agency. (2013b). Achieving excellence through continuing professional development: A CPD framework for early childhood educators. Retrieved from child carelink.gov.sg/ccls/uploads/CPD_Guide_5_FA.pdf

Early Childhood Development Agency. (2017). Key moves to further transform the early childhood sector. Retrieved from ecda.gov.sg/PressReleases/Pages/ KEY-MOVES-TO-FURTHER-TRANSFORM-THE-EARLY-CHILDHOOD-SECTOR.aspx

Economist Intelligence Unit. (2012). Starting well: Benchmarking early education across the world. Retrieved from lienfoundation.org/sites/default/files/sw_report_2.pdf

Khoo, K. C. (2010). The shaping of child care and preschool education in Singapore: From separatism to collaboration. *International Journal of Child Care and Education Policy, 4*, 23–34.

Lee, K. Y. (2012). *From third world to first: The Singapore story, 1965–2000* (Vol. 2). Singapore: Marshall Cavendish International Asia Pte Ltd.

Legatum Institute. (2016). Legatum prosperity index 2016 Singapore. Retrieved from prosperity.com/globe/singapore

Lim, S., & Lim, A. (2017). Governmentality of early childhood issues in Singapore: Contemporary Issues. In N. Rao, J. Zhou, & J. Sun (Eds.), *Early childhood education in Chinese societies* (pp. 185–215). Dordrecht, The Netherlands: Springer.

Lim-Ratnam, C. (2013). Tensions in defining quality pre-school education: The Singapore context. *Educational Review, 65*(4), 416–431.

Ministry of Education. (2009). Report of the Primary Education Review and Implementation committee. Retrieved from planipolis.iiep.unesco.org/en/2009/report-primary-education-review-and-implementation-peri-committee-5141

Ministry of Education. (2013). Nurturing early learners: A curriculum for kindergartens in Singapore. Educators' guide: Overview. Retrieved from moe.gov.sg/docs/default-source/document/education/preschool/files/nel-edu-guide-overview.pdf

Ministry of Health. (2016). Speech by Minister for Health, Mr Gan Kim Yong, at the MOH Committee of Supply debate 2016. Retrieved from moh.gov.sg/content/moh_web/home/pressRoom/speeches_d/2016/speech-by-minister-for-health--mr-gan-kim-yong--at-the-moh-commit.html

Ministry of Social and Family Development. (2016). Policy on protection & welfare of children. Retrieved from msf.gov.sg/policies/Strong-and-Stable-Families/Nurturing-and-Protecting-the-Young/Child-Protection-Welfare/Pages/Policy-on-Protection-Welfare-of-Children.aspx

Ministry of Social and Family Development. (2017). Strengthening the ecosystem of support for persons with disabilities and their families (Press release). Retrieved from msf.gov.sg/media-room/Pages/Strengthening-the-Ecosystem-of-Support-for-Persons-with-Disabilities.aspx

National Population and Talent Division. (2017). Marriage and parenthood package summary of measures. Retrieved from heybaby.sg/having-and-raising-children/enhanced-baby-bonus

Ng, J. (2011). Preschool curriculum and policy changes in Singapore. *Asia-Pacific Journal of Research in Early Childhood Education, 5*(1), 91–122.

Nyland, B., & Ng, J. (2016). International perspectives on early childhood curriculum changes in Singapore and Australia. *European Early Childhood Education Research Journal, 24*(3), 465-476. doi:10.1080/1350293X.2015.1102416

Parliament of Singapore. (1991). *Parliamentary debates: Official report. (1991, January 15). Shared values (Vol. 56).* Singapore: Govt. Printer. Retrieved from eservice.nlb.gov.sg/item_holding_s.aspx?bid=5809358#http://eservice.nlb.gov.sg/item_holding_s.aspx?bid=5809358.

Prime Minister's Office Singapore (PMO). (2012). Prime Minister Lee Hsien Loong's National Day Rally 2012 speech. Retrieved from pmo.gov.sg/newsroom/prime-minister-lee-hsien-loongs-national-day-rally-2012-speech-english

Prime Minister's Office Singapore (PMO). (2017). Prime Minister Lee Hsien Loong's National Day Rally 2017 speech. Retrieved from pmo.gov.sg/national-day-rally-2017

Quah, J. (2016). *The role of the public bureaucracy in policy implementation in five ASEAN countries.* Cambridge, UK: Cambridge University Press.

Singapore Budget. (2016). Head I Ministry of Social and Family Development. Retrieved from singaporebudget.gov.sg/data/budget_2016/download/23%20MSF %202016.pdf

Tan, C. T. (2017). Enhancing the quality of kindergarten education in Singapore: Policies and strategies in the 21st century. *International Journal of Child Care and Education Policy, 11*(7). doi:10.1186/s40723-017-0033-y

World Health Organization. (2014). World health statistics 2014. Retrieved from apps.who.int/iris/bitstream/10665/112738/1/9789240692671_eng.pdf?ua=1

CHAPTER 8

Acting on New Narratives

Sharon Lynn Kagan and Eva Landsberg

Titled *The Early Advantage 1: Early Childhood Systems That Lead by Example*, this volume has presented the stories of six unique jurisdictions whose early childhood efforts are exemplary. The intent in this chapter is to render their similarities and differences explicit by drawing out cross-cutting themes. In looking across the five countries and the Hong Kong Special Administrative Region, we aim to synthesize some of the volume's key lessons, particularly those that will support leaders as they seek to design, construct, and implement their services to young children and their families, as well as their ECEC systems.

Although the audience for this volume is leaders, reviewing the vast literature on leadership and social change is well beyond the purview of this chapter. Yet two points related to leadership must be rendered at the outset. First, most leadership texts underscore the salience of visionary leadership, often presented as thinking ahead of the curve, or creating inventive ways of addressing the future (Senge, 1990; Wheatley & Frieze, 2010). Recalling the theme that opened this book, this means that leadership involves the act of thinking anew, of creating new narratives—a feat accomplished by leaders in the jurisdictions included herein. The second dimension of leadership suggests that new thinking must be accompanied by generative actions that produce positive social change. Leaders, by definition, are those who think differently and act collaboratively and persuasively toward an end (Kanter & Sherman, 2017; Schein, 2011). In other words, leaders act on new narratives; they dare to think and act beyond what exists.

Our review affirms that the architects of these six jurisdictions' ECEC systems were leaders who did just that: They thought and acted differently, both from the past *and* from one another. Framed by their cultural and social backgrounds and their contemporary economic and political realities, they extruded ECEC systems from their unique circumstances. As a result, no two jurisdictions' ECEC systems look precisely the same; they are distinctive and compelling in their fidelity to their contexts.

Although this chapter expands considerably on jurisdictional differences and the contexts that framed them, it also notes striking cross-jurisdictional similarities. Among these and salient to the organization of this chapter, three new narratives seem to undergird the leaders' thinking and subsequent actions across jurisdictions. Each new narrative builds on the past but represents a tilt of the armature to present a new vision in the kaleidoscope. Whether unconscious or strategic, subtle or grandiose, these shifts in thinking have precipitated enhanced services to young children and ushered in systemic change. The three narratives (re)framing contemporary ECEC address new understandings and actions related to: (a) the role of contexts in contouring ECEC systems; (b) the infrastructures that guide ECEC systems; and (c) the outputs desired from ECEC systems. Each is discussed below, backed by examples from the six diverse jurisdictions.

NEW NARRATIVE I:
CONTEXTUAL VARIATION COMES TO ECEC SYSTEMS:
New Understandings and Actions Related
to the Role of Contexts in Contouring ECEC Systems

For decades, scholars have pointed to the many ways that distinct political and cultural contexts have differentially shaped the provision and pedagogy of ECEC around the globe. Indeed, political context has had demonstrable effects on the very rationale for services for young children, be it in the aftermath of World War II, when war-torn European countries turned to pro-family policies, or in the United States' War on Poverty, which ushered in striking new commitments to children. So profound is the impact of context on American ECEC policy that some scholars opine that it has been little more than a handmaiden to the social context, with episodic and poor-quality services provided only as a result of greater social need (e.g., wars, economic depressions), rather than as an embedded commitment to young children (Cahan, 1989; Steiner, 1976).

Cultural contexts shape the nature of early childhood pedagogy: Why is it normative to value individual achievement in one preschool setting but collective accomplishment in another? Why are ratios of 35 children to one adult deemed acceptable in one country but irresponsible in others? Why do some children play outdoors for hours, even in remarkably cold temperatures, while others spend barely minutes outside in magnificent weather? Acknowledging the role of cultural and contextual variation, classic postmodernists and many others have long been concerned with the over-homogenization of services for young children, insisting that natural variations must be honored in pedagogy and practice (Dahlberg, Moss, & Pence, 1999; Rao, Zhou, & Sun, 2017; Tobin, Wu, & Davidson, 2009). Moreover, transcending early childhood, scholars have addressed how cultural context profoundly influences one's sense of self and social structures (Nisbett, 2003; Shore, 1996), with the entire area of cultural psychology ascending in prominence.

Simultaneous to the bevy of contextual work that is taking place, systems thinking has emerged as an important construct in understanding and managing complex organizations and institutions. Flood and Jackson (1991) suggest that a system is an interlinked, complex network of parts that, when taken together, is greater than the sum of its parts. The system is so intertwined that a minor change in one subsystem reverberates to all subsystems. Yet despite its complexity, the system follows a fairly linear process, in which inputs are transformed into outputs and outcomes, all within a broader social context. Applied to early childhood education, systems work has taken several forms. It has sought to conceptualize services to young children in a broadened frame (Bruner et al., 2004; Kagan & Cohen, 1996), and it has identified the characteristics thought to evoke effective systems. These early efforts defined the essential elements somewhat acontextually, so that such elements were proffered to apply across contexts and settings.

Presently, and as these six jurisdictional analyses suggest, a new narrative is emerging. Once conceptualized as a model composed of required elements or fixed policies or structures, ECEC systems work was predicated on the assumption that the reproduction of these essential ingredients would formulaically yield quality systems, which in turn would evoke higher-quality programs and better child outcomes. Felled by scores of failed replications, this singular model approach is now being replaced by the reality that multiple ECEC systems approaches can and do work. These approaches, rather than aiming to evoke cookie-cutter solutions, are grounded in a far more nuanced narrative that understands and honors the realities and contributions that emerge from diverse contexts. Thus, rather than a fixed and formulaic model of an ECEC system, this study clearly evinces diverse approaches to designing, funding, implementing, monitoring, and governing ECEC, with differences reflective of unique operational and temporal contexts.

Operational Contexts

This volume suggests that despite very different social, political, and historical traditions, ECEC systems can be successfully implemented amidst a wide variety of contexts. The jurisdictions in this study span the globe, across cultures and diverse governmental structures, from highly centralized to federalized. They differ considerably in geographic size, ranging from Singapore and Hong Kong to Australia, and in population size and density. Despite these variations, successful ECEC systems are taking hold in all, under diverse guises.

Although there is no one preferred context, some patterns of approaches have been revealed. First, it appears that smaller, centralized jurisdictions are often more agile in their implementation. Second, among the limited set

Figure 8.1. Suggested Typology of CED Operational Approaches

NORDIC APPROACH Finland	• Heavy public funding for ECEC services
	• Heavy public provision of ECEC services
	• National framework; freedom of implementation; focus on children's agency
	• Limited, if any, national formal child monitoring
	• Limited, if any, formal program monitoring
	• Heavy public funding for health care and child protection
ASIAN APPROACH Hong Kong Korea Singapore	• Moderate to heavy public funding for ECEC services
	• Mixed public-private provision of ECEC services
	• National framework; structured pedagogy
	• Limited national formal child monitoring
	• Moderate to heavy formal program monitoring
	• Heavy public funding for health care and moderate to heavy funding for child protection
ANGLO APPROACH Australia England	• Limited to heavy public funding for ECEC services
	• Mixed public-private provision of ECEC services
	• National framework; moderately guided pedagogy
	• Moderate to heavy national formal child monitoring
	• Heavy formal program monitoring
	• Heavy public funding for health care and moderate to heavy funding for child protection

of six jurisdictions, three operational approaches to CED services emerge. No heuristic is perfect, but the suggested typology presented in Figure 8.1 offers a lens through which to view how the six jurisdictions' cultural contexts cluster and are manifest in diverse operational approaches. This clustering suggests that contextual variation profoundly shapes the nature of policies and services.

Nordic Contexts/Approaches. These countries are characterized by the existence (however tacitly) of strong social contracts that are accompanied by substantial investments in citizen well-being, including a commitment to CED services. In most cases, these countries heavily subsidize and provide CED services for young children, including significant investments in publicly funded family leave and pre- and perinatal services. In ECEC classrooms, national frameworks guide pedagogy, but teachers are accorded a great deal of freedom in implementing their programs. There is little emphasis on formal program monitoring; conversely, there is significant focus on, and respect for, children's agency, irrespective of age. In this volume, Finland is an example of this context and approach to CED.

Asian Contexts/Approaches. While public funding is increasing, these countries rely more heavily on markets, both philosophically (as a funding ideology) and practically (as a source of funding). ECEC programs exist in the public and private sectors, with the private sector boasting both for-profit and nonprofit programs. Although parental leave policies exist, there is often limited public funding for education and care services for young children from birth to age 3, with the exception of Korea; when such supports exist, they are typically not well funded. There is often a well-defined national framework for ECEC and some reliance on formal program monitoring. This is accompanied by a more structured pedagogy than is operative in the Nordic and Anglo countries examined in this study. Generally, there is heavy public funding for health care and moderate-to-heavy funding for child protection. In this volume, Hong Kong, the Republic of Korea, and Singapore are examples of this context and approach to CED.

Anglo Contexts/Approaches. In these countries, governments provide variable funding for ECEC, ranging from somewhat limited to very heavy support, with programs provided by both the public and private sectors. Less robust than in the Nordic countries but still quite strong, publicly supported family leave and pre- and perinatal services exist. A national framework guides pedagogy and is accompanied by public monitoring apparatuses; indeed, there is heavy reliance on and use of program monitoring and some use of formal child monitoring, along with transcendent support for formative assessment to guide pedagogy. There is heavy public funding for health care and moderate-to-heavy funding for child protection. In this volume, Australia and England are examples of this context and approach to CED.

Temporal Contexts

Just as countries' policies for young children have been shaped by their historical, geographic, and political contexts, temporal contexts contour services dramatically. At the most general level, all of the countries represented herein have a working knowledge of the repertoire of new sciences and have used these to justify, create, and/or expand services for young children and their families. They all have policy leaders who understand the importance of investing in young children for the economic and social benefits that accrue to the society at large and to the individual families and children. They all boast robust economies that are dependent on ongoing social capital to sustain, if not expand, their economic positions. Ensconced in a global world, the six countries also fully understand the importance of intra- and international connectedness via economic and technological linkages. In short, even in countries with durable commitments to young children, new knowledge and new social conditions have propelled ECEC to prominence on national agendas.

Although all the countries in the study are experiencing significant social and demographic changes, they are manifest differently. Increased immigration to the Nordic and Anglo countries has led to ECEC being regarded as a means to instill core societal values and foster an equal foundation for all children. Broadly, these countries are not only changing their policies to foster greater equity but are altering their programs so that notable attention is being accorded to cultivating the home values and languages of diverse populations. Meanwhile, the study's Asian countries, which often have smaller geographic footprints combined with aging populations and low fertility rates, regard ECEC as a crucial foundational investment in human capital. In these countries, an expanded emphasis on family support has taken hold. This, combined with a longstanding commitment to education, has led to renewed interest and investment in ECEC.

Context, both historical and contemporary, affects ECEC boldly. In some ways, as countries are exposed to similar data and experience similar changes, they face comparable challenges. Yet how they conceptualize these challenges and the options they exercise to address them vary, with that variation often firmly molded by their cultural values and sociopolitical contexts. This analysis suggests that new narratives are being constructed, with definitions of context broadening, and with responses to them being more individually legitimized as each country uniquely contours its ECEC system.

NEW NARRATIVE II: FROM PROGRAMS TO SYSTEMS AND THE ASCENDANCE OF INFRASTRUCTURE: New Understandings and Actions Related to the Infrastructure That Guide ECEC Systems

When early childhood services were first promulgated, the focus was on increasing the provision of direct services that actually touch the lives of young children. Programmatic in orientation and structure, this historic approach—with some limited exceptions—has led to the proliferation of direct services emerging under diverse auspices, often with their own unique professional standards, certifications, regulations, and quality standards. Challenging enough if the early childhood field existed within the purview of a single discipline or ministry, the situation is rendered far more complex because services for young children are associated with and accountable to multiple ministries, frequently including education, health, and welfare. Hence, the very strength of early childhood—its multidisciplinary nature—coupled with a traditionally somewhat limited interpretation of the nature of services and what it takes to evoke high quality, means that early childhood has been programmatically and somewhat narrowly conceptualized.

That is changing, and changing rapidly. In each of the six countries highlighted in this volume, ECEC is understood not only as programs, but as the marriage of programs with an infrastructure that supports them. Wise policymakers and practitioners have come to see that merely funding programs will not overcome the historic legacies of fragmentation. As a result, each country has conceptualized infrastructure somewhat differently—and perhaps has not labeled it "infrastructure"—but all have made significant investments in it. They recognize that in order to be maximally effective, investments in elements of the infrastructure that support the programs—finance, pedagogical quality, transitions, workforce development, data use, and engagement and support strategies—are necessary. Moreover, they appreciate that *multi*disciplinary does not mean *inter*disciplinary. They understand that to evoke effective ECEC, they must link the separate disciplines, converting them from multi- (many) to inter- (integrated) disciplinary. In this section, we address how the six countries have reconceptualized ECEC by focusing on, and making significant investments in, elements of the infrastructure.

Governance

In all six countries, there have been considerable efforts to overcome historic disciplinary schisms in the ECEC field. Typically, these efforts have been achieved through some form of consolidation, either structural and/ or functional. *Structural consolidations* are those that: (a) consolidate the majority of ECEC services under an existing ministry; (b) form an entirely new ministry or structure; or (c) create a new mechanism to span the boundaries of current disciplines and ministries, often referred to in the literature as boundary-spanning mechanisms (BSMs) and often existing in addition to line ministries. Alternately, there are efforts to consolidate functions across ministries; these *functional consolidations* involve developing common approaches to curriculum, pedagogy, professional development, monitoring, and/or financing. Some countries rely on structural consolidation to accomplish functional consolidation; in other cases, functional consolidations seem to suffice. Whichever strategy is used, all the countries in this study affirm the need to bring greater coherence to their early childhood policies, across ministries and disciplines, fully recognizing that new narratives must create new approaches to governance.

Structural Consolidations. Structural consolidations are now quite common, with many countries electing to consolidate their ECEC services within their education ministry. For example, Australia, England, and Finland have consolidated the majority of the delivery of their ECEC services under their respective ministries of education. Singapore, meanwhile, has implemented a different approach to structural consolidation through its establishment of a new entity, the Early Childhood Development Agency (ECDA), which centralized the governance of education and welfare as it impacts young children. A third, potentially less durable approach to structural consolidation is the development of BSMs that plan or coordinate services. Examples are seen in Australia, where the Council of Australian Governments (COAG) coordinates federal and state/territorial efforts, and in Hong Kong's Joint Office for Kindergarten and Child Care Centers, which is staffed by members of both the education and welfare departments and seeks to harmonize ECEC services for children aged 3–6.

Even structural consolidation does not always fully overcome changes in the policy zeitgeist, and there often remain some residual tensions between "care" and "education." For instance, in England, the political focus has recently shifted from child development/education to one that privileges parental employment, with new policies favoring a day care strategy.

Functional Consolidations. Less intense and potentially less durable, functional consolidations do not create new or realign existing structures, but rather consolidate certain specified functions so that they apply across funding streams and auspices. These consolidations vary by country. The Republic of Korea—where a split governance system persists—has enacted numerous functional consolidations through the Nuri Initiative, which harmonized the curriculum for all children aged 3–5 across settings, established an integrated fee subsidy system, and is in the process of consolidating its quality assurance (monitoring) system. Another example of functional consolidation can be found in Hong Kong, where the curriculum for all children aged 3–6 has been harmonized across settings and monitoring services for 3- to 6-year-old children have been synchronized across ministries.

Linking Structural and Functional Consolidations. Although presented above as different approaches, structural consolidation often precipitates functional consolidations; in fact, the structures have often been established with the primary goal of harmonizing functional consolidations. In Singapore, structural consolidation via ECDA enabled the consolidation of regulatory authority for center-based care and education. The establishment of this structural entity also produced numerous functional consolidations, including aligned curriculum and common regulations.

Finance

The study countries share some important commonalities with regard to how they fund and finance their ECEC services for young children. Except in small jurisdictions that are city-states (i.e., Hong Kong, Singapore), ECEC funding is typically generated at the national level and then dispersed to local levels for administration; local levels often provide resources as well. In many cases, national and local funding emanates from diverse ministries with only limited cross-agency integration. Predictably, Hong Kong and Singapore are exceptions and represent high levels of funding integration.

Although governments in all study countries contribute to ECEC, countries that have made a substantial political commitment to young children typically make larger investments. Contouring this, public investment is rarely consistent across all ages of children; more resources are usually devoted to children over age 3. With the exception of Republic of Korea, none of the study countries offers complete public funding for early education or care programs for children under 3.

In no country is the government the exclusive ECEC funder. All instead combine public and private resources, often relying on parental fees and private philanthropy to a far greater extent than they do for primary and secondary education. Private funding is often encouraged to bolster the number and nature of ECEC services provided, as well as to stimulate innovation and responsivity to parental needs. Some study countries strategically seek to increase private-sector engagement in ECEC by using public funds to incentivize private for- and nonprofit provision. In England and Finland—countries often associated with large-scale public funding—public funds may be used in private (often for-profit) centers. When public funds are used in the private sector, typically some form of accountability, notably government monitoring, is exerted.

Countries also vary in how they balance demand- and supply-side funding strategies, with most countries using both, often simultaneously. Government-supported demand-side funding takes the form of subsidies, typically to parents, enabling them to select the type of service(s) they desire. Demand-side funding is often employed to enhance the market's diversity. Increasingly, however, countries are favoring supply-side strategies, in which public funds are given directly to providers. This permits greater government control over fees and how funds are used, thus incepting more consistent quality and more equitably distributed services. Supply-side funding is also attractive to governments that wish to incentivize service provision to traditionally underserved or high-needs populations. Interestingly, the movement to supply-side funding is taking hold even in countries where demand-side strategies have prevailed for decades, such as Hong Kong.

Most of the study countries provide special grants to support context-specific needs. For instance, they may use special funding to pilot new programs or efforts, or to support at-risk children or children who live in remote areas. In Hong Kong and Singapore, where physical space is at a premium, capital funding efforts constitute an important component of supply-side funding. In countries facing rapid ECEC expansion, special funds are used to support professional development to build workforce capacity, as in England, Hong Kong, and Singapore.

Perhaps more than in other areas of the infrastructure, all six countries face common financing issues: how to balance costs and quality in the market, how to render quality services affordable and accessible, and how to sustain funding over time so that it is used most efficiently. Not yet fully resolved in any country, these questions continue to challenge governments in their efforts to create and sustain well-functioning ECEC systems.

Pedagogical Quality

Throughout the six jurisdictions studied, there is a strong, and often recently renewed, emphasis on the quality of the pedagogy to which young children are exposed. In Australia, for example, quality has been the umbrella rationale for the creation of new entities, new structures, and new visions. Notably, embedded in its National Quality Framework (NQF), Australia has created an Early Years Learning Framework (EYLF) that seeks to advance quality pedagogy throughout the country. And Australia is not alone. Framework documents that establish clear visions for ECEC also exist in England (The Early Years Foundation Stage, or EYFS), Korea (Nuri Curriculum), Singapore (The Early Years Development Framework and Nurturing Early Learners), Hong Kong (Guide to Pre-Primary Curriculum), and Finland (the national curricula for children from birth to 6).

Common characteristics shape these frameworks and curricula. All share approaches that foster child-centered and holistic pedagogy, the active engagement of families, and the need for quality personnel. Designed to cultivate quality, continuity, and consistency, the frameworks and curricula have been developed with input by ECEC professionals and, in some cases, parents. Though all exist at the national level, they encourage varying degrees of adaptation at the provider level. As might be suspected, their implementation ranges from mandated to suggested, with some jurisdictions (e.g., England, Hong Kong, Korea) making funding contingent on demonstrated compliance with the framework. Most countries accompany their frameworks with mechanisms that monitor its implementation.

Despite these overarching similarities, however, differences in the frameworks are also apparent. In some, the content of desired child outcomes is quite global, whereas in others, the outcomes are more specific. In some countries, the frameworks exist for only one age group (typically the year[s] closest to entry to formal school); increasingly, however, frameworks exist for children from birth to formal school entry. Both England's and Korea's early years frameworks are notable for their purposeful links with the primary school curriculum.

In some of the countries, the implementation of child-centered pedagogy is complicated by two forces. Consonant with the importance of context noted earlier, the first focuses on parents and the second focuses on pedagogical personnel. In the first case, which is particularly pronounced in the Asian study countries, many parents voice a preference for academically oriented content and pedagogy, fearing that their preschool-aged children will not be ready for premier primary schools. This pressure for more academically oriented learning approaches in ECEC has been attributed in part to Confucian ideology emphasizing academic success, combined with the powerful voice parents can and do exert through their market choices.

The second contouring focus finds expression in the postmodernist ideologies that favor more adaptive approaches to quality in which curriculum is evolved, rather than prespecified or prepackaged. This is manifest, for instance, in critics' reproach of the formal pedagogy engendered by the EYFS early learning goals in England. In this postmodernist understanding of quality, the transcendent influence of culture suggests the need for more locally constructed approaches to pedagogy. This often comes in stark contrast to national efforts to produce more standardized framework documents, although many framework documents accord flexibility to practitioners.

Transitions

There is growing recognition of the need to support young children and their families as they traverse multiple early childhood settings, programs, and services, particularly in their movement from the home to an ECEC setting, and from the ECEC setting to formal school. As noted previously, many of the study countries have made national-level efforts to create broad curricular and pedagogical alignment so as to reduce ruptures in learning as children move between these settings. This has been especially successful *within* the early years, by creating alignment through national curriculum frameworks that guide all or most ECEC settings. For instance, mandatory curricula in England and Korea (the EYFS and Nuri, respectively) ensure that children receive consistent learning experiences even as they move between child care, pre-primary, and/or kindergarten. Increasingly, this is being matched by attention to alignment between ECEC and primary school. Although no study country has yet created a single consistent curriculum that covers the span of 0–8 years, most countries have begun to purposefully connect learning goals and standards in early years curricula with those of primary schools, with Korea as a clear example. In some Asian countries, however, this is complicated by the sharp contrast between the child-centered, play-based national ECEC curricula and the more academically focused, rigid curricular enactment associated with primary school.

Beyond aligning pedagogy, the study countries demonstrate remarkable innovation in devising creative transition strategies. One popular approach is the transition statement/profile, which is prepared for each child by an ECEC teacher and shared with their primary school teacher in order to guide curricular planning and facilitate linkages between the two settings. In three of Australia's largest states, these "transition statements" are mandatory; in England, notably, the EYFS profile is a national requirement. Location sharing, in which ECEC classes are located on the site of primary schools, is another creative approach seen in England, applying to all Reception classes (mandatory for 5-year-olds). In a comprehensive approach to transition, Singapore has made significant strides, with the establishment of formalized links between Early Years Centers and government-run kindergartens, and the co-location of these kindergartens within primary schools. Fortifying its commitment to transition, Singapore's innovative Circle of Care pilot initiative establishes preschool "clusters" grouped around an anchor primary school, formalizing the working relationships among teachers, administrators, social workers, and counselors in these settings and encouraging visits between schools. Overall, though many transition strategies continue to be developed solely on a local level by ECEC and primary school teachers, state or national government involvement in developing and promoting such efforts is growing.

Workforce Development

Given the rapid ECEC expansion taking place in most of the study countries, the need to increase the size of the workforce is legion. Moreover, the workforce challenge is exacerbated as a result of the need for, and the renewed focus on, quality. Although efforts to inculcate capacity in the workforce are taking hold, insufficient attention to compensation is impeding the success of such efforts. All countries express concern that without attention to compensation issues, the status and longevity of personnel are seriously compromised and delimit the quality of services provided to children. Several reasons exist for this; in Hong Kong, for example, the market has not driven up wages and may, in fact, conspire to deflate them. Even in countries like Finland, where ECEC professionals are accorded much respect, compensation falls below that of primary or secondary teachers and contributes to reduced personnel retention rates. In short, despite recognition of their importance, workforce issues remain trenchant in all six countries.

Nonetheless, diverse efforts are taking place to improve the quality of the workforce, with most countries using a combination of pre- and inservice strategies. With regard to preservice strategies, many countries have sought to raise entry-level requirements without reducing workforce attraction or retention, two acute problems that plague the field. This attempt has required a careful balancing act on the part of national governments. Some, such as Australia, England, and Singapore, have established clear workforce qualification requirements that apply across most or all ECEC settings, thus making preservice training more coherent and more transferable as teachers move within the field. For instance, Singapore's innovative skills framework outlines three distinct ECEC career paths that transcend any particular setting or program. These pathways include both traditional preservice training at universities and nontraditional routes of entry, such as apprenticeships. Meanwhile, Hong Kong has taken steps to increase professional requirements for ECEC staff by tying teaching qualifications to participation in financial schemes, such as the erstwhile PEVS or FQKEP. Using a less structured strategy to prepare and induce teachers, Finland makes the ECEC field quite attractive to incoming personnel by according high respect, trust, and creative flexibility to ECEC professionals.

Raising staff abilities requires attention not only to those preparing to enter the field, but to those already working; this is accomplished through inservice training or continuing professional development (CPD). Traditionally, CPD has not been a matter of national policy and has been left to municipalities or employers. Today, however, perhaps propelled by the expansion of the ECEC workforce, this is changing. In Korea, there are many examples of both centralized and locally sponsored professional development opportunities. For example, professional learning communities for kindergarten teachers, incentivized by Local Offices of Education, operate as small, voluntary peer groups in which teachers meet to conduct action research on curriculum and pedagogy. In Finland, where professional development has primarily been left to the municipal level, a new, national-level "professional development ECEC task force" has been instantiated to operate within and across regions and municipalities. Singapore's aforementioned skills framework outlines clear pathways for progression within the profession, tied to government money that subsidizes up to 80% of inservice CPD costs. England includes professional development as part of its EYFS. Yet despite these advances, few countries have the dedicated infrastructure in place to collect monitoring data on national-level workforce participation in, and effectiveness of, CPD.

Data-Driven Improvement

This analysis suggests that most countries are ramping up their collection and use of data related to young children and programs. This increase is primarily motivated by the desire to foster programmatic and service improvement and inform within-country reform. Consequently, special attention is being accorded to generating and using data that emanate from country-based programs and country-based scholars, rather than international work. These desires notwithstanding, across and within countries, different kinds of data, emanating from different sources, are used.

All the involved countries are increasingly reliant on empirical research, although in some (notably Australia, Hong Kong, and Singapore), much of the research continues to come from international, rather than domestic, sources. To reduce this overreliance (and hence potential inapplicability), author recommendations call for the establishment of a dedicated research entity and a related country-based research capacity. Even Korea and England, which are noteworthy for their more developed research infrastructures, still cite the need to make use of data more effectively. With regard to data that evaluate existing programs, countries understand its importance and often seek to evaluate programs that are governmentally launched; however, the degree to which such evaluations are universal, and the degree to which such data are actually used and publicized, are not always optimal. First, because some of the studies and evaluations emanate from a single ministry or discipline, the transferability of information among diverse ministries is limited. Second, sometimes existing data may not be easily or legally accessible to all who might benefit from the findings.

Beyond research and evaluation data, in general, countries are establishing increasingly sophisticated monitoring systems that track and use information related to the nature and quality of ECEC programs. In Australia, ACECQA oversees the implementation of the National Quality Framework, dispatching officers to evaluate ECEC programs on a regular basis. Ratings are made public, thus promoting informed choices on the part of parents—a strategy similarly seen in Korea, Hong Kong kindergartens, and England. England's sophisticated inspecting/monitoring framework is conducted by Ofsted, the same trusted monitoring agency responsible for inspecting higher levels of schooling. Inspections occur at least every four years, with a focus on assessing service quality (through observation and document scrutiny) alongside regulatory compliance (e.g., health and safety requirements, staff-to-child ratios). In contrast, and representing a marked exception to the trend of increased program monitoring, Finland has widespread trust in government and in its education system, so that data on program quality are not routinely collected.

In contrast to data on programs, the collection and use of data on young children—with the exception of routinely collected health data—is far less prevalent and far more controversial. The collection and use of education-related child data is constrained by numerous factors: (a) a lack of consistently specified child outcomes; (b) a widespread perception that young children are not reliable test-takers; (c) a perspective that tests designed for young children often test the wrong things; and (d) a value premise that proffers ECEC as a universal right, not a service that must validate its existence via test results. Despite these prevailing issues around child data, Australia uses a national Early Development Census of children as they enter formal schooling. This "snapshot," conducted every three years, provides data on child development outcomes that can then be used to inform policy. England supports a national developmental assessment when the children are 2, accompanied by another national assessment when the children are 5. This latter assessment consists of a profile of each child based on the 17 early learning goals that are specified in the national curriculum. Compiled by teachers based on observations and interactions, along with children's work and discussion with family members, the anonymized data are collected on the national level and used to inform policymakers and regulations. The profiles are also used by teachers as formative assessments, intended to guide pedagogical improvement. Indeed, across the study countries, observing and recording children's behavior, with data kept at the teacher level and used to plan and guide teaching, is considered both justified and beneficial. Such formative assessments are routinely conducted in all six jurisdictions.

Engagement and Support Strategies

Early childhood policy is frequently guided by direct engagement with consumers and providers, as well as the general public. This is both an important sustainability strategy and a way to promote families' involvement in the lives of their children, both within ECEC programs and children's homes. Meaningful engagement of families, however, has proved universally challenging. In Singapore, for example, there is no national legislation promoting parental involvement in ECEC, despite the nation's emphasis on honoring families as children's first teachers. In Finland, parents have traditionally been accorded a great deal of choice in selecting activities and services for their children, yet new proposals, driven by budget concerns, may limit these options for lower-income and minority families. In Australia, the invigorated market approach to child care is shifting the conception of parents being considered partners in ECEC governance to parents being consumers *of* ECEC—a trend fostering an entirely different conception of engagement somewhat at odds with the emphasis on partnerships with families that is expressed in the NQF and the EYLF.

   With regard to engaging family members in the lives of their children outside formal ECEC programs, countries employ diverse strategies. In Singapore, programs such KidSTART and FamilyMatters! empower parents with knowledge and skills to nurture healthy and positive family relationships. Using health services as an entree, many countries provide parenting education during children's wellness checkups. The distribution of printed or digital materials to expectant mothers and families is common, but more targeted interventions also exist. In Australia, dual-generational programs focus on Indigenous and disadvantaged communities, aiming to involve parents and children together in programming that simultaneously fosters children's learning and development while providing support and education to parents regarding the early years. In Hong Kong, the Grandparenting Scheme engages grandparents in child care courses so that they will be versed in contemporary approaches to the care and guidance of their grandchildren.

Within the ECEC services themselves, there are also diverse examples of parent engagement. National mandates exist in Hong Kong, where the FQKEP guidelines stress the importance of parental engagement and encourage parent-teacher associations. Korea has a very clear mandate for parental engagement, in that all child care and kindergarten centers are required to establish and operate parent boards; cities may establish parent monitoring groups as well. The Finnish approach to ECEC also privileges parental participation, manifest in different ways, most notably through the engagement of families in the construction of the nationally mandated Individual Education Plan, developed for each child through collaboration between teachers, parents, and the children themselves.

As one reviews these diverse efforts, the emergence of a new narrative that focuses not only on direct services is clearly evidenced. The above examples provide ample evidence that countries concerned with the development of their young children recognize the importance of focusing efforts on diverse elements of the infrastructure: governance, finance, pedagogical quality, transitions, workforce, data, and engagement. Manifest and affirmed in action, the emerging narrative underscores a broader vision of ECEC, one that honors the infrastructure and strategically supports multi-disciplinary approaches to all its elements.

NEW NARRATIVE III:
EXPANDING THE DEFINITION:
New Understandings and Actions Related to
the Outputs Desired from ECEC Systems

In the past, as noted in Chapter 1, support for ECEC was predicated on three primary rationales: an empirical rationale, a social needs rationale, and an obligation-rights rationale. In accordance with these rationales, three categories of outputs were generally, though differentially, acknowledged as suitable outcomes for ECEC. Rooted in an empirical rationale, for example, outputs were characterized as those identifiable (and researchable) characteristics that accrue to those receiving the services. These were measured in terms of services received, or, with the advent of the global accountability movement, by gains in children's performance and or their well-being. The social needs rationale, meanwhile, prompted a focus on providing services in times of crisis, with the sentiment that the services should either address a broader social need or be terminated when the crises ended. As such, the outcomes were adult-driven or temporary, respectively. Last, the primary outcome of the obligation-rights rationale was the (primarily public) provision of services for all children.

Today, the advent of globalization, the emergence of new sciences, and overall recognition of the potency of ECEC has led to a totally new context, one in which services for young children have burgeoned and countries are not only motivated by the rationales suggested above, but have come to regard ECEC as an essential elixir of social advancement. In some countries, services once regarded as temporary are now part of the durable social fabric, and services that were once regarded as necessary for the few are now seen as essential for all. This explosion, then, is the manifestation of changed ideas about the role ECEC plays in many societies.

Not minor, these shifts have been accompanied by dramatic changes not only in the way countries envision their contexts (Narrative I) and their infrastructures (Narrative II), but in how they conceptualize the desired outcomes of ECEC. Indeed, a new narrative is taking hold. At one level, in many countries, new accord is being granted to the importance of child outcomes, undergirded by the thinking that ECEC is not an automatic right or entitlement but must demonstrate its capacity to yield child outcomes. Child outcomes, measured by children's performance in the short and long terms and once primarily associated with literacy and numeracy, have been expanded to include aspects of children's social, emotional, and physical development, with attention to approaches to learning and self-regulation gaining currency.

On another level, the new narrative also represents a change in thinking regarding outcomes' nature and beneficiaries. Historically, desired outcomes were lodged primarily with humans, notably children and families; if children and families benefited, outcomes were realized. The new narrative suggests a more nuanced understanding that focuses on both humans and the system. It suggests that child and family outcomes are contingent on the existence of a system (not simply a single program) that can evoke such outcomes. Thus, this new narrative does not diminish the importance of child and family outcomes; rather, it bulwarks them with new commitments to establish, document, and monitor systemic outputs associated with high-quality, equitably distributed, efficiently delivered, and durably sustained services. In other words, as we hold ourselves accountable to clearly specified goals for child and family outcomes, we must do the same for the system that produces those outcomes. Hence, the new narrative recognizes that child and family outcomes are bolstered by four linked systemic goals: quality, equity and equality, efficiency, and sustainability, each of which is being (re)defined and manifested in the jurisdictions considered.

Quality

The emergence of new narratives is particularly evident when addressing quality. As noted in Chapter 1, quality has been traditionally conceptualized as a pedagogical condition associated with programs, classrooms, or teachers, one that is premised on the understanding that high-quality contexts will produce more pronounced outcomes for children. To that end, quality measures for programs, classrooms, and teachers have been created and implemented in most study countries. Historically, however, quality was far less frequently associated with all elements of the infrastructure presented in the prior section. New understandings reflect the fact that quality outcomes for children, the traditional bellwether of success, occur only when quality is achieved in supportive areas—that is, the infrastructure. In light of bedrock data attesting to the importance of quality to child outcomes, contemporary policymakers in the six study countries readily acknowledge that investments in the infrastructure are the insurance policy for quality. Although the countries differ in how they approach quality enhancement, all understand that quality is contingent on the infrastructure and are making investments that operationalize that sentiment.

Of course, the importance of quality services has been acknowledged for decades. What is notable and new, however, is the expanded vision of the accelerators of quality. No longer limited to pedagogical inputs such as group size, ratios, and teacher quality, the new narrative squarely positions quality as a systemic output, conditioned on numerous inputs related to governance, finance, data, and engagement. Indeed, many countries in this analysis are collecting data on these broadened outputs and are using the data to improve their ECEC systems. Data on children are being joined by data on systemic variables to reflect a more robust picture of ECEC and the children and families it serves.

Such an expanded vision does not mean that all services will be of quality, automatically and instantaneously. Implementing quality enhancements is difficult in and of itself; when it is coupled with changing commitments to equality and equity, efficiency, and sustainability, as presented below, implementation is further complicated. What is important, however, is the burgeoning recognition of, and commitment to, a broadened vision of quality enhancement, one that incorporates all elements of the infrastructure. The study countries' experiences suggest that ideas about quality are being significantly expanded to frame a new narrative that addresses systemic visions of quality.

Equity and Equality

For the involved countries, equality of access to services has been the rationale for, or is emerging as a new priority for, ECEC service provision. In addition to the focus on equality of access, however, a simultaneous call for equity is taking hold. As noted in Chapter 1, an equality stance suggests that all children deserve and should be provided with ECEC services; an equity stance goes further, suggesting that because children are not all equal in need, the services they should receive are not either. To be truly equal, some children need more or different services. The emerging narrative reflects this stance, suggesting that services must be equally available and equitable in focus and orientation so that those in greater need receive more, and/or more tailored, services. In other words, there is clear recognition that equal service provision may not be equitable; the emerging narrative, therefore, is rooted in both equality *and* equity.

Despite an intellectual ethos that supports equal and equitable service provision, the six study counties are nevertheless all struggling to make this a reality. However, desirable, equal—much less equitable—access to services does not exist. Finland, England, and Korea do come close with regard to equal service access for segments of their populations. In Finland, for example, ECEC services for children from birth to age 5 are provided by municipalities as part of the universal services organized by the government. Access to these services, however, which was once guaranteed at public expense for all, is now being reduced for children whose parents are neither students nor in the workforce, therein delimiting the universality of equal access. In England, where services are funded by the government for all children, 3- to 4-year-old children of working parents are funded for 30 hours per week, compared to half that time for children of nonworking parents, a disparity that clearly advantages children of working parents. In Korea, Nuri vouchers are intended to provide free half-day ECEC to all children aged 3–5, but inadequate government funds and additional fees for "extracurricular" care induce inequalities that result in children from wealthier families having greater access and opportunity.

Adopting an equity stance, Australia, Hong Kong, and Singapore, along with Finland, demonstrate particular concerns for traditionally underserved populations. Australia has focused on developing unique funding mechanisms for Indigenous communities, who have historically been both disadvantaged and underserved. Hong Kong and Singapore, both heavily marketized countries, seek to foster greater equity of access for children from low-income and vulnerable families by providing additional targeted financial subsidies and/or integrated support services (covering health, welfare, and education). Finland, noted above for its emphasis on equality, also demonstrates an equity stance through its strong investment in children with disabilities. For each child, an individualized support plan is developed through collaboration between welfare, health care, and education workers, along with parents, and ample financial benefits and disability allowances are provided in order to ensure equitable ECEC opportunities.

Although no country achieves complete equality in terms of its access to services or equity in terms of the range of services provided for children of all ages, some commonalities exist. With the notable exception of Korea, younger children are served with far less regularity than are children closer to formal school entry age. Moreover, in all study countries, fewer per capita resources are expended on children in their earliest years when compared with children in primary and secondary schools. In some countries—England, for example—per capita expenditures for children in the Reception year (i.e., the year immediately prior to primary school) are roughly equivalent to those expended in Grade 1, and in other jurisdictions as well a trend exists toward enhanced per capita expenditures as young children approach formal schooling. Nonetheless, inequality between financial investments in ECEC and formal schooling perpetuates inequities in services delivered and runs counter to Heckman's findings that early investments are the most efficient (Heckman, 2006).

Recognizing these deficits, countries are more seriously tackling differences with regard to age and, in some cases, with regard to inequities in services. For example, Australia employs a unique funding strategy to provide programs for Indigenous children and their families, ensuring that the services are culturally responsive and meet children's comprehensive needs. In Singapore, the Integrated Child Care Program and the Early Intervention Program for Infants and Children provide dedicated, specialized care and education to children with mild to severe disabilities. Thus, while the equity-equality debate is far from resolved, the above examples demonstrate that countries are now recognizing that their responsibility covers *all* young children and that they must enhance equitable services across age, economic status, ability, language, and culture. In short, equality and equity are enjoined in the emerging narrative.

Efficiency

Some countries in the study are seeing the expansion of public funds into ECEC, whereas others are developing new and inventive financing strategies to more heavily engage parents and the private sector in financing services. Regardless of which is operative, the transcendent message is that resources are precious and must be used judiciously; no country, no matter how richly or poorly endowed, desires inefficient resource usage. As a result, efficiency is an emerging rationale in the development of ECEC systems. Efforts to enhance efficiency are manifest throughout the country stories, particularly in

202 The Early Advantage: Early Childhood Systems That Lead by Example

the efforts being made to consolidate governance structures and functions. Such consolidation makes the complex field of ECEC more comprehensible for parents and families while also fostering efficiencies by curtailing the duplication of administrative functions. Through consolidation, space can be more effectively utilized and services can be more effectively linked, reflecting the holistic orientation of child development and the need to eliminate service redundancies.

Such a focus on efficiency, replete with the structural and functional changes it occasions, does not come easily. A field already in turmoil, due to the contextual and temporal factors discussed earlier, is now also being asked to re-contour its conventions and ways of doing business. For frontline workers, this is often associated with increased pressure and recurrent demands to do more with less. In some countries, where the change is too formidable and the rewards insufficient, ECEC personnel turnover and retirement are rising. For those who stay, the efficiency focus eventuates in adaptations and in the (sometimes tacit) acknowledgment that a different intellectual zeitgeist, one that privileges efficiency, undergirds the field.

The growing inclusion of the for-profit sector—in Finland, for example— is an efficiency strategy to curtail public expenditures; it is also often regarded as an automatic compromise of quality. In some countries this has been the case. Yet as some countries in this study have shown, efficiency does not need to be equated with quality sacrifice. Through inventive strategies, such as the incentivization of high-quality efforts in the private sector and/or enhanced regulation, quality and efficiency can be simultaneously fostered, if the effort is carefully conceptualized. The emerging ECEC narrative promotes efficiency as both necessary and doable.

Sustainability

Although not the case in all the study countries, there is concern that current commitment to ECEC has not been, and will not be, durably sustained over time. Many countries experience an ebb and flow in their dedication of public funds to ECEC. Others experience changes in the relative priorities accorded to different segments of the ECEC field (e.g., a focus on one age group or population, at the expense of others). Sustainability challenges have traditionally been exacerbated by insufficient understanding of the importance of the early years, along with various contextual realities. Today, via the popularization of new sciences and new research evidence, coupled with the meaningful engagement of political elites and families, the constituency for ECEC is being broadened, with a newfound focus on sustainability. Although such strategies tacitly acknowledge that ECEC is not (yet) deemed a permanent right, they advance an understanding that here-today, gone-tomorrow efforts are inefficient and unlikely to foster quality or equity. As such, the sustainability of programmatic and infrastructure efforts has become an acknowledged end goal of early childhood strategists. The study countries are therefore advancing a long-haul vision, with the understanding that stability of context and commitments is essential to a durable, well-functioning ECEC system. Sustainability, then, has become part of the new ECEC systems narrative.

This third new narrative is revolutionary. It shifts the end goal of ECEC from focusing solely on child outcomes as the exclusive metric by which success is determined to a broadened vision, one that heartily acknowledges the essentiality of quality, equity, efficiency, and sustainability. In so doing, it acknowledges the necessity of systemic perspectives and investments. As such, it stands as the proverbial seal on the emerging narratives that are characterizing innovative and exemplary ECEC systems.

NEW NARRATIVES AND A NEW ERA

The purpose of this comparative analysis of six jurisdictions' ECEC systems was not comparison or ranking. Rather, the goal was to learn from them: to better understand why and how they work, and to extract lessons that might be applicable in widely diverse contexts.

Of course, one could regard the efforts under way across the globe as highly idiosyncratic endeavors, spearheaded by bold pioneers—worthwhile, yet hard to replicate and/or doomed for termination once the extant political will and human energy for them dissipates.

Yet this volume suggests something quite different. It beckons the reader to consider that we find ourselves living in a new era, framed by new knowledge, new narratives, and new actions. It suggests that rather than an episodic scurry of efforts, today's commitments to young children are far more grounded, durably framed as an equity rationale, as a social and economic development rationale, or both. They are seriously motivated, and for the most part increasingly well designed and well documented. They are building on lessons from past experience, using data to reform themselves, and evoking a spirited sense of direction.

This is not to suggest that there are no hurdles along the way. As Johann Wolfgang von Goethe noted, "Thinking is easy, acting is difficult, and to put one's thoughts into action is the most difficult thing in the world." In an era of resource constraints, the countries in this analysis are coping with service retrenchments or compromises. Political parties and regimes change, eliciting altered priorities. And social contexts continue to grow in complexity, rendering equitable improvements all the more challenging. As highlighted throughout this volume, social change—and responses to it—cannot, and does not, emerge overnight; rather, it is evolutionary.

Mostly, however, the new narratives described in this volume present a significant revolution in thought. At their most simplistic level, they underscore the importance of context, infrastructure, and outcomes, abetted by vigorous research. At another level, they suggest a reformation of the way young children and the services accorded them are being regarded. The thinking evinced by these new narratives is nuanced, comprehensive, and inventive. It is driven by a social impetus and routed via implementation pathways that reject rigidity, formulaic interpretations, and one-size-fits-all mentalities. Conversely, it honors diversity, invention, comprehensiveness, inclusivity, and variation. In short, the new narratives, when taken together, reveal a new zeitgeist in thinking, one that dramatically alters how societies regard their commitments to young children. Acknowledging that a revolution in thinking must precede evolutionary action, this volume suggests that ECEC is well positioned for the future. It is our hope that the strategies and examples presented herein, fortified by this new thinking, will evoke invigorated efforts on behalf of young children. It is to that aim that this work is dedicated.

REFERENCES

Bruner, C., Stover-Wright, M., Gebhard, B., & Hibbard, S. (2004). *Building an early learning system: The ABCs of planning and governance structures*. Des Moines, IA: Child & Family Policy Center, State Early Childhood Policy Technical Assistance Network (SECPTAN) in collaboration with the Build Initiative.

Cahan, E. D. (1989). *Past caring: A history of U.S. preschool and education for the poor (1820–1965)*. New York: National Center for Children in Poverty.

Dahlberg, G., Moss, P., & Pence, A. (1999). *Beyond quality in early childhood education and care: Postmodern perspectives*. Philadelphia, PA: Falmer Press, Taylor & Francis Inc. Retrieved from files.eric.ed.gov/fulltext/ED433943.pdf

Flood, R. L., & Jackson, M. C. (1991). *Critical systems thinking*. Chichester, England: John Wiley.

Heckman, J. J. (2006). Skill formation and the economics of investing in disadvantaged children. *Science, 312,* 1900–1902.

Kagan, S. L., & Cohen, N. (Eds.). (1996). *Reinventing early care and education: A vision for a quality system*. San Francisco, CA: Jossey-Bass.

Kanter, R., & Sherman, A. (2017). *The happy, healthy nonprofit strategies for impact without burnout*. Hoboken, NJ: Wiley.

Nisbett, R. E. (2003). *The geography of thought*. New York, NY: Free Press.

Rao, N., Zhou, J., & Sun, J. (Eds.) (2017). *Early childhood education in Chinese societies*. Dordrecht, The Netherlands: Springer.

Schein, E. (2011). *Helping: How to offer, give, and receive help*. San Francisco, CA: Berrett-Koehler.

Senge, P. (1990). *The fifth discipline: The art and practice of learning organizations*. New York, NY: Currency.

Shore, B. (1996). *Culture in mind: Cognition, culture and the problem of meaning.* New York, NY: Oxford University Press.

Steiner, G. Y. (1976). *The children's cause.* Washington, DC: Brookings Institution.

Tobin, J. J., Wu, D. Y. H., & Davidson, D. H. (2009). *Preschool in three cultures revisited: Japan, China, and the United States.* Chicago, IL: University of Chicago Press.

Wheatley, M., & Frieze, D. (2010). Leadership in the age of complexity: From hero to host. Retrieved from margaretwheatley.com/articles/Leadership-in-Age-of-Complexity.pdf

Country Fact Sheet—Australia

Population

Country size/geography:[1] 7,692,024 km^2
Population density:[2] 3.1/km^2
Total population:[3] 24,127,000
Children under 18:[4] 5,41,000
Children under 6:[5] 1,870,000
Total fertility rate (TFR):[6] 1.81
Population diversity:
　　Ethnic/racial diversity: Not available
　　Languages spoken:[7] 80% speak only English at home; 20% speak two
　　　or more languages at home.

Employment Rates

Overall labor force participation:[8] 77%
Female labor force participation:[9] 71.6%
Maternal labor force participation:[10] 62.9%

Economic Conditions

GDP per capita:[11] $45,821 ($63,462 AUD)
Social expenditures as % of federal budget:[12] 19.1%
Child poverty rate:[13] 12.8%
GINI:[14] 0.334

Parental Leave[15]

Duration for mothers/fathers: Eighteen weeks paid leave for eligible
　employees who are primary caregivers of children and two weeks for
　eligible partners. In addition, all employees are entitled to 12 months of
　unpaid parental leave providing they have worked for their employer
　for at least 12 months.

Wage replacement for mothers/fathers: Payments are at the national minimum wage of $501.80 per week ($695 AUD) and are made directly to the employee. Eligibility includes a work test and an individual adjusted income of $108,303 ($150,000 AUD) or less. Dad and Partner Pay provides eligible working fathers or partners with up to two weeks' pay at the rate of the national minimum wage. Dads or partners have to be on unpaid leave or not working to receive the payment.

Schooling/Literacy[16]

Ages/years of compulsory attendance: Across most states and territories, attendance is compulsory between the ages of 6 and 15–17. School education comprises 13 years (including the first preparatory year at age 5).

Secondary school completion rates: Seventy-two percent achieve Year 12 completion.

Governmental Expenditures for Children Under 6

Child care:[17] $5,124,000,000 ($7,096,736,665 AUD)
Early education:[18] $1,050,000,000 ($1,454,249,317 AUD)
Total educational expenditure:[19] $6,174,000,000 ($8,550985,981 AUD)
Unit cost per child in pre-primary education:[20] $2,700 ($3,739 AUD)
Funding of ISCED 0 as a % of GDP:[21] 0.6% (public)

Governmental Auspices for ECEC Services

Responsible ministries: Federal ECEC is under the Department of Education and Training; state/territory ECEC is generally under the education departments. Key roles in ECEC are also provided through additional ministries in Western Australia (through the Department of Local Government and Communities) and the Australian Capital Territory (through the Chief Minister, Treasury, and Economic Development Directorate).

BSM/coordinating mechanisms:[22] The Council of Australian Governments (COAG) is a forum of first ministers of the Commonwealth Government and state and territory governments. The COAG Education Council is a forum for education ministers (including those responsible for ECEC) of the Australian Government, state, and territory governments for strategic policy and information sharing at the national level.

Service Access

Percent of children who have access to:

    Comprehensive health screenings:[23] All Australian states and territories
        provide initial access to health screenings for children and families.
        National data on participation are not collected.

    Comprehensive health services:[24] In major cities, 95.4 general
        practitioners are available for every 100,000 residents. In outer
        regional, remote, and very remote areas, 80.9 general practitioners
        are available per 100,000 residents.

    Child care (including family child care):[25] 42.6%

    One year of pre-primary education:[26] 91.4%

    More than one year of pre-primary education:[27] 15%

Required ECEC Service Indicators[28]

Staff qualifications: In center-based services: In services educating and caring
    for children preschool age or under, at least 50% of the educators
    required to meet ratio requirements must have or be working toward
    at least an approved diploma-level qualification. All other educators
    who are required to meet ratio requirements must have or be working
    toward at least a Certificate III level qualification. *In family day care
    services:* Coordinators must have at least an approved diploma-level
    education and care qualification. Educators must have or be actively
    working toward at least an approved Certificate III–level education and
    care qualification.

Ratios and group size: In center-based services: Staff-to-child ratio must be
    1:4 for children birth to 24 months, 1:5 for children 25 to 35 months,
    and 1:11 for 36 months up to and including preschool age (there are
    exceptions across states and territories). The maximum group size is
    not regulated. *In family day care services:* Staff-to-child ratios must be
    1:7 with a maximum of four children under school age. The maximum
    group size is not regulated.

Mandated monitoring system: The National Quality Framework (NQF)
    includes an assessment and ratings process. Regulatory authorities
    monitor and enforce compliance with the National Law and
    Regulations, and their Authorized Officers rate the services against
    a National Quality Standard consisting of seven quality areas, using
    a customized assessment tool. The assessment and rating applies to
    services under the NQF. Tasmania and Western Australia have chosen
    to continue regulating kindergartens (preschools) under relevant state
    education legislation, but they ensure that state-based requirements
    for these services correspond with those of the NQF. ACECQA, the
    national agency overseeing this process, reports results to the COAG

Education Council. As part of the assessment and rating process, services are obligated to develop and implement a Quality Improvement Plan.

Notes

1. Geoscience Australia. (2017). Area of Australia: States and territories. Retrieved from ga.gov.au/scientific-topics/national-location-information/dimensions/area-of-australia-states-and-territories

2. ABS. (2017). Regional Population growth Australia 2016. Population Density. (Catalogue No. 3218.0. Retrieved from abs.gov.au/AUSSTATS/abs@.nsf/Latestproducts/3218.0Main%20Features752016

3. Australian Bureau of Statistics. (ABS). (2016). Australian Demographic Statistics, June 2016 (Catalogue No. 3101.0). Retrieved from abs.gov.au/AUSSTATS/abs@.nsf/Lookup/3101.0Main+Features1Jun%202016?OpenDocument

4. Ibid.

5. Ibid.

6. ABS. (2015). Births, Australia, 2015 (Catalogue No. 3301.0). Canberra, Australia: Author.

7. ABS. (2012). *Reflecting a nation: Stories from the 2011 census, 2012–2013* (Catalogue No. 2071.0). Canberra, Australia: Author.

8. OECD. (n.d.) LFS by sex and age—indicators [Dataset]. Retrieved from stats.oecd.org/Index.aspx?DatasetCode=LFS_SEXAGE_I_R

9. Ibid.

10. OECD. (2016). *OECD Family Database LMF1.2.A: Maternal employment rates*. Paris, France: OECD Publishing. Retrieved from oecd.org/els/family/LMF_1_2_Maternal_Employment.pdf

11. OECD. (2016). Country statistical profile: Australia. oecd-ilibrary.org/economics/country-statistical-profile-australia-2016-2_csp-aus-table-2016-2-en

12. OECD. (2016). Social expenditure—aggregated data [Dataset]. Retrieved from stats.oecd.org/Index.aspx?DataSetCode=SOCX_AGG

13. OECD. (2016). *OECD Family Database CO2.2.A: Child income poverty rates*. Paris, France: OECD Publishing. Retrieved from oecd.org/els/soc/CO_2_2_Child_Poverty.pdf

14. OECD. (2010). Income distribution and poverty [Dataset]. Retrieved from stats.oecd.org/Index.aspx?DataSetCode=IDD

15. Department of Social Services (DSS). (2017). *Paid Parental Leave Scheme.* Canberra, Australia: Author. Retrieved from dss.gov.au/our-responsibilities/families-and-children/programmes-services/paid-parental-leave-scheme

16. Steering Committee for the Review of Government Service Provision (SCRGSP). (2016). *Report on Government Services 2016: Child care, Education and Training* (Vol. B). Canberra, Australia: Productivity Commission. Retrieved from pc.gov.au/research/ongoing/report-on-government-services/2016/childcare-education-and-training

17. Ibid.

18. Ibid.

19. Ibid.

20. OECD. (2016). *OECD Family Database PF3.1: Public spending on child care and early education.* Paris, France: OECD Publishing. Retrieved from oecd.org/els/soc/PF3_1_Public_spending_on_child care_and_early_education.pdf

21. Ibid.

22. Council of Australian Governments. Council of Australian Governments. Retrieved from coag.gov.au/; Education Council (n.d.). Education Council. Retrieved from scseec.edu.au/Council.aspx

23. Australian Health Ministers' Advisory Council (AHMAC). (2011). *National framework for universal child and family health services.* Canberra, Australia: Author.

24. SCRGSP. (2016). Report on Government Services 2016: Health (Vol. E) (Table E.2). Retrieved from pc.gov.au/research/ongoing/report-on-government-services/2016/health/rogs-2016-volumee-health.pdf

25. SCRGSP. (2016). *Report on Government Services 2016: Child care, Education and Training* (Vol. B). Canberra, Australia: Productivity Commission. Retrieved from pc.gov.au/research/ongoing/report-on-government-services/2016/child care-education-and-training

26. Ibid.

27. OECD. (2016). *OECD Family Database Chart PF3.2.F: Enrollment rates for 3-, 4- and 5-year-olds in pre-primary education or primary school.* Paris, France: OECD Publishing. Retrieved from oecd.org/els/soc/PF3_2_Enrolment_childcare_preschool.pdf

28. Australian Children's Education and Care Quality Authority (ACECQA). (2017a). *Guide to the Education and Care Services National Law and the Education and Care Services National Regulations 2011.* Sydney, Australia: Author.

Dollar amounts reported in this case study report are U.S. dollars, with Australian dollars bracketed for Australian readers. The conversion followed the U.S. Bureau of Fiscal Service Treasury Department protocols, using the current quarterly conversion rate of exchange (September 30, 2017). On this exchange rate AUD$1.2760 is equivalent to US$1. The convention used for a billion is a thousand million.

Country Fact Sheet—England

Figures refer to England unless specified as United Kingdom (where disaggregated data are not available).

Population

Country size/geography:[1] 133,000 km^2 (making up the largest part of the
  248,500 km2 total size of the United Kingdom)
Population density:[2] 401 per km^2
Total population:[3] 55,268,100
Children under 18:[4] ~11,300,000
Children under 5:[5] ~3,300,000
Total fertility rate (TFR):[6] 1.81
Population diversity:[7]
  Ethnic/racial diversity: White British (79.7%), Asian/Asian British
    (7.8%), White non-British (5.8%), Black/Black British (3.5%),
    Mixed/multiple ethnic group (2.2%), Others (1%)
  Languages spoken: English (92%), other European languages (3.7%),
    South Asian languages (2.5%), other languages (1.8%)

Employment Rates (UK)

Overall labor force participation:[8] 78.2%
Female labor force participation:[9] 73%
Maternal labor force participation:[10] 60% for lone mothers, 72% for married/
  cohabiting mothers
Maternal with young children under 6:[11] With children under 3: 39% for lone
  mothers, 65% for married/cohabiting mothers. With children aged
  4–10: 61% for lone mothers, 74% for married/cohabiting mothers

Economic Conditions (UK)

GDP per capita:[12] $43,123
Social expenditures as % of government budget:[13] 49%
Child poverty rate:[14] 11.2%
GINI:[15] 0.36

Parental Leave

Duration for mothers/fathers:[16] 52 weeks statutory leave (39 of which are paid) for mothers, one to two weeks paid leave for fathers. A mother can also choose to end her maternity leave, and the two parents can take the remaining leave and pay as shared parental leave and pay.
Wage replacement for mothers/fathers:[17] Ninety percent of average weekly earnings before tax for first six weeks, and $190.98 (£140.98) or 90% of average weekly earnings (whichever is lower) for next 33 weeks.

Schooling/Literacy

Ages/years of compulsory attendance:[18] 11 years of compulsory "schooling" from age 5 to age 16, plus two additional years of compulsory "education" (either academic or vocational) which does not have to take place in a school, until the age of 18
Secondary school completion rates: Upper secondary 61%,[19] lower secondary 99.86%[20]

Governmental Expenditures for Children Under 6

Child care and early education:[21] $3.6 billion (£2.7 billion)
Total educational expenditure:[22] $94 billion (£69.3 billion)
Unit cost per child in pre-primary education:[23] ~$7,000 (UK)
Funding of ISCED 0 as a % of GDP:[24] 0.8% (UK)

Governmental Auspices for ECEC Services

Responsible ministries: Department for Education (sometimes working in partnership with Department of Health and Department of Work and Pensions)
BSM/coordinating mechanisms: None, as all ECEC services fall under responsibility of Department for Education

Service Access

Percent of children who have access to:
  Comprehensive health screenings:[25] All children have free access to routine examinations, hearing tests, and immunizations; 93.6% of children aged 0–1 complete primary immunization courses.
  Comprehensive health services: All children have free access to all health services run by the National Health Service, unknown how many attend.
  Child care (including family child care):[26] All children have access. Sixty percent of 0–2-year-olds and 93% of 3–4-year-olds receive

some form of child care; almost 100% of 5-year-olds are in statutory Reception class in primary schools.

One year of pre-primary education: It is a statutory requirement for children to attend Reception class (considered part of ECEC) in the term in which they turn 5, so some children attend for a full school year in a statutory capacity, whereas others will attend in the same classrooms but in a nonstatutory way before turning 5. For this reason, almost all children attend Reception for the whole school year.

More than one year of pre-primary education:[27] From the age of 3, all children are entitled to 30 hours of free child care per week; 93% of 3-year-olds and 96% of 4-year-olds access the funded entitlement.

Required ECEC Service Indicators

Staff qualifications:[28] The manager of group settings must hold at least a Level 3 qualification (specific to ECEC and obtained through Further Education at age 16–18), and at least half of the other members of staff must hold a Level 2 qualification (general vocational qualification obtained in secondary education at age 16–18). Teachers of nursery and Reception classes (in primary schools) must hold a Level 6 qualification (obtained through bachelor's degrees or postgraduate teacher training courses)

Ratios and group size:[29] For children under 2, 1:3 (one member of staff must hold a Level 3 qualification). For children aged 2 to 3, 1:4 (one member of staff must hold a Level 3 qualification). For children aged 3 to 5, 1:13 (if a member of staff holds a Level 6 qualification) or 1:8 (if staff holds Level 3 qualification). For children in Reception class (aged 4-5+), 1:30 (teacher must hold Level 6 qualification). The vast majority of Reception classes have one teaching assistant at Level 3.

Mandated monitoring system: Office for Standards in Education (Ofsted) is a nonministerial governmental agency reporting to the Department for Education, and inspects all educational institutions (e.g., schools, ECEC centres, education management in local authorities). The Early Years Foundation Stage (EYFS) framework specifies both the curriculum and the required characteristics of structural quality for all ECEC providers. Ofsted inspects providers based on the extent to which they meet the statutory requirements that are outlined in the EYFS framework.

Notes

1. Area of England and the UK. (n.d.). Retrieved from webarchive.nationalar-chives.gov.uk/20160108051201; ons.gov.uk/ons/guide-method/geography/beginner-s-guide/administrative/the-countries-of-the-uk/index.html

2. Population density figures for England. (2010). Retrieved from ons.gov.uk/peoplepopulationandcommunity/populationandmigration/populationestimates/datasets/populationdensitytables

3. Total population for England. (2016). Retrieved from ons.gov.uk/peoplepopulationandcommunity/populationandmigration/populationestimates/bulletins/annualmidyearpopulationestimates/mid2016#population-of-england-reaches-55-million

4. Population estimates for children in England. (2013). Retrieved from nomisweb.co.uk/census/2011/DC2101EW/view/2092957699?rows=c_ethpuk11&cols=c_age

5. Ibid.

6. Total fertility rate for England and Wales. (2016). Retrieved from ons.gov.uk/peoplepopulationandcommunity/birthsdeathsandmarriages/livebirths/bulletins/birthsummarytablesenglandandwales/2016

7. Detailed characteristics of census 2011. (2013). Retrieved from nomisweb.co.uk/census/2011/detailed_characteristics

8. Labor force participation figures for the UK. (2016). Retrieved from stats.oecd.org/BrandedView.aspx?oecd_bv_id=lfs-data-en&doi=data-00309-en

9. Ibid.

10. Full report–Women in the labour market. (2013). Retrieved from webarchive.nationalarchives.gov.uk/20160108012507; ons.gov.uk/ons/dcp171776_328352.pdf

11. Ibid.

12. UK GDP per capita. (2016). Retrieved from data.oecd.org/gdp/gross-domestic-product-gdp.htm

13. Social expenditure as percentage of total UK government expenditure. (2013). Retrieved from nomisweb.co.uk/census/2011/DC2101EW/view/2092957699?rows=c_ethpuk11&cols=c_age

14. UK poverty rate. (2014). Retrieved from data.oecd.org/inequality/poverty-rate.htm

15. UK GINI before adjustment for taxes and transfers. (2014). Retrieved from data.oecd.org/inequality/income-inequality.htm

16. England's parental leave policy. (2017). Retrieved from gov.uk/maternity-pay-leave/pay

17. Ibid.

18. School leaving age in England. (2017). Retrieved from gov.uk/know-when-you-can-leave-school

19. UK upper secondary school completion rates. (2012). Retrieved from oecd.org/unitedkingdom/EAG2012%20-%20Country%20note%20-%20United%20Kingdom.pdf

20. Percentage of UK population age 25+ with at least completed lower secondary education. (2014). Retrieved from data.worldbank.org/indicator/SE.SEC.CUAT.LO.ZS?locations=GB

21. Expenditure on education in England. (2016). Retrieved from gov.uk/government/uploads/system/uploads/attachment_data/file/630570/60243_PESA_Accessible.pdf

22. Ibid.

23. Funding of ISCED 0 as % of UK GDP. (2013). Retrieved from oecd.org/els/soc/PF3_1_Public_spending_on_child care_and_early_education.pdf

24. Ibid.

25. Percentage of UK children who have completed their primary immunization courses by their first birthday. (2016). Retrieved from digital.nhs.uk/catalogue/PUB21651

26. Child care and early years survey of parents 2014 to 2015. Retrieved from gov.uk/government/uploads/system/uploads/attachment_data/file/516924/SFR09-2016_Child care_and_Early_Years_Parents_Survey_2014-15_report.pdf.pdf

27. Percentage of UK children accessing funded entitlement (as of January 2017 when funded entitlement was 15 hours per week). Retrieved from gov.uk/government/uploads/system/uploads/attachment_data/file/622632/SFR29_2017_Text.pdf

28. Statutory framework for the early years foundation stage. (2017). Retrieved from foundationyears.org.uk/files/2017/03/EYFS_STATUTORY_FRAMEWORK_2017.pdf

29. Ibid.

Country Fact Sheet—Finland

Population

Country size/geography:[1] 390,908 km² (land area: 303,912 km²; freshwater area: 34,536 km²; seawater area: 52,460 km²)
Population density:[2] 18.1 per km²
Total population:[3] ~5.5 million people
Children under 18:[4] 1,071,905
Children 6 and under:[5] 411,555
Total fertility rate (TFR):[6] 1.57
Population diversity:
    Ethnic/racial diversity: No data available
    Languages spoken:[7] Finnish (approx. 89%), Swedish (5.3%), foreign language (6%). The most widely spoken foreign languages in Finland include Russian, Estonian, Arabic, Somali, and English.

Employment Rates

Overall labor force participation:[8] 72.5%
Female labor force participation:[9] 71.8%
Maternal labor force participation:[10] Only a few mothers with children under the age of 1 are in the workforce, compared with more than 50% of mothers with children between the ages of 1 and 2. When their youngest child is aged 3 to 6, a majority of mothers have returned to work. Nearly 90% of mothers of school-age children are working.

Economic Conditions

GDP per capita:[11] $43,363
Social expenditures as % of government budget:[12] 30.8%
Child poverty rate:[13] Approximately 3.7%
GINI:[14] 0.257

Parental Leave[15]

Duration for mothers/fathers: Pregnant women have the right to paid maternity leave lasting 105 working days. Fathers can take up to 54 days of paternity leave. Additional parental leave is available for 158 working days, with an extension of 60 working days for each child in the case of multiple births. Either the mother or father can take this leave. After the parental leave, parents have a right to take unpaid leave from work to care for a child until the age of 3 and are supported by a government-provided home care allowance during this period.

Wage replacement for mothers/fathers: Maternity, paternity, and parental leaves are government-supported. The financial support is means-tested, i.e., dependent on mothers' or fathers' income. The minimum payment by the central government for those with no or little income is about $28 (€23.73) per day. This can rise significantly; for instance, for an annual income of $71,000 (€60,000), the payment is about $136 (€115.66) per working day.

Percent using parental leave: Maternity leave is used by almost 100% of mothers. In 2014, 78% fathers took paternity leave for 1–18 days, while 34% of fathers took paternity leave lasting between 18 and 54 days. The additional parental leave is rarely used by fathers. Of the 89% of families that use the home care allowance, mothers are the ones to take the leave in 97% of instances. More than 55% of families use their home care allowance for less than 12 months. Sixteen percent of families use all 24 months of home care allowance in order to take care of their child at home before the child turns 3.

Schooling/Literacy[16]

Ages/years of compulsory attendance: Pre-primary education (for 6-year-olds), basic education (for children aged 7–16)

Secondary school completion rates: Nearly 100% of the population completes the basic education syllabus and receives a basic education certificate, typically at the age of 16.

Governmental Expenditures for Children Under 6

Child care and early education:[17] Most spending on ECEC comes from public funding. Annual ECEC expenditure per child for children under 3 is about $12,092 (€10,454). The same applies to children over 3 years old, where the expenditure per child is $10,477 (€9,057.66).

Child benefit: Finland has a child benefit scheme paid by the Social Insurance Institution of Finland (KELA) on a monthly basis, regardless of the child's guardian's income.

Total educational expenditure:[18] Public expenditure on education relative to GDP in Finland (excluding ECEC) is 6.8%.

Unit cost per child in pre-primary education:[19] The expenditure per child over 3 years old is $10,477 (€9,057.66).

Funding of ISCED 0 as a % of GDP: No data available

Governmental Auspices for ECEC Services

Responsible ministries: Ministry of Education and Culture, Ministry of Social Affairs and Health
BSM/coordinating mechanisms: No formal mechanisms

Service Access[20]

Percent of children who have access to:
   Comprehensive health screenings: 100%
   Comprehensive health services: 100%
   Child care (including family child care): 100%
   One year of pre-primary education: 100%
   More than one year of pre-primary education: 100%

Required ECEC Service Indicators

Staff qualifications: At least one third of the ECEC staff working with children aged 0–6 must have a bachelor's degree or equivalent in early childhood education, while the rest of the staff are required to have at least secondary or postsecondary nontertiary level education in health and welfare.
Ratios and group size: In center-based ECEC, the regulated staff-to-child ratio is one adult to four children ages 0 to 3 and one adult to eight children for children aged 3 to 5. In pre-primary education (6-year-olds), the ratio is one adult to 13 children or two adults to 20 children. In family day care, the regulated staff-to-child ratio is one adult to four children for full-time care, as well as one pre-primary or school-age child on a part-time basis. In group family day care, the ratio is two to three adults for eight to 12 children. In pre-primary education, the maximum permitted group size is 20 children for two adults, or alternatively 13 children and one adult.
Mandated monitoring system: At the local level, responsibility for monitoring ECEC program quality rests on municipalities and Regional Administrative State Agencies. At the national level, the responsibility for monitoring ECEC quality lies with the National Evaluation Center.

Notes

1. Official Statistics of Finland. (2017). Environment and Natural Resources. Retrieved from tilastokeskus.fi/tup/suoluk/suoluk_alue_en.html

2. Kuntaliitto.fi. (2017). Kuntien pinta-alat ja asukastiheydet. Retrieved from kuntaliitto.fi/asiantuntijapalvelut/kuntien-pinta-alat-ja-asukastiheydet

3. Official Statistics of Finland. (2017). Population structure. Helsinki, Finland: Statistics Finland. Retrieved from stat.fi/til/vaerak/2016/vaerak_2016_2017-03-29_kuv_002_en.html

4. Vipunen Education Statistics Finland. (2017). Population. Retrieved from vipunen.fi/en-gb/_layouts/15/xlviewer.aspx?id=/en-gb/Reports/Väestö%20-%20ikäryhmä_EN.xlsb

5. Ibid.

6. Official Statistics of Finland. (2017). *Births*. Helsinki, Finland: Statistics Finland. Retrieved from stat.fi/til/synt/index_en.html

7. Official Statistics of Finland. (2017). Population structure.

8. Official Statistics of Finland. (2017). Labor force survey. Retrieved from stat.fi/til/tyti/2017/06/tyti_2017_06_2017-07-25_tie_001_en.html

9. Eurostat. (2016). Europe 2020 employment indicators. Retrieved from ec.europa.eu/eurostat/documents/2995521/7240293/3-26042016-AP-EN.pdf/

10. Official Statistics of Finland. (2014). Labor force survey. Families and work 2013. Retrieved from tilastokeskus.fi/til/tyti/2013/14/tyti_2013_14_2014-10-07_kat_004_en.html

11. OECD. (2016). Gross domestic product. Retrieved from data.oecd.org/gdp/gross-domestic-product-gdp.htm

12. OECD. (2016). Social expenditure database—Expenditure for social purposes [Dataset]. Retrieved from oecd.org/social/expenditure.htm

13. OECD. (2016). OECD income distribution database—Income distribution and poverty [Dataset]. Retrieved from oecd.org/social/income-distribution-database.htm

14. OECD. (2016). Starting Strong IV. Early Childhood Education and Care. Data Country Note. Finland. Retrieved from /oecd.org/edu/school/ECECDCN-Finland.pdf

15. THL. (2017). Tilastotietoa perhevapaiden käytöstä. Retrieved from thl.fi/fi/tutkimus-ja-asiantuntijatyo/hankkeet-ja-ohjelmat/perhevapaatutkimus/tilastotietoa-perhevapaiden-kaytosta

16. Kumpulainen, T. (Ed). (2015). Key figures on early childhood and basic education in Finland. Publications 2015:4. Finnish National Board of Education. Tampere, Finland: Juvenis Print.

17. OECD. (2016). Starting Strong IV. Early Childhood Education and Care. Data Country Note. Finland.

18. Eurostat (2017). Educational expenditure statistics. Retrieved from ec.europa.eu/eurostat/statistics-explained/index.php/Educational_expenditure_statistics#Public_expenditure

19. OECD. (2016). Starting Strong IV. Early Childhood Education and Care. Data Country Note. Finland.

20. All children in Finland are guaranteed the right to these services by law. Health services are guaranteed under the Child Welfare Act (417/2007); child care under the Child Home Care and Private Care Allowance Act (1128/1996); and pre-primary education under the Act on Early Childhood Education and Care (36/1973).

Country Fact Sheet—Hong Kong

Population

Country size/geography:[1] 1,106 km² on the southeast coast of the People's Republic of China (PRC) in the South China Sea
Population density:[2] 6,790 persons per square kilometer of land area
Total population:[3] 7.3 million people
Children under 18:[4] 1,015,710
Children under 6:[5] 344,901
Total fertility rate (TFR):[6] 1,234 live births per 1,000 women
Population diversity:[7]
  Ethnic/racial diversity: Chinese (92%), Filipino (2.5%), Indonesian (2.1%), Caucasians/whites (0.8%), Indian (0.5), Nepalese (0.3%), Pakistani (0.2%), Thai (0.1%), Japanese (0.1%), Other Asians (0.3%), Others (0.9%)
  First languages spoken: Cantonese (88.9%), Putonghua (1.9%), English (4.3%)

Employment Rates[8]

Overall labor force participation: 60.8% (3,954,798)
Female labor force participation: 54.5% (1,937,925)
Maternal labor force participation: Not available

Economic Conditions

GDP per capita:[9] $42,066 (HK$328,117)
Social expenditures as % of government budget:[10] About 40.67%
Child poverty rate:[11] 21.7%
GINI:[12] 0.54

Parental Leave

Duration for mothers/fathers: 10 weeks for mothers, 3 days for fathers
Wage replacement for mothers/fathers: Not available

Schooling/Literacy

Ages/years of compulsory attendance: Six years for primary school (aged 6 to 12) plus three years for junior secondary school (aged 12 to 15)
Secondary school completion rates:[13] 99.7%

Governmental Auspices for ECEC Services

Responsible ministries: Education Bureau, Labour and Social Welfare Bureau, Food and Health Bureau
Service auspices: Joint Office for Kindergartens and Child Care Centers, Curriculum Development Council, Social Welfare Department
BSM/coordinating mechanisms: Joint Office for Kindergartens and Child Care Centers (3 to 6 years); Social Welfare Department (0 to 3 years)

Service Access

Percent of children who have access to:
   Comprehensive health screenings:[14] All have access; 95% take up
   Comprehensive health services:[15] All have access; 99% take up
   Child care (including family child care): No data available
   One year of pre-primary education: No legal entitlement but estimated that 100% attend one year of pre-primary education
   More than one year of pre-primary education:[16] No legal entitlement but nearly 100% attend more than one year of pre-primary education

Required ECEC Service Indicators

Staff qualifications: Must be holders of qualifications recognized by the Social Welfare Department or Educational Bureau. Qualified Kindergarten Teacher certificate or equivalent or above for children above 3 years
Ratios and group size: Ratio varies from 1:5 (for children up to 2 years) to 1:11 (for children aged 3 to 6) since September 2017. No minimum group sizes, but there are minimum prescribed space requirements per child.
Mandated monitoring system: All programs are regulated and licensed by the Social Welfare Department, Educational Bureau, or the Joint Office for Kindergartens and Child Care Centers.

Notes

1. Government of the Hong Kong Special Administrative Region. (2017). Hong Kong in figures (2017 edition). Retrieved from statistics.gov.hk/pub/B10100032017 AN17B0100.pdf

2. Ibid.

3. Ibid.

4. Census and Statistics Department. (2017). 2016 Population by-census: Main tables. Retrieved from bycensus2016.gov.hk/en/bc-mt.html

5. Ibid.

6. Census and Statistics Department. (2015). Hong Kong monthly digest of statistics: The fertility trend in Hong Kong, 1981 to 2014. Retrieved from statistics.gov.hk/pub/B71512FB2015XXXXB0100.pdf

7. Census and Statistics Department. (2017). 2016 Population by-census: Summary results. Retrieved from bycensus2016.gov.hk/data/16bc-summary-results.pdf

8. Ibid.

9. Census and Statistics Department. (2016). Gross Domestic Product. Retrieved from statistics.gov.hk/pub/B10300012016QQ03B0100.pdf

10. The Government of the Hong Kong Special Administrative Region. (2017). 2017–18 budget: Government revenue and expenditure. Retrieved from budget.gov.hk/2017/eng/io.html

11. Oxfam Hong Kong. (2016). Hong Kong Poverty Report (2011–2015): Inequality breeds poverty. Retrieved from oxfam.org.hk/content/98/content_31062en.pdf

12. Hong Kong Council of Social Service. (2017). Social indicators of Hong Kong. Retrieved from socialindicators.org.hk/en/indicators/children/29.14

13. Census and Statistics Department. (2017). 2016 Population by-census: Summary results. Retrieved from bycensus2016.gov.hk/data/16bc-summary-results.pdf

14. Department of Health. (2016). Health facts of Hong Kong 2016 edition. Retrieved from dh.gov.hk/english/statistics/statistics_hs/files/Health_Statistics_pamphlet_E.pdf

15. Ibid.

16. Education Bureau. (2017). Student enrolment statistics, 2016/17 (Kindergarten, Primary and Secondary Levels). Retrieved from edb.gov.hk/attachment/en/about-edb/publications-stat/figures/Enrol_2016.pdf

Country Fact Sheet—
Republic of Korea

Population

Country size/geography:[1] 100,339 km²
Population density:[2] 509.2 per km²
Total population:[3] 49,855,796 Korean residents and 1,413,758 foreign residents
Children under 18:[4] 9,375,887
Children under 6:[5] 3,153,489
Total fertility rate (TFR):[6] 1.172
Population diversity:

> *Ethnic/racial diversity:*[7] Korean (96.6%); Composition of foreign residents: Korean ethnic Chinese (37.1%), Chinese (15.7%), Vietnamese (12.6%), Thai (4.9%), Filipino (4.8%), American (3.9%), Central Asian (3.2%), Japanese (1.6%), Others (Europeans, Latin American, etc.)(16.2%)
> *Languages spoken:* Not available

Employment Rates

Overall labor force participation:[8] 63.3%
Female labor force participation:[9] 56.2%
Maternal labor force participation:[10] 46.4% of women with children under age 6 are employed in the workforce.

Economic Conditions

GDP per capita:[11] $29,332
Social expenditures as % of government budget:[12] 59.9% (Education 14.7%; Health, Welfare, and Labor 32.4%; R&D 4.8%; Security 4.5%; Culture 1.8%; Environment 1.7%)
Child poverty rate: Not available
GINI:[13] 0.304

Parental Leave

Maternity/paternity leave
> *Duration for mothers/fathers:*[14] 90 days for mothers, 5 days (3 of which are paid) for father
> *Wage replacement for mothers/fathers:*[15] Employer fully pays the first 60 days of maternity leave. In the final 30 days, the government pays up to a maximum of approximately $1,364 (KRW 1,500,000) for every child, with the rest paid by the employer. The employer pays for the first three days of paternity leave.

Parental leave
> *Duration for mothers/fathers:*[16] Each working mother and father can take a leave of up to one year for each child age 8 and under.
> *Wage replacement for mothers/fathers:*[17] For the first three months of parental leave, 80% of salary is covered (minimum of $636, KRW 700,000; maximum of $1,364, KRW 1,500,000). For the remaining nine months, the government covers 40% (minimum of $454, KRW 500,000; maximum of $909, KRW 1,000,000). Due to low numbers of fathers taking parental leave, however, the government has increased the parental leave benefit of the second user (typically the father) to cover 100% of the salary in the first three months, up to a maximum of $1,818 (KRW 2,000,000).

Schooling/Literacy

Ages/years of compulsory attendance: Nine years of compulsory school (6 years in primary school and 3 years in middle school)
Secondary school completion rates:[18] 98.9%

Governmental Expenditures for Children Under 6

Total educational expenditure:[19] Approx. $51 billion (KRW 56.4 trillion), covering from early childhood to higher education
Unit cost per child in pre-primary education:[20] Estimated at approximately $420 (KRW 460,000) per month, for 20 to 25 hours/week.
Funding of ISCED 0:[21] Approximately $12.7 billion (KRW 14 trillion) for child care and kindergarten.

Governmental Auspices for Early Years Services

Responsible ministries: Ministry of Education, Ministry of Health and Welfare
BSM/coordinating mechanisms: Office of National Policy Coordination, Prime Minister's Secretariat

Service Access

Percent of children who have access to:
> *Comprehensive health screenings:* All children have access, unknown how many attend
> *Comprehensive health services:* All children have access, unknown how many attend
> *Child care (ages 0–5):*[22] No legal entitlement. Enrollment increases to age 2 (31.9% at age 0, 72.5% at age 1, 87.8% at age 2), then declines (53.9% at age 3, 37.9% at age 4, 32.5% at age 5).

Kindergarten (ages 3–5):[23] No legal entitlement, but between 35.8% (age 3) and 58.2% (age 5) have access to kindergarten.

One or more years of pre-primary education: In total, 89.7% of 3-year-olds, 91.1% of 4-year-olds, and 90.7% of 5-year-olds have access to ECEC, either in a center or kindergarten.

Required ECEC Service Indicators

Staff qualifications:[24] Minimum entry qualification for kindergarten teachers is a degree from a 2- or 3-year college with a specialization in the early childhood education department. Minimum entry qualification for child care teachers is one year of training after high school graduation.

Ratios and group size: For child care centers,[25] staff-to-child ratio varies depending on children's age: 1:3 (under 1 year), 1:5 (1-year-olds), 1:7 (2-year-olds), 1:15 (3-year-olds), 1:20 (4- to 5-year-olds). For kindergartens[26], Local Offices of Education set ratios (from 15 up to 30 children per teacher), with no regulation from the national level.

Mandated monitoring system: All ECEC services are regulated and licensed on a voluntary basis by the Early Childhood Education Act (kindergartens) and Child Care Act (child care centers). Participation rates exceed 90% because participation is linked to government subsidies.

Notes

1. Ministry of Land, Instruction, and Transport. (2017, April). Country size increases 15 times of Yeouido over one year (Press release). Retrieved from molit. go.kr/USR/NEWS/m_71/dtl.jsp?lcmspage=1&id=95079092

2. Statistics Korea. (2016). Population density by population census. Retrieved from kosis.kr/eng/statisticsList/statisticsList_01List.jsp?vwcd=MT_ETITLE&parentId =H#SubCont

3. Statistics Korea. (2017). Population/household—Population Census General-ization—Total Population in 2016 census. Retrieved from kosis.kr/eng/statisticsList/statisticsList_01List.jsp?vwcd=MT_ETITLE&parentId=H#SubCont

4. Ministry of Interior and Safety. (2017). Number of children under 18. Retrieved from mois.go.kr/frt/sub/a05/ageStat/screen.do

5. Ibid.

6. Statistics Korea. (2017). Vital statistics of Korea—Total fertility rate. Retrieved from kosis.kr/nsportalStats/nsportalStats_0102Body.jsp?menuId=10&NUM=1033

7. Statistics Korea. (2017). Foreign residents. Retrieved from kosis.kr/index/index.jsp

8. Statistics Korea. (2017). Economically active population survey. Retrieved from kosis.kr/eng/statisticsList/statisticsList_01List.jsp?vwcd=MT_ETITLE&parentId =H#SubCont

9. Ibid.

10. Statistics Korea. (2017). Working mothers with a child under 6 years old. Retrieved from kosis.kr/statHtml/statHtml.do?orgId=101&tblId=DT_1ES4J003& vw_cd=&list_id=B19_8&seqNo=&lang_mode=ko&language=kor&obj_var_id= &itm_id=&conn_path=MT_ZTITLE

11. Bank of Korea. (2016). GDP per capita. Retrieved from kosis.kr/nsportalStats/ nsportalStats_0102Body.jsp?menuId=17

12. Open Fiscal Data. (2017). Budget by sector. Retrieved from openfiscaldata. go.kr/portal/theme/themeProfile2.do

13. Statistics Korea. (2016). Gini coefficient. Retrieved from kosis.kr/nsportalStats/ nsportalStats_0102Body.jsp?menuId=13&NUM=1138

14. Labor Standards Act. (2014). Article 74 (Protection of Pregnant Women and Nursing Mothers). Retrieved from law.go.kr/eng/engMain.do

15. Act on Equal Employment and Support for Work-Family Reconciliation (2015). Article 18-2 (Paternity Leave). Retrieved from law.go.kr/eng/engMain.do

16. Ministry of Employment and Labor. (2016). Financial support for maternity leave and parental leave. Retrieved from moel.go.kr/policy/policyinfo/woman/ list5.do

17. Act on equal employment and support for work-family reconciliation. (2017). Article 19 (Child Care Leave). Retrieved from moel.go.kr/policy/policyinfo/ woman/list5.do

18. Framework act on education. (2015). Article 8 (Compulsory Education). Retrieved from law.go.kr/eng/engMain.do

19. Open fiscal data. (2017). Budget by sector. Retrieved from openfiscaldata. go.kr/portal/theme/themeProfile2.do

20. Choi, E. Y., Kim, N. Y., Choi, Y. K., & Eom, M. Y. (2016). *Estimation of unit cost for early childhood education.* Korea Institute of Child Care and Education. Retrieved from kicce.re.kr/kor/publication/02_03.jsp?mode=view&idx=21747& startPage=0&listNo=96&code=report05&search_item=&search_order=&order_ list=10&list_scale=10&view_level=0

21. Park, J. A., Park C. H., & Eom, J. W. (2015). *Estimating finance of ECEC for mid- and long-term.* Korea Institute of Child Care and Education. Retrieved from kicce.re.kr/kor/publication/02.jsp?mode=view&idx=18986&startPage=10& listNo=95&code=report01&search_item=&search_order=&order_list=10&list_ scale=10&view_level

22. Ministry of Interior and Safety. (2016). Number of children 0 to 5. Retrieved from mois.go.kr/frt/sub/a05/ageStat/screen.do; Ministry of Health and Welfare.

(2016). Statistics on child care, p. 98. Retrieved from mohw.go.kr/react/jb/sjb0303
01vw.jsp?PAR_MENU_ID=03&MENU_ID=0321&CONT_SEQ=339611&page=1

23. Ibid; Korean Educational Statistics Service. (2017). Statistical yearbook of
education 2016, children by age. Retrieved from kess.kedi.re.kr/eng/index

24. Early Childhood Education Act. (2017). Article 22 (Qualifications for
Teaching Staff), Annexed Table 2, Retrieved from law.go.kr/eng/engLsSc.do?menuId=
1&query=education&x=0&y=0#liBgcolor32

25. Ministry of Health and Welfare. (2016). A guide to child care 2016, p.
59. Retrieved from central.child care.go.kr/ccef/community/data/DataImgSl.jsp?
BBSGB=42&BID=271954&flag=Sl

26. Kim, E., Lee, J. H., Park, E. Y., & Kim, J. (2016). Strategies for improving the
environment of ECEC: Focusing on teacher-child ratio, pp. 36–37. Retrieved from
kicce.re.kr/kor/publication/02.jsp?mode=view&idx=21531&startPage=0&list-
No=103&code=report01&search_item=&search_order=&order_list=10&list_
scale=10&view_level=0

Country Fact Sheet—Singapore

Population

Country size/geography:[1] 720 km² urban city-state located at the tip of peninsular Malaysia

Population density:[2] 7,796 per km²

Total population:[3] 5,612,300, of which 70.6% are residents (Singapore citizens and permanent residents) and 29.4% are non-residents

Children under 18:[4] ~727,000

Children under 6:[5] ~247,000

Total fertility rate (TFR):[6] 1.20

Population diversity:

   Ethnic/racial diversity:[7] Chinese (74.3%), Malay (13.4%), Indian (9.1%), Other (3.2%)

   Languages spoken:[8] English (36.9%), Mandarin (34.9%), Chinese dialects (12.2%), Malay (10.7%), Tamil (3.3%), other languages (2.0%)

Employment Rates[9]

Overall labor force participation: 68%

Female labor force participation: 60.4%

Maternal labor force participation: Not available

Economic Conditions

GDP per capita:[10] $52,680 (SG$73,167)

Social expenditures as % of government budget:[11] Social Development budget is 47% (including education; national development; environment; culture, community, and youth; social and family development; communication and information; and manpower)

% of GDP spent on social protection[12] = 4.2%

Child poverty rate: Not available

GINI:[13] 0.458 (0.402 after adjustment for government taxes and transfers)

Parental Leave

Duration for mothers/fathers:[14] 16 weeks for mothers, two weeks for fathers. Option for fathers to use four of the 16 weeks of mother's leave.

Wage replacement for mothers/fathers:[15] Employer pays first 8 weeks of maternity leave; government pays an additional 8 weeks (for first and second child) or 16 weeks (for third child onward) up to maximum of $1,800 (SG$2500) per week. Shared parental leave and paternity leave is provided by the government (maximum of $1,800 (SG$2500) per week).

Schooling/Literacy[16]

Ages/years of compulsory attendance: Ten years of compulsory school from age 7 to 16.

Secondary school completion rates: 96.9% (the number of students who continued to postsecondary education).

Governmental Expenditures for Children Under 6

Total educational expenditure:[17] $9.14 billion (SG$12.7 billion, 17.7% of the overall budget) covering all public primary, secondary, tertiary, and university education.

Unit cost per child in pre-primary education: Not available

Funding of ISCED 015: The government spent $626 million (SG$870 million) on preschools in 2017; this total does not include all aspects of ECEC provision such as health care and welfare.

Governmental Auspices for Early Years Services

Responsible ministries: Ministry of Social and Family Development, Ministry of Health, Ministry of Education

Responsible agency: Early Childhood Development Agency

BSM/coordinating mechanisms: No formal mechanisms

Service Access

Percent of children who have access to:

    Comprehensive health screenings:[18] All children have access, unknown how many attend

    Comprehensive health services:[19] All children have access, unknown how many attend

    Child care (including family child care):[20] No legal entitlement but between 21% (below age 2) and 91% access child care depending on the age of the child

One year of pre-primary education:[21] No legal entitlement but 90%
attend the year prior to entering primary education, and 99% have
at least one year of preschool education

More than one year of pre-primary education:[22] No legal entitlement
but 90% of children attend more than one year of preschool
education

Required Service Indicators

Staff qualifications:[23] Minimum certificate (one-year post-secondary
qualification) or diploma (two-year postsecondary qualification)
depending on position. Additional advanced diplomas required for
leadership positions.

Ratios and group size:[24] Ratio varies from 1:5 (for children up to 2 years)
to 1:25 (for children at 6 years of age in the pre-primary year). No
minimum group sizes, but there are minimum prescribed space
requirements per child.

Mandated monitoring system: All programs are regulated and licensed by
the Child Care Centers Act[25] or the Education Act.[26] Regulation and
licensing of all centers will be harmonized under the Early Childhood
Development Centers Act.

Notes

1. Singapore Department of Statistics. (2017). Latest data population & land
area. Retrieved from singstat.gov.sg/statistics/latest-data#16
2. Ibid.
3. Ibid.
4. Immigration and Checkpoints Authority, Singapore Department of Statistics.
(2017). M810091—Births and fertility rates, annual. Retrieved from tablebuilder.
singstat.gov.sg/publicfacing/createDataTable.action?refId=3733
5. Ibid.
6. Singapore Department of Statistics. (2017). Latest data births & deaths. Retrieved from singstat.gov.sg/statistics/latest-data#18
7. Singapore Department of Statistics. (2017). Singapore in figures 2017. Retrieved from singstat.gov.sg/docs/default-source/default-document-library/publica-
tions/publications_and_papers/reference/sif2017.pdf
8. Singapore Department of Statistics. (2015). General household survey.
Retrieved from singstat.gov.sg/docs/default-source/default-document-library/publi-
cations/publications_and_papers/GHS/ghs2015/ghs2015.pdf
9. Singapore Department of Statistics. (2017). Latest data labour & productivity. Retrieved from singstat.gov.sg/statistics/latest-data#4
10. Singapore Department of Statistics. (2017). Latest data gross domestic
product (GDP). Retrieved from singstat.gov.sg/statistics/latest-data#1

11. Singapore Budget. (2017). Analysis of revenue and expenditure financial fear 2017. Retrieved from singaporebudget.gov.sg/data/budget_2017/download/FY2017_Analysis_of_Revenue_and_Expenditure.pdf

12. Handayani, S. W. (2014). Asian Development Bank sustainable development working paper series no. 32 measuring social protection expenditures in Southeast Asia: Estimates using the social protection index. Retrieved from adb.org/sites/default/files/publication/42753/sdwp-032.pdf

13. Singapore Department of Statistics. (2017). Key household income trends, 2016. Retrieved from singstat.gov.sg/docs/default-source/default-document-library/publications/publications_and_papers/household_income_and_expenditure/pp-s23.pdf

14. Ministry of Manpower. (2017). Employment practices: Leave. Retrieved from mom.gov.sg/employment-practices/leave

15. Government-Paid Leave. (2017). Annex A. Retrieved from profamilyleave.gov.sg/Documents/PDF/AnnexA.pdf

16. Ministry of Education. (2017). Education statistics digest 2017. Retrieved from moe.gov.sg/docs/default-source/document/publications/education-statistics-digest/esd_2017.pdf

17. Singapore Budget. (2017). Analysis of revenue and expenditure financial year 2017.

18. Health Promotion Board. (2014). Health booklet. Retrieved from health-hub.sg/sites/assets/Assets/Programs/screening/pdf/health-booklet-2014.pdf

19. Ibid.

20. Early Childhood Development Agency (personal communication, October 31 2017).

21. Ibid; Early Childhood Development Agency. (2016). Statistics on Singaporean children who have not attended preschool. Retrieved from msf.gov.sg/media-room/Pages/Statistics-on-Singaporean-children-who-have-not-attended-pre-school.aspx

22. Early Childhood Development Agency (personal communication, October 31 2017).

23. SkillsFuture Singapore. (2016). Skills framework for early childhood care and education: A guide on occupations and skills. Retrieved from skillsfuture.sg/-/media/Initiatives/Files/SF-for-ECCE/SF_ECCE_Guide_2016.pdf

24. Early Childhood Development Agency. (2015). Guide to setting up a child care center. Retrieved from ecda.gov.sg/documents/ccls/CCC_Guide.pdf

25. Singapore Statutes Online. (2012). Child Care Centers Act. Retrieved from sso.agc.gov.sg/Act/CCCA1988

26. Singapore Statutes Online. (2009). Education Act. Retrieved from sso.agc.gov.sg/Act/EA1957?ValidDate=20091201&ProvIds=xv-

About the Contributors

Alfredo Bautista, Ph.D., Contributing Author, Singapore. Alfredo Bautista is research scientist and lecturer at the Center for Research in Child Development, National Institute of Education, Singapore. Prior to this, Alfredo completed his Ph.D. in psychology at Universidad Autónoma de Madrid (Spain), and subsequently worked as a postdoctoral researcher at the University of Victoria (Canada) and Tufts University (United States). He joined the National Institute of Education in October 2013, where he runs several research projects as principal and co-principal investigator. His research focuses on teacher professional development and the analysis of instructional practices, which is disseminated in mainstream journals in psychology and education. He currently works with preschool educators and primary/secondary music teachers, in close collaboration with Singapore's Ministry of Education.

Rebecca Bull, Ph.D., Co-Principal Investigator, Singapore. Rebecca Bull is principal research scientist at the Center for Research in Child Development, National Institute of Education, Singapore. Prior to this role, Rebecca was a reader in psychology at the University of Aberdeen, Scotland. Recognized internationally and nationally for her scholarship related to children's cognitive development and learning, Rebecca is the author of numerous articles published in prestigious journals within cognitive, developmental, and educational psychology. Her research focuses on the factors that result in individual differences in children's cognition and self-regulation, and how these skills subsequently impact on learning in the classroom. Rebecca is the recipient of international and national research grants from the United States, United Kingdom, and Singapore, including funding for the first large-scale study of early childhood education in Singapore, the Singapore Kindergarten Impact Project (SKIP). Working closely with the Ministry of Education and Early Childhood Development Agency in Singapore, Rebecca's work focuses on the impact of early childhood environments and teacher-child interactions on children's development in the kindergarten years, with a view to raising the quality of early childhood education across the preschool sector.

Lily Fritz, Contributing Author, England. Lily Fritz works as a research assistant to Professor Kathy Sylva as part of the Families, Effective Learning and Literacy research group at Oxford University's Department of Education. Before joining the University of Oxford, Lily worked for an educational social enterprise and as a teaching assistant in a school. Lily received her B.A. (Hons) in Modern and Medieval Languages at the University of Cambridge before completing an MSc in Child Development and Education at the University of Oxford with distinction.

Bridget Healey, Contributing Author, Australia. Bridget Healey is a research assistant at the National Center for Children and Families. Prior to this, she was a senior policy officer leading early childhood education policy initiatives in the Victorian Department of Education and Training, Australia, where she was instrumental in delivering the statewide Victorian Early Years Learning and Development Framework (2016) and implementing the National Quality Framework. Bridget holds a master's degree in education policy from Teachers College, Columbia University.

Sharon Lynn Kagan, Ed.D., Principal Investigator. Sharon Lynn Kagan is the Virginia and Leonard Marx Professor of Early Childhood and Family Policy and co-director of the National Center for Children and Families at Teachers College, Columbia University, and professor adjunct at Yale University's Child Study Center. Recognized internationally and nationally for her accomplishments related to the care and education of young children, Kagan is a prolific public speaker, author of 300 articles and 14 books, a member of over 30 national boards or panels, and has worked with over 75 countries around the globe to establish early learning standards, public policies, and teacher education strategies.

A recipient of international and national honorary doctoral degrees, Dr. Kagan is past president of the National Association for the Education of Young Children and a past president of Family Support America. She has served as chair of the National Education Goals Panel Technical Planning Group for Goal One; a member of the Clinton Education Transition Team; a Distinguished Fellow for the Education Commission of the States; and a member of numerous National Academy of Sciences, foundation, and administration panels. She was made a Fellow of the American Educational Research Association (AERA) in 2010, elected to membership in the National Academy of Education in 2012, and awarded a Fulbright Fellowship in 2016. She is the only woman in the history of American education to receive its three most prestigious awards: the 2004 Distinguished Service Award from the Council of Chief State School Officers (CCSSO), the 2005 James Bryant Conant Award for Lifetime Service to Education from the Education Commission of the States (ECS), and the Harold W. McGraw, Jr. Prize in Education.

Kristiina Kumpulainen, Ph.D., Co-Principal Investigator, Finland. Kristiina Kumpulainen is professor of education, specializing in preschool and early primary education, at the Faculty of Educational Sciences, University of Helsinki. Prior to her present position, she has acted as the Director of Information and Evaluation Services at the Finnish National Agency for Education. Recognized internationally for her scholarship in learning and pedagogy, Kumpulainen is the author of over 100 articles and 10 books. Her research interests focus on young children's learning, development, and well-being in their social ecologies in and out of formal education, dialogic learning, agency and identity, multiliteracies, and professional development of teachers. She is the recipient of numerous research and development grants. A leader in shaping the conceptual thinking of the future of Finnish education policy and practice, she is a regular keynote speaker at national and international conferences and venues. For the National Center on Education and the Economy's Comparative Study of Early Childhood Education in Selected High Performing Countries, she is the lead scholar from Finland.

Eva Landsberg, Contributing Author, National Center for Children and Families. Eva Landsberg is a research assistant at the National Center for Children and Families at Teachers College, Columbia University. Prior to joining NCCF, she conducted research on early childhood education policy at the Children's Defense Fund in Washington, D.C., specifically focusing on the intersection of poverty and early education. She also worked as a teaching assistant in an early education center. She received her B.A. in history from Yale University.

Carrie Lau, Contributing Author, Hong Kong. Carrie Lau is assistant professor, Faculty of Education, The University of Hong Kong. Her research focuses on language and literacy development, English as a second language, and early childhood development and education. She is interested in the role of home environments and classroom practices in the language and literacy development of children learning English as a second language. Her recent projects include the development of a classroom assessment tool to measure the quality of English language teaching in early childhood settings and the evaluation of early childhood education policies in Hong Kong. She has received grants from government and nongovernmental organizations. In addition, she is involved in professional organizations that aim to promote the well-being of children through research and advocacy efforts.

Mugyeong Moon, Ph.D., Co-Principal Investigator, Republic of Korea. Mugyeong Moon is director of the Office of International Research, Korea Institute of Child Care and Education, in the Republic of Korea. Before working at KICCE, Moon was head of the Early Childhood Education

Division, Graduate School of Education, Ajou University. Moon has been a principal investigator and author of numerous publications, including more than 80 policy research reports granted by the Korean government and National Research Council. Moon's expertise and research interests include early childhood policy, multicultural education, teacher education, and curriculum development. Recent research projects include integrating early childhood education and care, national frameworks and work issues of ECEC teachers, improving the consultation system of the Nuri Curriculum, standard unit cost for kindergarten education, and more.

Moon served as a vice chair (2009–2011) and the national coordinator (2007–2012) for the OECD Early Childhood Education and Care Network Project and as an expert committee member (2009–2010) on the UNESCO World Forum on ECCE representing Asia. A founding member of PECERA (Pacific Early Childhood Education Research Association), Moon is a vice-chair of PECERA Korea. She also serves as a steering committee member of ARNEC (Asia Regional Network of Early Childhood) (2011 to present). Moon led and participated in numerous committees and task force teams for the Korean government policy development.

Grace Murkett, Contributing Author, England. Grace Murkett is a research assistant at the Department of Education, University of Oxford. She earned a B.A. (hons) in psychology at Bath University. Following this, she worked in the Families, Effective Learning and Literacy research group at Oxford on early education studies. She is currently teaching English in Latin America and plans a career in education.

Tom Peachey, Contributing Author, Australia. Tom Peachey is a consultant with ACIL Allen Consulting, Australia's largest independently owned economics and policy consulting firm. In this role he advises government and nongovernment organizations in early childhood, education, health. and human services sectors. Before joining ACIL Allen, Tom worked for over 10 years in executive and management roles with government, principally in strategic policy roles. He has led or been involved with the development of state and national early childhood development plans. Tom has an executive master's degree in public administration.

Nirmala Rao, Ph.D., C.Psychol., FBPS, Co-Principal Investigator, Hong Kong. Nirmala Rao is Serena HC Yang Professor in Early Childhood Development and Education, Faculty of Education, The University of Hong Kong. A developmental and chartered (educational) psychologist by training, she has been recognized internationally for her research on early childhood development and education in Asian cultural contexts. She has participated in international meetings as an expert/specialist, written advocacy materials, and undertaken consultancies for UNICEF, UNESCO, the World Bank,

DFID, OECD and the Brookings Institute. Professor Rao has published widely and has authored over 100 international peer-refereed journal articles, books, book chapters, and research reports and presented more than 50 invited papers on early childhood development and education, child development and educational policy, and educational psychology in different parts of the world. She has been the recipient of numerous research grants from governments and international nongovernmental organizations. She also serves on the editorial board for several journals and is currently an associate editor of *Child Development*. She was a member of the steering committee for the 2017 *Lancet* Series on early child eevelopment. In addition, she has held significant administrative leadership roles at The University of Hong Kong within the faculty and as dean of the Graduate School.

Kathy Sylva, Ph.D., Co-Principal Investigator, England. Kathy Sylva is Honorary Research Fellow and professor of educational psychology at the University of Oxford. After earning a doctorate in developmental psychology at Harvard, she moved to England for postdoctoral research with Jerome Bruner at the University of Oxford Department of Experimental Psychology. Her research interests fall into two themes. She has conducted several large-scale studies on the effects of early education and care on children's development, acting as a lead researcher on the Effective Pre-school and Primary Education study (EPPE/EPPSE), which followed 3,000 children from pre-school entry to the end of compulsory schooling. She co-led the national Evaluation of Children's Centres in England, another large-scale study on the effects of early childhood services on development. Her second interest is in programs aimed at enhancing parents' capacity to support their child's learning and behavior. She has led three randomized controlled trials to evaluate parenting interventions. Kathy has published seven books and 200 papers/technical reports on early education/care, early literacy, and support for families. She was specialist adviser to the U.K. Parliamentary Committee on Education 2000–2009, the Scottish Parliament Education Committee in 2007, the U.K. Review of the early childhood curriculum in 2011, the National Expert Panel on "Standards for Early Years Teachers" in 2012, and the House of Lords Enquiry into "Affordable Child care" in 2015. She has honorary doctorates from the University of Gothenburg, the Open University, and Oxford Brookes University. She was awarded the Order of the British Empire (OBE) in 2008, and in 2014 the British Education Research Association's Nisbett Award for outstanding contribution to educational research.

Collette Tayler, Ph.D., Co-Principal Investigator, Australia. Collette Tayler passed away on December 1, 2017. Previously, she was professor and chair of early childhood education and care (ECEC) in the Melbourne Graduate School of Education at the University of Melbourne, Australia. She was the project leader of the Australian Research Council E4Kids longitudinal study, a chief investigator within the Australian Research Council's National Science of Learning Research Centre, and leader of the 3a (Abecedarian Approach Australia) research and development suite of projects. Prior to these roles, Tayler was head of the School of Early Childhood at the Queensland University of Technology. Recognized nationally and internationally for her research and development on the promotion of children's learning from birth to age 8 years, Tayler studied the contexts, child experiences, teaching strategies, and relationships within homes, early childhood centers, and schools. Her research projects included culturally and linguistically diverse urban, regional, and remote communities across Australia, and these projects are collectively concerned with the effective provision of a comprehensive ECEC system to support Australian families and young children. With John Bennett for the OECD, Tayler analyzed ECEC systems across 20 OECD countries, co-authoring the report *Starting Strong II* (OECD, 2006) which had international influence on the policy direction and provision of contemporary early childhood systems.

A leader in shaping the Australian Early Childhood Quality Framework for the reform of ECEC provision (2009–2016), Tayler was appointed as deputy chair of the Australian Children's Education and Care Quality Authority, which oversees the implementation of the systemic reform across the Australian jurisdictions. She was a Fellow of the Australian College of Educators and served the Victorian government through ministerial appointments, including to the Victorian Children's Council, the Board of the Victorian Curriculum and Assessment Authority, the Education Minister's Expert Panel for Schools, and the Minister for Families and Children Expert Panel for Early Childhood Development.

Index

Note: **Bold** page numbers indicate chapter authors.